THE SPYING GAME

Bruce Bennett AO was Emeritus Professor of the University of New South Wales at the Australian Defence Force Academy in Canberra. In 2005–6 he was Group of Eight Professor of Australian Studies at Georgetown University in Washington DC.

A Rhodes scholar, he was a graduate of the Universities of Western Australia, Oxford and London and also a Doctor of Letters from the University of New South Wales. Bennett was a Fellow of the Australian Academy of the Humanities. He held visiting appointments at universities in Asia, Europe and North America and has served on the Australian National Commission for UNESCO and the Australia–India Council.

His books included *An Australian Compass* (1991), *Spirit in Exile* (1991), *The Oxford Literary History of Australia* (1998), with Jennifer Strauss, *Australian Short Fiction* (2002), *Homing In* (2006) and he was co-editor of the anthology *Of Sadhus and Spinners: Australian Encounters with India* (2009).

THE SPYING GAME
AN AUSTRALIAN ANGLE

BRUCE BENNETT

AUSTRALIAN SCHOLARLY

A number of these chapters first appeared in journals:

An earlier version of 'Secret Agents and the Search for Truth' was published in *JEASA: Journal of the European Association for Studies on Australia*. Festschrift in Honour of Prof. Werner Senn, Vol. 1, 2009, and is reproduced here with the editor's permission.

'Exploration or Espionage? Flinders and the French' was first published in *JEASA*, 2.1, May 2010, and is reproduced here with the editor's permission.

'Under Cover: Projections of British and Australian Secret Intelligence' is a revised version of the paper 'Under Cover: Projections of British and Australian Secret Intelligence' in *Under Cover* eds. Kerr and Warner, Adelaide, Lythrum Press, 2008, pp. 25–35 and is reproduced here with the editor's permission.

An earlier version of 'Traditional Myths and Problematic Heroes: The Case of Harry Freame' was published in *Asiatic*, 4.2, June 2008, pp. 10–20, and is reproduced here with the editor's permission.

A version of 'A Wilderness of Mirrors: Perspectives on "The Spying Game" in Australian Literature' was delivered at the ASAL Conference on 'Spectres, Screens, Shadows, Mirrors' at the University of Western Australia, 3–6 July 2006.

An earlier version of 'Memory, Identity and Imagination in Secret Intelligence: Christopher Koch's *The Memory Room*' was published in *Antipodes,* USA, December 2009 and is reproduced here with the editor's permission.

'Spies, Lies and Intelligence: Reconfiguring Asia-Pacific Literatures' was first presented at the 12th Biennial Symposium on Literatures and Cultures of the Asia-Pacific Region at the University of the Philippines, Quezon City, 23–5 November 2007.

'Of Spies and Terrorists: Australian Fiction after 9/11' was first presented at the European Association of Commonwealth Language and Literature Studies, Venice, 25–9 March 2008.

© Bruce Bennett 2012

First published 2012
Australian Scholarly Publishing Pty Ltd
7 Lt Lothian St Nth, North Melbourne, Vic 3051
TEL: 03 9329 6963 FAX: 03 9329 5452
EMAIL: aspic@ozemail.com.au
WEB: scholarly.info

A Cataloguing-in-Publication entry for this title is available
from the National Library of Australia

ISBN 978-1-921875-68-7

Design and typesetting by Art Rowlands
Printing and binding by BPA Print Group

Contents

Transnational Challenges

Acknowledgments

The research which has led to this book was driven by a persistent curiosity about 'the spying game', which interested me in its broad human perspectives rather than its technical aspects. The interest was fed by the experience and imaginings of men and women in a number of countries. In the course of writing these essays and commentaries, I have met and talked with many individuals who are or have been engaged in espionage or related activities. A number of these conversations were off the record. The majority were broad-ranging discussions with authors or former intelligence agents who have made it their business to engage with the world of secret intelligence and reflect on its significance.

The work would not have been possible without a Discovery Project grant from the Australian Research Council and the support of the University of New South Wales at the Australian Defence Force Academy in Canberra. Research assistance by Susan Cowan, Marina Bollinger and Patricia Bennett was especially helpful. Administrative support by David Lovell, Jo Muggleton and colleagues in the School of Humanities and Social Sciences was also appreciated.

Australian scholars with whom I held discussions about the human implications of spying include Des Ball, Frank Cain, Derrill de Heer, Peter Boyce, Denis Blight, John McFarlane and Brian Toohey. I had a number of informative conversations with Phillip Knightley in London and Sydney. In Britain, I was fortunate to join an Intelligence seminar led by Christopher Andrew at Cambridge University. I also benefited from the knowledge and insights of Nigel West.

A period at Georgetown University, Washington DC in 2005–6 enabled me to consult holdings in the wonderful Lauinger Library and to meet with George Tenet, Paul Pillar, Nicholas Scheetz and Hayden

Peake. Alan Tidwell at the Center for Australian and New Zealand Studies was a source of support and encouragement. A 'spy retreat' in the mountains of Virginia enabled me to meet David Major, Oleg Kalugin and a number of retired intelligence officers from the old 'East' and 'West'.

These acknowledgements would not be complete without mention of the many writers who have increased my interest and curiosity in the secret worlds of international spying. They include biographers, historians and novelists. The latter range from Rudyard Kipling and Joseph Conrad to Graham Greene and John le Carré. In the neglected area of Australian literature, I have been fortunate to read and discuss work with writers including Christopher Koch, Nicholas Hasluck, Frank Moorhouse, Michael Wilding, Warren Reed, Satendra Nandan, Tom Keneally and Peter Porter. In the Philippines, Butch Dalisay gave me some valuable insights and Santosh Sareen in India introduced me to some of the relevant literature.

A number of the papers and essays from which this book derives were tested at international conferences and first published in books or journals in Europe, North America, Asia or Australia. I thank the editors of these publications for their interest in this work and for their permission to publish in revised form here. The place of first publication is given on the copyright page. I also wish to acknowledge Nick Walker at Australian Scholarly Publishing for his positive attitude and active support for the publication of this book.

Above all, I acknowledge the existence in our history and imagination of those who work under the radar in their search for knowledge and understanding that may, in the end, lead to more peaceful and fulfilling international relations.

Bruce Bennett
Canberra
February 2012

Introduction

The kinds of people recruited by intelligence agencies vary widely across time and in different countries. A cartoon in Britain in the late 1980s captures some of the clichés of its time. An older man sits at a careers desk interviewing an awkward-looking young man: 'You're a deceitful, cunning poofter, Smithers – ever thought of joining MI5?'[1] An advertisement for the Australian Secret Intelligence Service in the early twenty-first century seems to set its sights higher, ambiguously promising 'Extraordinary Work for Extraordinary People'.[2] Advertising for spies, like dramas about them, often hovers between the comic put-down and an appeal to the mystique of the unknown.

Though I have never been a spy in any official sense, it is possible that I was considered for such a role. After completing a three-year stint at Oxford University in the late 1960s, I was interviewed in Canberra for a position in Australia's foreign service and told I had been successful. Having been simultaneously offered a university lectureship in Western Australia, I opted for the latter and was allowed to delay a final decision on the foreign affairs position for a year. I enjoyed university teaching and decided to stay with it, seeing a more stable and satisfying future there. But I sometimes wish, and imagine, that foreign affairs had turned my head just that bit more and given me a chance to immerse myself in the world of international diplomacy and secret intelligence. When I moved east to teach at the University of New South Wales at the Australian Defence Force Academy in Canberra in the last decade of the twentieth century, it was clear that a number of my best students were proceeding into careers in military intelligence and my previous brush with foreign affairs sparked a developing interest in the world they were entering.

In 1992–3, peaceful prospects were in the air. UN peacekeeping activities were strongly promoted and there was talk of the Australian Defence Force in more combined, 'purple' operations. Educating young officers of both sexes in leading peacemaking forces seemed a worthwhile challenge alongside the traditional training for defence and attack. The collection and analysis of secret intelligence seemed part of a new, more peace-oriented international community. But before a decade was out, a catastrophe had occurred in New York and a whole new lexicon of terror enveloped our imagination. Traditional humanities in the universities would have to reassert their relevance in a variety of new shapes and forms.

My dual interest in serious literature and the gathering and analysis of secret intelligence means that I am always on the lookout for intriguing books and stories – including popular novels and movies, but with a preference for those with greater literary ambitions than the spy/thriller genre dominated by James Bond and Jason Bourne. While I enjoy the tautness, tension and excitement of the spy/thriller genre at its best, I am more deeply attracted to Kipling's *Kim*, Conrad's *The Secret Agent*, Maugham's *Ashenden*, Durrell's *The Alexandria Quartet* or the best of Graham Greene and John le Carré. Why? Because in such books I find complexities of human desire, motivation and behaviour explored in suitably complex and life-like ways. Films, too, vary from the straightforward thriller genre to recent cinematic classics such as *Breach* or *The Lives of Others* which extend our understanding of patriotism, twisted motives, loyalty and betrayal. Perhaps they appeal to deeper levels of the spy in all of us.

But while British, American and Soviet empires have produced plentiful supplies of heroes, villains and stirring tales, Australians have typically averted their gaze from their country's involvement in 'the second oldest profession'. Does this reflect a sense of shame among a people who would like to consider their country more innocent than in fact it has been in the ways of the world? As I began to research this field from a cultural and historical standpoint, I discovered that the Australian continent and its inhabitants have been engaged in espionage since the earliest European imaginings of a southern landmass. Cartographic spies were called upon to copy or steal the maps of fellow navigators from other countries competing for the discovery of new lands. Spanish,

Portuguese, Dutch, French and British navigators depended not only on publicly accessible maps but also on what could be gleaned (or stolen) from others. Networks of secret agents operated to bribe or otherwise obtain maps held under lock and key (and often seal) by countries or companies intending to control the sea-lanes. The cat-and-mouse games between British and French navigators in the early nineteenth century, in which Matthew Flinders became embroiled, illustrate the kinds of deception involved in these imperialist contests.

While different kinds of espionage operated before and during colonial occupation, an entirely new phase of spying activity began when Australia became a nation in 1901. Although a nation, Australia was still inextricably part of the British Empire – but, some dreamed, a country with scope to become a 'new Britannia' some day in these southern seas. Inevitably, our institutions of spying (or intelligence gathering) would be based on those of Britain; and these influences would persist for at least three-quarters of the twentieth century before American influences and practices became dominant. But the very early years of the twentieth century also revealed emergent Australian perspectives on the troubled Pacific where European empires vied for control of the islands and Japan began to flex its military muscles. Moreover, as Australia's second prime minister Alfred Deakin remarked, Japan was 'next door' to Australia while British headquarters were a world away. While small-scale spying missions were planned to obtain military intelligence on Samoa or New Caledonia (in both British and Australian interests), Australians also took account of the Russo–Japanese war and suspicious Japanese activities were monitored off the Queensland coast.

In these studies, I have chosen to probe selected areas of espionage interest while remaining alert to wider contexts of geography, history and politics. My chief interest has been 'the spying game' in its international dimensions rather than its internal security aspects, though the two often interact. Many records are sketchy or non-existent. Many actors who should have voices will not talk. Much is distorted or disguised. But my interest is less in the operational details of spying missions than in some of the men and women who have engaged in these activities, the international implications of what they do and what happens to them as human beings. Literary and cinematic texts as well as biographies, histories or political accounts can play a part in such investigations, and they contribute to an underlying question of this book: what are the roles of reason and imagination in secret intelligence? How do apparently normal people get involved? What happens to them?

The kinds of spying under consideration in these studies range from that of a scout in the trenches of Gallipoli to a female figure sketching military installations in First World War France – who turns out to be an Australian man in drag paid by the British secret service. From the lone-ranger type of agent in the field to the scholarly collector and analyst of strategic information, Australians have played many roles in intelligence. In this, they have been influenced by their own experience and choices inflected by ideologies, outlooks and individuals whom they have met at home or in other countries. Almost always, they are trans-national figures. Some have been patriots, some traitors to their country's interests.

I have generally avoided the easy categorisation of heroes and villains in these essays (though I have occasionally tested the applicability of these terms which are often simplistic and formulaic). But a general question is raised as to the status of secret agents or spies: for example, why has the status of hero been accorded to intelligence operatives in certain countries (e.g. the US, Soviet Union, Israel) but almost never in Australia? Part of the answer may lie in Britain's 'ownership' of this field and their projection of a state of fascinated ambivalence about the world of espionage which led to a spy thriller genre that dominated the literary field for much of the twentieth century. By the same token, the CIA has been a seed-bed of popular heroes in the US until 9/11 changed all that. By bringing some of Australia's actors in the spying game out of the shadows, the studies in this book may develop greater interest and understanding of our historic and cultural involvement in this field of international activity.

While spying had played a part in the lives of some Australians in the early decades of the nation's existence, this usually occurred in collaboration with the British secret service, as in the case of Charles Howard ('Dick') Ellis who entered the British SIS after the First World War and became a secret agent in Germany and Eastern Europe. Ellis went on to play an influential role in the foundation of Australian intelligence after the Second World War but was plagued by claims that he was a 'traitor of major proportions' who had passed secrets to both the Germans and the Russians. One of Ellis's chief accusers was Peter Wright, the author of *Spycatcher*, who retired to Tasmania and famously boasted of his career at MI5 as a carnival of break-ins and bugging beyond the reach of law.

The Second World War provided opportunities in the field of intelligence for hundreds of Australians. Nancy Wake was a spy and saboteur for the French resistance against the Nazi invaders. Peter Ryan secretly reported on Japanese troop movements behind the lines in Papua New Guinea in 1942–3. The Japanese Australian Harry Freame was perhaps the most problematic of this trio. A legendary scout during the Anzac landing at Gallipoli in the First World War, Freame reported to Australian intelligence on the Japanese community in Australia in the Second World War and was apparently killed while carrying out secret work for the Australian government in Tokyo in 1940.

Although Cold War espionage was generally more intense and wide-ranging in the northern hemisphere than in Australia, the defection of Soviet intelligence officers Vladimir and Evdokia Petrov in 1954 carried its own drama and produced significant intelligence on KGB activity in Australia together with new information on the international front including the first hard evidence that British spies Burgess and Maclean were in Moscow.[3]

What gained most media attention in Australia after the Petrovs' dramatic defection was an alleged 'nest of traitors' who had obtained state secrets and passed them to the KGB. But who *were* some of these individuals? I focus on the Petrovs themselves and men such as the 'Rhodes Scholar spy', Ian Milner, and his co-accused Ric Throssell. Such stories raise questions not only of guilt or innocence but of identity and motivation – what has undermined or sustained such individuals during the 'hot' and 'cold' wars of our times?

As well as being actors in some of the world's major spy dramas, Australians have also been reporters, commentators and analysts. The doyen of journalists in this field is Phillip Knightley who, with Murray Sayle and Bruce Page, was a member of the London *Sunday Times* Insight team who investigated the pre-eminent spy of twentieth century Britain, Kim Philby, after he had fled to Russia. Knightley remained persistently on this case and finally obtained six days of interviews with Philby in Moscow in 1988, several months before

Philby died. Knightley's book, *Philby: KGB Masterspy*, provided the template for subsequent work on this notorious individual and gave Knightley insights into the KGB and its operations which led to subsequent important publications.

Although some writers of spy fiction, including Greene and le Carré, have also worked in intelligence, many have not. Australian novelist Christopher Koch has met, talked with and corresponded with secret agents and become intrigued with the world they inhabit for its many insights into human motivation and behaviour in the force-field of international politics. Others who have presented aspects of the spying game in their work, such as Nicholas Hasluck, Frank Moorhouse, Blanche d'Alpuget, Robert Drewe, Janette Turner Hospital and Andrew McGahan, have observed not only the duplicity and deceit but also the search for truth that their profession requires, and occasionally impels.

Despite the apparent end of the Cold War, interest in espionage and its effects seems to be mounting among journalists, novelists and film-makers. A profusion of spy thrillers is complemented, on a smaller scale, in serious literary fiction – the main focus of this book. In Australia, this interest is highlighted in recent major novels by Nicholas Hasluck and Frank Moorhouse. Hasluck's novel *Dismissal* (2011) examines the continuation of Cold War allegiances into Australian politics in the 1960s and '70s and the dismissal of a Prime Minister.[4] With forensic finesse, Hasluck examines motives and follows an intriguing international trail of leaks, lies and betrayals ranging from the Petrov affair to atomic testing in the Pacific.

Moorhouse's *Cold Light* (2011) shows its protagonist, Edith Berry, in Canberra after her return from interwar diplomatic and administrative work in Geneva for the League of Nations. Edith cannot recapture in Australia's fledgling capital the intrigue, excitement or sophistication of interwar Europe, with its Bloomsbury-style sexual ambiguities and spying opportunities. Instead, Edith the adventuress, becomes enmeshed in a new nation's architectural planning, its ideological battles with communism and the birth of a uranium industry. Recurrent features of Moorhouse's novel, as of Hasluck's, are the watching, following, analysing, reflecting and interpreting activities of the spy. The human dramas in both novels focus on questions of trust and betrayal. In one of Edith's canny bouts of self-questioning, she reflects that:

> The world – life – was based on unremitting suspicion, right down to children and parents, husbands and wives. Parents spied constantly on their children and vice-versa – the reading of correspondence and journals, keyhole listening. Respite came only from establishing that suspicion was unfounded … We spend our lives seeking someone we can trust.[5]

In the light of Edith's complex private and public lives, these are significant reflections. But where do they lead? 'Safety lay in candour', Edith muses, 'the open personality in an open society'.[6] But the novel shows this to be a utopian ideal.

Although a gulf may seem to be fixed between the counter-espionage practices of the Cold War and the counter-terrorism of our post-9/11 world, the parallels are remarkable. While contemporary telecommunications, computers and signals intercepts are immensely more sophisticated than earlier methods of selecting and reading suspicious letters, as in the First World War, or even the wizardry of *Spooks* or Bourne's micro-chips and memory transplants, many of the purposes and requirements of contemporary human intelligence remain the same. Secret intelligence in Australia, as in other countries, often tests our reason, imagination and beliefs.

An alternative title for this book could be 'The Spy in Us All' for we all seek out (and perhaps share) some of a spy's attributes – alertness, curiosity, a desire to explore the unknown, to uncover secrets. Yet my investigations in this field suggest different perspectives from our different countries of origin, our histories, our political and moral imperatives and our preparedness to 'break rules' in the service of particular causes. Australia has played a classic role as a middle power in waiting, watching and sometimes stalking great powers in pursuit of goals which have changed over time. From the shadows, we too have our stories to tell.

One
Points of Departure:
Spies and Families

'I spy with my little eye'. The spying game begins at an early age in many families and is often thought to have educational value. To observe closely, and report on people, objects and situations, sometimes mischievously or misleadingly, is thought to sharpen one's powers of observation and language use. Stretching the imagination is also part of the game: what might we have spied if we had looked around the corner?

Childhood games of hide and seek or listening to conversations we are not meant to hear take us further inside the spy's domain. If we lie awake at night overhearing our parents' whispered anxieties and secrets, as Graham Greene did, we could be in training to be both a spy and a novelist.[1]

Books for children reflect some of these interests and preoccupations. Enid Blyton's famous five are often waiting behind rocks to spot smugglers and uncover their secrets. Biggles and other Second World War adventurers are on the lookout for German accents or other signs of foreigners in Britain as well as fighting the Hun in the skies over Europe. In the early twenty-first century, the spying game has become more generically fixed in novels by Charlie Higson and Anthony Horowitz for early teenage boys which draw on James Bond as their inspiration.[2] Deborah Abela's *Max Remy Superspy* series appeals to both girls and boys.

One of the least explored aspects of the spying game among adults is its impact on actual families, especially children. Yet a small but growing literature indicates that having a parent who is a dedicated intelligence officer or secret agent committed to the spying game can have profound effects on sons and daughters. Because the tradition of both Western and Eastern bloc intelligence services since the early twentieth century has generally placed men in dominant roles, it is more difficult to analyse the impact of women who are spies on their husbands, partners or children. Yet there are some instances where this can be observed.

Women as Spies

While Mata Hari, the spy as seductress, highlights some popular stereotypes of the woman as spy,[3] the American Elizabeth Bentley evokes a different set of prejudices and expectations. Bentley embraced communism in the 1930s and fell in love with a KGB agent who initiated her into the world of espionage. At the commencement of the Second World War, Bentley was directing operations of the two largest spy rings in America and sending much valuable intelligence to Moscow. When she defected in 1945 and told her story to the FBI, and at public hearings and trials, Bentley was dubbed by the press the 'Red Spy Queen'.

She did not however fit popular stereotypes. Bentley's biographer has discerned some fundamental contradictions at the core of her identity:

> Her family had some of the deepest roots in America, yet she herself was rootless, a woman who never found a home or belonged to a place, geographic or spiritual. Brought up by strait-laced New Englanders to tread carefully in their sedate footsteps, she had an undeniable wild streak that led her someplace else entirely. She was an emotionally distant woman, yet she made a white-hot connection that changed her life. She was a woman who craved attention and ran from it, who purposely sought the spotlight and then couldn't stand the heat, who escaped into anonymity and then couldn't stand the quiet.[4]

Unlike Mata Hari, who wrote to her daughter on the eve of her execution by a French firing squad in 1917, Elizabeth Bentley had no children, so her personal influence on another generation could not be tested. After the investigations and trials that brought her into the public spotlight, and contributed to the hysteria of the McCarthy era,

Bentley found her chief solace in alcohol, a frequent source of comfort and nightmares among ex-spies.

Along with wider societal changes, the role of women in spy agencies has changed dramatically since the mid-twentieth century. Stella Rimington, the first woman to be appointed Director-General of MI5, has remarked that Vernon Kell, the first head of British intelligence in the early twentieth century had a simple prescription for women in his agency: 'I like my girls to have good legs'. By the 1990s, Rimington says gender-free recruitment was more complicated:

> For our cadre intelligence officers we wanted people with a good brain, good analytical skills, the ability to sort out information and put it in order and to express themselves well orally and on paper. But coupled with that they needed to be self-starting, with a warm personality and ability to persuade. And we needed people who would be good on their feet in difficult and possibly dangerous operational situations, where they could not seek advice. We also wanted common sense, balance and integrity. It's quite a tall order.[5]

Recruited by British intelligence when she was in India, Rimington worked her way up to the most responsible job in her agency while raising her two daughters. Her autobiography reveals the conflicting loyalties and priorities involved in running counter-espionage operations in Europe while arranging the home lives and schooling of her daughters and trying to protect them from the repercussions of her work. Rimington's well-developed sense of the need for confidentiality means that her autobiography does not extend to her influence on her daughters, or theirs on her, though she says that at age eleven one daughter 'knew that I did something secret for the government'. Nowadays, Rimington adds, 'all she will say about those sort of experiences is that they made her independent'.[6]

In some situations, however, the repercussions of 'secret work' on family life can be traumatic, as the case of CIA spy Valerie Plame reveals. Plame had grown up in a military family. Her father was a lieutenant colonel in the US Air Force who worked for the National Security Agency for three years. By 2002, in her late thirties, Plame was married to former Ambassador Joseph Wilson and was the mother of two-year-old twins. She had revealed her employment with the CIA to Wilson only after they began dating and became 'close'.[7]

Due to the nature of her work, many details about Plame's professional career are still classified, but her memoir *Fair Game* (2007), and the film based on the book, confirm that she worked for the CIA in a clandestine capacity relating to counter-proliferation of nuclear and other weapons.[8] Known as an international businesswoman, Plame's 'cover' roles included posing as an energy analyst for a private company. Plame's central workplace was CIA headquarters in Langley, Virginia, but her international work involved meeting with workers in the nuclear industry, cultivating sources and managing spies in a number of countries. The major trauma in her professional and personal career occurred in 2003 when a *Washington Post* journalist, Robert Novak, apparently briefed by Vice-President Dick Cheney's chief-of-staff I. Lewis 'Scooter' Libby, revealed her identity as a CIA operative. With her cover thus blown, Plame's twenty-year career as a spy was over, her sources in other countries were endangered and her precariously balanced family life was thrown into turmoil.

Most of the debates and publicity that surrounded Valerie Plame's 'outing' in 2003 were concerned with its political implications, in particular the roles of President George W. Bush, Vice-President Dick Cheney and White House staff. Critics and commentators have seen Plame's 'outing' as an attempt by the White House to discredit Plame's husband, Joseph Wilson, for reporting in the *New York Times* that the Bush administration had manipulated intelligence data to make the case for the invasion of Iraq. Plame's memoir *Fair Game* however, and the film which premiered in 2010, give closer attention to the *human* consequences of a spy's cover being blown in this way: 'My family had always valued public service and kept a quiet patriotism', Plame writes in her memoir, 'I thought that if I served in the CIA it would extend a family tradition. Still, I had my nagging doubts. Hadn't the CIA tried to kill Castro with an exploding cigar?'[9]

The film *Fair Game*, which stars Australian actress Naomi Watts as Plame, and Sean Penn as Wilson, explores some of the explosive consequences of the spying game on family life. As a reviewer notes, the director Doug Liman reveals an 'uneasy masquerade' in family life and seeks to locate 'the human element amid the clutter of spin, hypocrisy and partisan rhetoric … Like a le Carré novel, its story shows how things really work and how compromised lives can become when one must serve more than one master'.[10] The case of Valerie Plame remains intriguing for its insights into the way spying can be accommodated within a family's life and may cause disruption and even devastation when this way of living is lost. 'For someone who had lived under cover, assuming it as a part of my life and protecting it zealously,' Plame wrote, 'this instantaneous shift to being a public person brought great anxiety, manifested both emotionally and physically'.[11]

Fathers and Sons

Although the recent entry of women into major roles in professional spying makes it difficult to discern patterns or trends, it is possible to see some emergent themes in relations between fathers and sons. Sometimes this manifests in sons following (or trying to follow) in their father's footsteps – a kind of family tradition. Sometimes, by way of countervailing human relations, sons rebel against a father's way of life, or become curious or even intrigued enough to explore its implications, both negative and positive.

A dramatic instance of following in his father's footsteps was evident in 2009 when a 24-year-old son was charged with carrying on his jailed father's espionage efforts while his father was in jail. The father, Harold Nicholson, was a former senior CIA agent who was jailed in 1997 for 23 years after pleading guilty to selling secrets to the Russians. Espionage missions planned by his father from his prison cell took Nathaniel to San Francisco, Mexico City, Lima and Cyprus where he met Russian contacts. According to FBI agents, who had got suspicious and tracked Nathaniel's movements, he had received $35,000 for the secrets he sold. In a letter the FBI interpreted as confirming that his son had followed his father's career path, Harold Nicholson had written: 'You have been brave enough to step into this new unseen world that is sometimes dangerous but always fascinating. God leads us on our greatest adventures'.[12]

A common outcome among sons in search of their fathers is that they remain a mystery, an unresolved puzzle. Such is the case of journalist Jimmy Burns who asks: 'Was my father a British spy?'[13] He discovers that his father, a part-Chilean Hispanophile, was sent to Spain in 1940 to help keep Franco's Spain neutral in the Second World War rather than siding with Hitler and Mussolini. Kim Philby and Anthony Blunt, later revealed as Soviet agents working for British intelligence, tried to discredit Burns as a closet fascist.[14] Burns's research for his book involved access to documents held in MI5 for 67 years and show that his father Tom was involved in several successful covert operations against the Nazis in Spain and occupied France. The son's determined search for clues to the personality of his 'real' father reveals a duplicitous, womanising, hypocritical individual. No longer does the son harbour illusions about a romantic James Bond figure; he now sees his father 'not as a hero, but as a vulnerable and complex human being who served his king and country as best he could.' Whatever puzzles remain, the son is no longer restricted to a one-dimensional view of his father.

The modelling of sons on fathers is a recurrent theme in Vin Arthey's biography of the Soviet spy known as Rudolph Abel, who was exchanged in Berlin in 1962 for the captured American spy-pilot Francis Gary Powers.[15] Rudolph Abel was one of the cover names used by British-born William Fisher, whose father Heinrich, a German born in Russia, was involved in gun-running to Russian revolutionaries from northern England and Scotland and managed to avoid arrest. When Heinrich returned to Moscow in 1921 with his son, Willie, he was an ideal and willing candidate for recruitment by the Soviets. Willie had learned from his father, his biographer notes, 'how systems and politicians operated and he had been drilled into maintaining personal and political discipline'.[16] His dedicated career as a spy for the Soviets did not finish in 1962. After the prisoner exchange with Powers, Willie Fisher *alias* Rudolph Abel continued to work for the KGB until his death in 1971.

The Philbys – Father and Son

The most fully developed study of a father and son in relation to spying is Anthony Cave Brown's biography of H. St John Philby and his son Kim Philby, *Treason in the Blood*. As the book's title somewhat melodramatically indicates, Brown suggests a genetic tendency in father and son towards treason. In practice, thanks to his conscientious and painstaking research, Brown does indeed reveal intellectual and temperamental likenesses between the two Philby males who influenced each other while each rebelled in different ways against the British establishment values in which they were raised.

A famous Arabist, explorer and author, St John ('Montie') Philby has been described as 'the Professor Moriarty of the Colonial Office'.[17] A larger-than-life figure, he spent much of his life in the Middle East. When Philby decided his disagreements with the Colonial Office could not be reconciled, he resigned. His son's rebellion, on the other hand, entailed living a long double-life as a senior British intelligence officer with the Secret Intelligence Service. Philby was talked of as a potential head of that service, but was simultaneously a deep penetration agent for the Soviet Union. On the verge of being exposed, Philby decamped for Moscow in 1963 and lived there until his death in 1988.

When St John Philby resigned from his position as Chief British Representative in Jordan in 1924, he was just ahead of Colonial Office superiors who sought to sack him for maladministration and insubordination. Philby senior wrote to a friend that he could 'no longer go on working for the present High Commissioner who, being a Zionist Jew, cannot hold the scales even between Zionist and Arab interests'. Besides this, he added, 'Abdullah has rather let me down with his personal extravagance…'.[18] Brown remarks that Philby had 'sacrificed a brilliant career in order to expose the system being created by the British, the French, and the Zionists in the Middle East'.[19] In a revealing aside, he adds: 'He displayed the same honest glint that Kim would show later on. Perhaps the son learned the trick from the father, but whatever the case, it had the same effect: to create the impression of a strength of character that confounded the critics and enemies'.[20] This 'trick' element – the 'honest glint' in the eye of both father and son – deceived many apparently sophisticated men and women in government and diplomatic spheres across two generations.

An earlier biographer, Phillip Knightley, noted another feature of the father's behaviour that his son emulated to some degree: '[St John Philby's] married life was strange, to say the least – he always discussed his new mistresses with his wife yet she remained loyal to him'.[21] If the son was somewhat more secretive than his father in this area of this life, Kim also inherited his father's remarkable vivacity and ability to make women feel they loved him: this applied in varying degrees to his four wives and some of his mistresses, though the divided life of a spy avoiding detection, fuelled by alcohol and nightmares made him difficult to live with. Nevertheless Philby's second wife, English-born Aileen Furse, with whom he had five children, betrayed him to authorities when she wrote to the British Foreign Office in 1952 that Philby was 'the third man'. But she was not believed, her depression increased; she became an alcoholic and died in London in December 1957.[22]

Eleanor Brewer, Philby's third wife, was an American who, when she met him in Beirut was married to the *New York Times*'s foreign correspondent. Philby was a journalist for the London *Observer*. Eleanor was probably a controlled informant for the CIA, charged with discovering what she could about Philby while he was extracting information from her that would be useful to the KGB. As Brown remarks, 'Philby and Eleanor sought to use each other but ended up in love with each other'.[23] In her memoir *The Spy I Loved*, Eleanor records what initially attracted her to Philby:

> What touched me first about Kim was his loneliness… A certain old-fashioned reserve set him apart from the easy familiarity of the other journalists. He was then forty-four, of medium height, very lean, with a handsome heavily-lined face. His eyes were an intense blue… He had a gift for creating an atmosphere of such intimacy that I found myself talking freely to him. I was very impressed by his beautiful manners.[24]

Eleanor's sentimental memoir is interesting for its perceptions of Philby in the last phase of his career as a spy in the West (he fled Beirut in 1963) and for the initial phase of his exile – or 'homecoming', if it can be called that (though he had never been to Russia before) – in Moscow. Eleanor followed Philby to the Russian capital with two of his children but the relationship did not thrive in the new environment and she returned to the USA for good in 1965.

The final phase of Philby's familial life is described by his Russian fourth wife, Rufina, whom he married in 1971. In her memoir *Kim Philby: The Moscow Years,* Rufina credits their relationship with lifting Philby from his depression, nightmares, alcohol addiction and attempted suicide.

Of special interest here are Rufina's perceptions of Philby's sons and daughters who visited him in Moscow. Philby's most comprehensive biographer, Cave Brown, has presented a cynical picture of Philby's early attitude to family life, using it as a cover for his other activities when he is with Aileen and their four young children in Istanbul in 1947:

> All he wanted to do was to re-establish his reputation … a man of great ability doing secret work for the [British] government who was well and happily married with a brood of charming children.[25]

In the last phase of his life in Moscow however, from his late 50s until his death in 1988 at the age of seventy-six, Philby was visited by most of his children. Russians who knew Rufina said they could not believe that his spying career had no consequences for his children in Britain, but they seem to have suffered little prejudice there. As for their occasional holidays in the Soviet Union, they reacted differently. Rufina may have had little rapport with Philby's children but she doubted that any of them understood why their father did what he did and preferred to avoid the subject (at least in her company). Yet to her, this Russian woman, they unanimously expressed the same view: 'He was a great father.'[26]

Although none of Kim Philby's children appear to have modelled themselves on him, his eldest son John was closest to his father and shared his political views. During one of his twelve visits to his father in Moscow, John stole two red Soviet flags from their flagstaffs and laid them over his father's bed, indicating his respect for his father's ideals.[27] Although not drawn to Communism, John was a socialist. He trained as a carpenter in England and his father seemed to admire his eldest son for making his own, quite different way in life. In the only interview John gave about his father, John Philby seemed to regard his father as an almost heroic figure: 'I couldn't quite understand what he had done, but I couldn't condemn it.'[28]

The Walker Family Business

The most remarkable case of a family of spies may be that of the Walker family in America. John Anthony Walker, a retired US Navy Chief Warrant Officer, was convicted of spying for the Soviet Union from 1968 to 1985. The remarkable aspect to this case is that Walker had made spying a family business, having recruited his older brother Arthur and his only son Michael, who also worked for the US Navy, as partners in espionage. In addition, Walker tried to recruit his daughter Laura, who was in the Army, but she turned him down. Instead he called in his best friend, Jerry Whitworth, a Navy communications expert with high security clearance. All members of this spy ring passed their documents and information through John Walker to Soviet agents and were paid handsomely for their efforts. The Walkers and Whitworth helped the Soviets to decipher more than a million encrypted naval messages.

After eighteen years of amply rewarded spying for the Soviet Union, at the height of the Cold War, John Walker was 'betrayed' to the FBI by his ex-wife, Barbara, who had known for some years of Walker's activities.[29] *The New York Times* reported in 1987 that this group was regarded as 'the most damaging Soviet spy ring in history'.[30]

Whereas John Philby could derive comfort in the belief, or illusion, that his father was an ideological spy, driven by a strong and sustained belief in communism, Michael Walker could find no such rationalisation for his father's selling of secrets to the Russians. At the beginning, his father John Walker felt he needed the money; later, he wanted more. Similar motives seem to have imbued the other members of this ring with a bizarre sense of loyalty, engaged together in an illegal activity. Despite the nationalistic ideals of the armed services to which they had each pledged loyalty, these men succumbed to the more powerful impulse of personal greed.

A reading of Kim Philby's various writings beside interviews and statements by the Walker family reveals Philby's much greater intellectual control and sophistication, confirming his sobriquet 'master spy'. The Walkers, driven by their different financial and marital insecurities, alcohol and relatively unsophisticated educational background, represent some of the tensions of middle Americans of their time seeking economic advancement, excitement and meaning.

The mixed motives of John Walker's divorced wife, Barbara, without whose intervention her family might have remained 'free', in their way, are indicative. Barbara was resentful at John's failure to pay her alimony and the fact that he had acquired a young girlfriend and luxuries such as a boat and a small aeroplane. Her comments at first made FBI agents suspect that Barbara might have invented the spy charges out of anger, seeking revenge on her husband.[31] Yet Barbara had her complications too, having enjoyed an extended sexual relationship with John's older brother, Arthur, apparently not knowing that he was spying for her ex-husband. After speaking to the FBI, Barbara told Arthur what she had done and later claimed that she had wanted to give John a chance 'to run'. Moreover, she did not realise that, by telling the FBI what she had been concealing about her former husband since 1968, she would lose all connection to her son, Michael, who was sentenced to a jail term and turned against her.[32] Fortunately for American justice, Barbara Walker's contorted stories, her emotional instability, dependence on alcohol and mixed motives did not prevent the FBI's further, conclusive investigations.

A petty thief in his teenage years, John Walker had boasted that once a thief always a thief. If he had worked in a bank, he boasted, he would have stolen money. With access to secret documents, these were a suitable, lucrative alternative. His older brother Arthur (or 'Art') who had been the 'good boy' of the family, excelling at school and in the Navy, helped his troubled younger brother find a position in the Navy, despite his criminal record. Art's affair with Barbara however drove an emotional wedge between the two brothers and sibling rivalry continued after John's arrest and Arthur's questioning by the FBI, during which he denied knowledge of John's spying activities or spying himself. But Arthur was not a good liar: polygraph tests showed that he lied persistently in answer to these questions. Ironically, he received a longer prison sentence than his younger brother.

An interesting aspect of the trial proceedings was Arthur's realisation that most attention was focussed on his younger brother: this made him feel jealous and a little envious. In confessional mode, he tried to explain how he responded to John's request to steal secret documents:

> I knew what I was doing was wrong. But I just couldn't turn him in, and then the next thing that I did was let him talk me into getting him some documents. I don't know how to put this except to put it in religious terms. Once you start sinning, you either stop sinning or you just keep going and going and you carry this guilt around, subconsciously perhaps … It eats on you, and it would be nice to tell someone, but who can you tell?

Who? Just John. It was strictly John and I, and I would remain pretty upbeat with John when I saw him because I didn't want to disappoint him.[33]

Convicted of espionage, John's son Michael Walker was sent to gaol for 25 years because of his relatively minor role in the conspiracy and was released on parole in 2000. His father John and uncle Arthur Walker and Jerry Whitworth all received life sentences. However, thanks to his plea bargain John received one life sentence while his 'good' older brother was sentenced to three life terms and a $250,000 fine. It is difficult to imagine a reunion of this family of spies in this world.

Larry J. Kolb's Father

In the still hazardous but somewhat more secure zone of spying for (rather than against) one's country, it is possible to discern other patterns of family relations. Larry J. Kolb's 'confessions of a reluctant spy', for example, shows the depth of his indebtedness to his father even as he tries to distance himself. He writes:

My father was a senior United States intelligence official, or, if you prefer the lurid: a spymaster. I grew up all over the earth, and from when I was very young I had spies for uncles. By the time I was eleven, I'd learned to sit on the stairs in the dark and listen to my father and his men downstairs drinking into the night and saying things they thought no-one else would hear. I grew up knowing secrets. I grew up knowing my family's telephones were monitored. Our mail was intercepted. I grew up understanding everyone has the capacity to betray.[34]

Written from a safe house in Florida while he awaits resolution of problems with 'a certain foreign power' that has announced 'it wants to have a word with me', Kolb reflects widely and deeply on his initial rejection of a career in the CIA and his later recruitment and acceptance of a position there.

Kolb's memoir reveals the would-be secret world that a boy has glimpsed in the family home when his 'uncles' visit. Here is the older self describing that scene:

> They were watchers, listeners, fixers, buggers, burglars, bagmen, interrogators, polygraphers, safecrackers, photo analysts, photo doctors, pencil pushers, graph plotters, gunrunners, sheep-dippers. They were even seducers, and elicitors, and code clerks, and forgers. They were codebreakers and talent spotters and reports officers. And a few of them were the uncles every kid has who can make quarters come out of their ears. But one thing they were not was spies. Not a one of them. Not if you asked them.[35]

Larry Kolb's father had graduated from military intelligence, as a colonel on General Eisenhower's staff, to post-war US intelligence, as many others in post-war intelligence did. An early lesson the boy learns from his father is the great pains a spy must take to look ordinary: 'I don't want anything that draws attention to myself',[36] says the father. An observant and inquisitive boy, Larry is given snippets of information and advice on being an effective spy. High among these is the compartmentalising of knowledge: 'So it's my job,' his father asserts, 'to make sure my own men know as little as possible. No more than what they need to know, and the less the better'.[37] If they are captured by a hostile interrogator, they will not be able to give away vital information that could lead to the deaths of other agents.

An inevitable consequence of the limited knowledge available to actual secret agents in the field, and a frequent source of frustration, is that the stories they construct are always incomplete. Growing up in a spy's household, as Larry Kolb does, enables him to learn the terminology and grammar of espionage before he can understand their meaning and consequences. Later, he understands the frustration of the spy as storyteller:

> The information is almost always incomplete. The files are almost always ripe with code names and other obliquities no one has yet deciphered... I was frustrated as hell that I could never quite get to the bottom of a story from beginning to end.[38]

Nevertheless, he comes to a generic view of spy stories: that they are fundamentally tragic because they reveal that 'spying is an exercise in betrayal'.[39]

Many of Larry Kolb's father's assertions and precepts haunt his son. 'The greatest dangers to a spy aren't physical, but psychological' is one of them. But the greater psychological crisis for the father occurs not in the field but with his retirement from active service in his mid-50s. Having turned down a senior role in intelligence in Vietnam, Kolb senior is totally unprepared for retirement and his son feels the weight of a son's responsibility when a friend of his father's tried to recruit him with the line: 'Sons of intelligence men make good intelligence men. And the agency likes to hire them. They're easier to check out. Known commodities.'[40] Thereafter, as a successful international businessman, and more belatedly as a spy for the CIA, he finds that his father's words and precepts continue to haunt him, despite the knowledge that his father never seemed to enjoy his work and that 'his secret life hadn't exactly been a boon for him or his families'.[41] Nor has the son made a happier life for himself than his father's, as he shows when he describes his escape from the covert world he was born into to a state of anonymous and frustrated exile on a beach in Florida.

John H Richardson and Son

While the occupations of parents probably influence all children to some extent, the work of spies or secret agents seems to generate more anxiety and confusion among sons and daughters than most jobs. John H. Richardson's investigative memoir *My Father the Spy* explores this phenomenon in a personal way. Using personal journals, his own recollections and those of his older sister, letters, declassified government documents and recollections of ex-agents, Richardson writes a deeply personal, psychologically rich portrait of a father who had become an abstraction to his children. Seymour Hersh has endorsed *My Father the Spy* as 'the most compelling and complex book I've ever read on CIA family life, with all of its difficulties and contradictions'.[42]

John Richardson senior's career traces a contrasting trajectory to that of his son. In the early years of the Second World War, when he was an idealistic student of literature and sociology, Richardson senior was recruited into military intelligence and sent to Italy and Austria to hunt spies and saboteurs. In the early Cold War years he joined the CIA, recruiting spies for the United States in post-war Europe, manipulating governments in Greece, the Philippines, South Vietnam and South Korea. By contrast, in *his* early teenage years his son had turned to drugs and petty crime: at 16, military intelligence informs his father that John

Jr is a 'known user' of LSD. He is jailed in Hawaii for selling drugs. In Seoul he gets into a fight with military intelligence. His father believes that the 'honour' of the CIA is smeared by his son's behaviour. Despite the tactics and behaviour required by his profession, Richardson senior still believes in superior motives and chivalric notions of warfare.

At a distance, when the father is away on postings, or up close when the family is with him overseas or at home, he is a distant presence – 'planet Dad'. But the mystique that attaches to popular views of the spy do not apply to a rebellious, sceptical son: 'when you are a child in a house of secrets, you tend to find little glamour in mysteries. Secrets are just the papers on your father's desk.'[43]

The major crisis in this family's life occurs when John Richardson senior's CIA career as a spy is brought to an abrupt conclusion at the age of fifty. Richardson is head of station in Saigon in 1963. He has a major falling-out with US Ambassador Henry Cabot Lodge and is recalled to Washington. For the first time, a CIA station chief is publicly identified (a precursor in some respects of Valerie Plame's dilemmas) and rumours abound in the media about the reasons for Richardson's dismissal. The word 'insubordination' is bandied about. In a televised press conference, President Kennedy says he has looked through the record carefully and the CIA has done nothing but support policy. But for Richardson, his son reports 'it was the sound of a career ending'.[44] As a sop, he is given a job back at Langley training young spies. In a bizarre turn, Richardson buys a block of land next to CIA headquarters and builds a big white house on it. He becomes progressively more hard-line conservative.

The fascinating aspect of *My Father the Spy* is the son's account of his father's emotional turmoil, which is hidden from public view, over events in Vietnam following his departure, notably the deaths of Diem and the Ngo brothers. The former CIA station chief attends a wake in Washington for the Diem regime and writes an account of the night:

> We all joined in expressing concern over how Vietnam – and the United States – would face the problems ahead without Diem's strength and leadership, and in wondering how our Government could have been so blind as to have contributed directly to his overthrow and death.[45]

Had the ex-CIA chief in Saigon conspired in this coup and the deaths of Diem and his brother? Late in his father's life, his son, rehabilitated and now a writer, obtains glimpses of his father's dilemma in Vietnam, especially when the Ambassador reads him the fateful telegram from President Kennedy ordering an end to the Diem regime 'unless you have overriding objections'.[46] Richardson tells his son that it was the biggest regret of his life that he did not resign at that point instead of obeying his superiors. Ambassador Lodge had said he did not have an aeroplane available to take President Diem out of the country and this allowed the deaths to occur.[47] Deniability of involvement and responsibility is a crucial feature of such covert operations.

Australian writer Morris West's novel *The Ambassador* (1965) which was completed in Saigon in October 1963, contains a depiction of a CIA chief in Saigon in the early 1960s called Harry Yaffa. In an author's note to the novel, West warns that readers who seek to 'identify the actors in this drama with real personages' will find themselves 'betrayed into anomalies'. Nevertheless many readers have assumed that, despite anomalies, Harry Yaffa is a version of John H. Richardson. West describes Yaffa as:

> Short, pudgy, dapper and benign. His hands were soft and beauti-fully manicured. His silk shirt was elegantly cut with a monograph woven in blue thread under his left breast. His voice was soft. His manner was full of charm and deprecation. He was reputed to be devious, ruthless and without moral scruples of any kind.[48]

Unlike John Richardson junior's portrait of a conflicted individual with severe doubts about his country's policies in South Vietnam, West's CIA chief is certain about the need for a change of government. West's novelistic character is an amalgam of stock images of CIA spies and popular media images of John H. Richardson. In West's novel, it is the idealistic and conflicted American ambassador in Saigon who draws sympathy from the reader for the difficult situation in which he is placed. It is the actual CIA chief's son who is left to defend the honour of his real life father by quoting from a review of West's popular novel:

> Only those readers with discernment and retentive memories will recall that Richardson departed Vietnam well before the

coup, and that his chief 'crime' appears to have consisted of counselling caution concerning the viability and the aftermath of certain drastic remedies that were prescribed by others.[49]

But the son admits that this review seems to have been written by a former CIA colleague who was concerned to improve the image of the CIA. A stronger and somewhat more objective analysis by Evan Thomas contends that 'The coup against Diem was orchestrated not by the CIA but rather by [Ambassador] Lodge and a cabal of Kennedy advisors in the State Department and the White House. The CIA at the time opposed getting rid of Diem because it could envision the political chaos in Vietnam that was to follow'.[50]

Despite such retrospective defences, which arise in large part from a son's determined efforts to fully know his father, he can never quite do so. The secretive life of the spy will always leave the 'real' person shrouded in mystery – or in politics. That is the frustration and appeal of the figure of the spy; and why he or she appears in such protean forms in literature and life. One thing seems certain: the lives of spies and their families are usually conflicted and are never predictable.

Two

Loyalty Tests:
Spies Under Review

Secrets are the lifeblood of spying. Without them, a spy's life would seem pointless: all that training to obtain by licit or illicit means the enemy's secrets would be without purpose. But is the corollary true? In the utopian situation of secrets no longer being possible, would knowledge of the truth always liberate? And whose truth would we trust? The CIA seems to profess firm belief with its gospel pronouncement in the foyer at Langley Park that 'the truth shall make you free'. Oddly perhaps, the Australian founder of WikiLeaks, Julian Assange, seems to agree, though his premises are clearly different from the CIA's. Having published over a million US military documents from the wars in Iraq and Afghanistan on the WikiLeaks website in 2010, Assange defended his action by saying that they revealed the 'truth' about these conflicts from a 'global' perspective. For better or worse, neither the CIA's nor WikiLeaks's claims on the truth are likely to satisfy many individual states or the international community. Despite those who are sceptical of its value, the spying game in its many guises seems bound to continue; and with it, the continual testing of perceived truth and loyalty.

Films, novels and memoirs continue to provide entertaining insights into the involvement of individuals in the clandestine struggles of the past century. Two films and two novels will be considered here which show how power-plays affect the pursuit of truth or villainy, and loyalties are tested. The films *Lust, Caution* and *The Lives of Others*, and the novels *A Captive in the Land* by James Aldridge and *The Prisoner of Mount Warning* by Michael Wilding explore different aspects of the spying game and its impact on individuals.

Lust, Caution

The film *Lust, Caution* was directed by Ang Lee and released in 2007: it explores espionage and its impacts on individuals and communities during the second Sino–Japanese War (also known in China as the War of Resistance against Japan, 1937–45). The film is based on a story by Chinese author Eileen Chang (1920–95) whose personal experience is drawn on in both the story and film.[1] The film's heroine Wang Chia-Chih is a college drama student who is recruited to a clandestine cell in Shanghai committed to resisting the Japanese occupation. She is given the task of seducing and entrapping Mr Yi, a Chinese collaborator who has risen to a powerful position in the Japanese security force. In Chang's story, Yi is 'a self-satisfied career spy and philanderer' and may have been drawn partly from Chang's first husband.[2] The story and the film both explore the ethics and motives of two kinds of spy – the apparently cold and calculating professional who works for the Japanese occupiers versus the amateur who sets out to spy on and destroy him but impulsively (perhaps perversely) sacrifices herself and her cause to save him.

Lust, Caution explores some of the issues implicit in E. M. Forster's often quoted remark: 'If I had to choose between betraying my country and betraying my friend, I hope I should have the guts to betray my country.' The trouble is that the young woman Jiuzhi becomes caught in the very honey-trap that she has devised, under instruction from her revolutionary cell, in order to entrap Mr Li. The theme of play-acting is important. In masquerading as a young married woman who enjoys shopping, playing mah-jongg, going to the theatre, flirting and making love to an older man, Jiazhi risks losing the identity that previously drove her actions. In this process, she comes to enjoy the role and inhabit it fully; and becomes a 'detached spectator' of the body's activities.[3] In the critical scene at the jewellery shop when Jiazhi's betrayal of her lover is planned to result in his assassination, she warns him and he escapes. But he shows no mercy. He orders the execution of his lover Jiazhi and her fellow underground supporters.

The implications of Jiazhi's betrayal of her cause and her colleagues are intriguing. What has happened to her love of country – the nationalist ideology – that had apparently inspired her and her fellow resistance workers? Has she been a bourgeois dreamer all along, always likely to bend like a reed towards the holder of power? Has she been misled by exotic sex? (The extended sado-masochistic sex scenes in the movie received an NC-17 rating in the US.) Ang Lee's direction shows the masochism and violence in these scenes morphing into mutual erotic pleasure. Pleasure and pain are intertwined. Yi is ruthless but we learn that he in some sense loves Jiazhi. Her main task was to inform on her lover's movements and to deliver him to his assassins. In this crucial task she fails. It is not surprising that Chinese nationalist critics were angry at the film's portrayal of an ultimately weak woman and an almost sympathetic collaborator and traitor; but this is the complex reality with which we are presented.

The 'truths' displayed in *Lust, Caution* extend beyond those that might be revealed by historical documents. They also test E. M. Forster's perceptions of the paramount importance of personal friendship. Jiazhi and Yi are not 'friends' in any conventional sense. Yet their sexual relationship seems to transcend the realities of international conflict. Personal vulnerabilities are tested in this film against communal beliefs and loyalties. The most 'human' spies are perhaps the least effective.

A Captive in the Land

The Cold War that followed hard on the heels of the Second World War was another theatre in which national allegiances and personal loyalties often found themselves in conflict. James Aldridge's novel *A Captive in the Land* (1962) captures these Cold War dissonances close to the time of their political prominence. An expatriate Australian journalist, war correspondent and novelist based in London, Aldridge obtained a wide readership with his novel, *The Diplomat* (1950), which was translated into twenty-five languages and was a bestseller in the Soviet Union. The novel explores human and political motives in an Anglo-American and Russian dispute over Iran and Iranian oil. Unusually for a novel from the West, it shows a sophisticated understanding of Marxism in its Soviet contexts. *A Captive in the Land* further reveals Aldridge's interest in the political and personal motives that drive Soviet and Western (especially British) relations.

The protagonist in *A Captive in the Land* is Rupert Royce, a rich but restless Englishman who has given away his wealth and is trying to live an 'ordinary' life. But an extraordinary event occurs when, working as a meteorologist, he parachutes from an aeroplane over the Arctic icecap. The wreck of the aircraft he had seen on the icecap contains a badly injured survivor whom Rupert nurses and eventually brings to safety. The survivor, Alexei Vodopyanov, later invites his saviour to Russia and Rupert's experience there, as a potential spy for the British, is an odyssey of attempts to uncover and understand the secrets of the Soviet Union – its bombs, submarines and radar equipment, but more fundamentally, the Russian mind, character or soul.

Rupert Royce's long period of enforced intimacy with his Russian friend in the Arctic makes him a figure of suspicion to his supposed allies, the British and American security forces. Meanwhile, the Russians try to conscript Rupert by making him an official hero of the Soviet people for his famous rescue. When he is invited to visit Alexei and his wife in Russia, Rupert is asked to gather intelligence for the British secret service. His genuine interest in the remnants of ancient Greek civilisation around the Black Sea will be his cover. He is given a pen and invisible ink for recording his observations. But Rupert does not accept money from the British, or indeed, after some equivocation, from the Russians when they later try to buy his loyalty. Royce thus remains an amateur spy, testing conflicting loyalties on his own pulse. In the tradition of Sherlock Holmes, he will act independently on the evidence and make his own judgments.

The briefing given to Rupert Royce by his potential British handler, Admiral J. B. Mille, indicates a traditional style of intelligence gathering based on close observation of people and places and seeking the 'truth' about a foreign power – to discover especially 'the true sources of this Soviet desire to win over the world to the communist ideology'.[4] This kind of intelligence gathering bears a curious resemblance to traditional notions of higher learning in the humanities; and is a reminder of emphasis on intellectual distinction in university studies in the foundation years of the CIA.[5] Cultural knowledge and understanding is at the core of this kind of intelligence gathering. But complications occur when Rupert becomes aware he is being 'shadowed' during his travels. Trust is difficult to establish when even Nina, Alexei's apparently independent-minded wife – to whom Rupert is physically and emotionally attracted, and finally succumbs – seems to be spying on him. From these personal, conflicted relations as much as from what he learns by more 'objective' means, Rupert intuitively recognises that he and Nina share a 'moral identity' which in some respects brings him closer to the Russian woman than to his own wife and country.

As is appropriate in a Cold War novel, the tensions in *A Captive in the Land* remain unresolved at the end. The novel resists the melodrama of assassinations and executions. After his crisis of identity in Russia, Rupert catches a train from Moscow to the West. He tears up the cheque the Russians have given him and smashes the invisible ink pen given to him by British intelligence, thus symbolically severing obligations to both sides. Leaving the complications of his Russian experience behind, he hopes to return to his 'one life' in England, but the thunder and storms of his experience in the Soviet Union still rumble.

Michael Wilding and *The Prisoner of Mount Warning*

The Cold War also reverberates in the short fiction and novels of Sydney-based writer Michael Wilding, but in a different key. Perhaps the distance in time and space from the centres of Cold War activity that engaged Aldridge in the 1950s have contributed to Wilding's more ironic and satiric representations of the spying game. Twenty-four years younger than Aldridge, Wilding is an Englishman in Australia who experienced the later stages of the Cold War through Australian and international reactions to the Vietnam War (or, as the Vietnamese call it, the American War). Wilding's left-wing orientation has contributed to a lively critique of American neo-imperialism and engagement with a youthful generation's attempts to liberate themselves from their parents' habits and preconceptions.

The title story of Wilding's selection *Under Saturn* (1988) features a protagonist who airs his conspiracy theories about the CIA, UFOs, break-ins and sexual entanglements. The narrative is carried forward chiefly by dialogue in which the main character's paranoia about the state of the world is projected onto sunny Sydney, a deceptively benign city where brutality and hypocrisy reign. How should the thinking young person react to these conditions? The alternatives of engaging politically or perhaps even spiritually are considered. But Wilding's character gloomily retreats from late Cold War challenges and the astrological sign of Saturn triumphs.

A later novel by Wilding[6] engages humorously and convincingly with Cold War reverberations in Australia in the 1970s and after. The novel is a comic and satiric fable about suppression of freedom, and the paranoia and plots which individuals and communities create when they feel suppressed or threatened. This is territory that Wilding had traversed previously in a variety of forms. The present writer had first-hand experience of the power of Wilding's fictions when he chaired a session on 'Plots' at an Adelaide Writers Festival in the late 1970s in which Wilding was a leading speaker. Wilding and his friends had spread a rumour that the author would be attacked in the marquee where he was programmed to speak. The tent was packed, the atmosphere tense when two motorcyclists in dark helmets roared across the adjacent parking area and skidded to a halt outside the tent. In slow motion, the dark helmeted figures advanced through the crowd and remained stationed, as enforcers or bodyguards, during Wilding's literary-political exposition of plots. His talk projected images of heroic revolutionaries, drug busts, CIA helicopters and other precursors of the later British TV series *Spooks*.

In *The Prisoner of Mount Warning*, Wilding exercises his talents in theatre of the absurd to trace the investigation of an alter ego, Plant, into the claims of one Edward Dorritt that the latter has been imprisoned and tortured in a form of sex-slavery by informants for the Australian security service. The fact that security services in both Britain and Australia have traditionally been more critical of left- than right-wing activists lends some credence to this situation. Dorritt's cover job was as a researcher and interviewer charged with compiling a survey of alternative presses and their publishers, editors and writers. This plot device enables the author, through his appropriately named Plant, to explore the observations, dreams and conspiracy theories of an alternative, 'liberated', often drug-inspired culture in northern New South Wales and Queensland, where writers and intellectuals who were active in the 1970s and '80s have retired to more agricultural pursuits.

The semi-deranged Dorritt is not really 'of' this culture. But like William Dorritt in Charles Dickens's novel *Little Dorritt* (1858), the latter-day Edward draws on a deep vein of fantasy to sustain him. Like Dickens's Dorritt too, Wilding's character suffers a breakdown that makes him an unreliable narrator of events. Wilding's Charles Dorritt takes a contemporary cure – a creative writing course – as therapy for his ailments. This gives him an apparent point of connection with his interviewees and he obtains such gems of observation from them as 'there's no left left'.[7] Ironically, these former sophisticates of the city bemoan the de-radicalisation of politics while upholding the virtue of protecting 'the last remnants of local agriculture' in the marihuana crops of northern New South Wales. In this culture, trippers are truth-tellers – or think they are. This is Wilding territory.

In the world conjured by Wilding in this novel, the power of storytelling is paramount. Stories of spooks from the popular media interweave with personal observations and memories. Thus when Plant interviews Rose to ascertain whether she and her friends have in fact kidnapped and imprisoned Dorritt, Plant has to grapple with the conundrum of stories within stories. Plant asks why Rose and her associates were suspicious of Dorritt:

> 'They thought he was some sort of, I don't know, infiltrator or something.'
> 'Infiltrator?'
> 'Informer, then.'
> 'Informing who?'
> 'Who knows? Drug squad. Secret service. Spooks incorporated. It could have been anybody.'
> 'So?'
> 'So, kidnapping, torture, drugs and sex-slavery, I guess. If that's how he saw it.'
> 'You're telling me you kidnapped him?'
> 'It was fashionable at the time,' she said.
> 'Fashionable?'
> 'The Red Brigades and the Tupamaros and the Baader-Meinhof and Patty Hearst. Even the media families were into it. Everybody was doing it. And writing about it. Novels. Movies. It was like a sort of theme of the times'.[8]

These Australian proto-revolutionaries see themselves as contributing to an international pattern. But are they puppets of some grand design? Or just deluded followers of fashion? In torture, if they were indeed into it, they were perhaps ahead of their times? Abu Ghraib, Bagram and Guantanamo came later. This does not rule out the possibility that Dorritt has indeed been the victim of sex slavery. But Dorritt is mixed up – is he a perpetrator of plots or their victim?

As befits the 'mystery' genre, *The Prisoner of Mount Warning* offers a denouement that doesn't quite tie things up. We learn that Dorritt's 'controller' is his thesis supervisor, Professor Oates, who hints to Plant that he is a recruiter and spymaster for the secret service. He prefers the 'great game' in the 'real' world to the mundane affairs of a university.[9] His role as a recruiter of potential intelligence officers among clever university students is very credible – the presence of academic recruiters in the universities at this time is well known. But is Oates deluded too? He certainly knows his English spy fiction and quotes Durrell, Oppenheim and Maugham. He reinforces the persuasive view that the 'great game' is intricately interlaced with literature – with stories that refer to real worlds and also to the way readers and writers distort and reinvent reality through the wealth of ambiguities available to sophisticated users of language. A myriad of memoirs and histories from the old East and West reinforce harsh realities of the Cold War and its aftermath. But literary texts like Wilding's demonstrate the continuing capacity for fertile storytellers to revisit with wit and humour those times and marvel at the languages they have spawned.

The Lives of Others

If the largely vicarious experiences of Michael Wilding's 1970s revolutionaries seem a long way from actual political repression, Florian Henckel von Donnersmarck's powerful dramatic film, *The Lives of Others* (2007) (*Das Leben der Anderen*),[10] offers an intense treatment of East Germany's repression of its own citizens in the 1980s and the reprisals that follow disobedience of that communist dictatorship's orders. With theatrical panache, von Donnersmarck has set his cinematic drama in the iconic year 1984, recalling George Orwell's novel depicting the deadening impact of a totalitarian state on its citizens. In *The Lives of Others*, viewers are confronted with individuals who watch over each other not for each other's good but to gain advantage and control. They represent a society saturated with spies and the corruption that follows from this.

Since the collapse of the Berlin Wall in 1989 and the beginning of the end of the Soviet Union in 1991, the role of the East German secret police, the Stasi, has been exhaustively reviewed. The most vivid accounts include British historian Timothy Garton Ash's *The File* (1997) and Australian writer Anna Funder's *Stasiland* (2003). Written like a novel, Funder's book casts the author as a character in her accounts of life in the former German Democratic Republic. But *The Lives of Others* adds another dimension to accounts in its dramatisation of the psychology of spying and its impact on the private lives of individuals. The film shows that spying can reveal surprising aspects of others' lives that can sometimes change the spy as well as those who are spied upon.

An early caption in *The Lives of Others* informs the vicarious viewer that the Stasi employs 100,000 people and 200,000 informers. Their goal is 'to know everything' about their targets. Captain Gerd Wiesler, who lectures at Stasi College, informs trainee officers that the most effective way of telling truth from lies is 'non-stop interrogation'. An apparently soulless servant of the state at this stage, Wiesler turns a blind eye to the effects of torture and manufactured evidence. But Captain Wiesler's transfer to a surveillance operation for the Ministry of Culture brings him into contact with a world of books and theatre which had previously eluded his notice.

When he is tasked with carrying out intensive surveillance of a famous East German writer, Georg Dreyman, Wiesler is at first punctilious and dedicated to the task. Captain Wiesler and a colleague listen in an attic above Dreyman's bugged apartment to all conversations that take place there and even to the love-making of Dreyman and his girlfriend, Christa-Maria Sieland, a well known actress. For Wiesler's dim-witted assistant this sexual activity is high entertainment and confirms why he prefers the surveillance of writers and artists to priests and other potential dissidents. 'These artists,' he says, 'they're always at it.'

The changes in Captain Wiesler are registered differently in subtle changes of expression and behaviour. These responses reveal the paid spy's frustration with the abuse of power by his superiors in the Stasi and a growing awareness of the poetry of art – of music, drama and literature, through the lives of these 'others' on whom he has been commanded to report. In one critical scene Wiesler, the spy, is shown reading a book of Brecht's poetry that he has 'borrowed' from Dreyman's apartment; in another he witnesses the way his target deals with grief after learning of a theatre-director friend's suicide as a result of cruel hounding by the Stasi: Dreyman turns to his piano and plays his friend's composition, 'Sonata for a Good Man'. Despite all the well-founded post-war scepticism in Germany about the civilising value of art, given its abuse by the Nazis, we glimpse here its power of transcendence through the eyes and ears of a Communist spy in another repressive regime.

Yet the vicarious experience of spying on others offers more disillusionment and despair than these scenes may suggest. The compromises that Georg Dreyman is forced to make to remain a practising artist in Communist East Germany are exceeded by those of his attractive actress-lover Christa, who has sex with a Party boss to retain her place in the theatre and to fund her drug habit. When Georg learns of this he appeals to her better self: 'You don't need him. Have faith in your talent.' She replies: 'You get in bed with them too,' and leaves for her assignation. Moved by their real-life dilemma, of which he is a privileged witness, the spy Captain Wiesler leaves his listening-post at the upstairs room soon after and discovers Christa in a nearby bar drinking to dull her pain. Wiesler addresses Christa as a fan of her as an actress and reinforces Georg's view that she is 'a great artist'. In reply, Christa says, 'You are a good man.' This is darkly ironic. Yet despite some of the contradictory events that follow, this exchange stands as a small beacon of hope against the general darkness of a repressive regime.

From this critical moment, Gerd Wiesler, the Stasi officer, becomes an active individual instead of a cog in the great machine of state security. When Christa betrays Georg by informing her interrogators of the hiding-place of a typewriter used to produce incriminating documents, Wiesler saves Georg (and thinks he is also saving Christa) by secretly removing the typewriter before his apartment is searched. Not knowing that her betrayal has been nullified, however, Christa rushes from the apartment and is killed by a passing vehicle.

The reprisals begin. Wiesler is told, 'Your career is over.' Having failed the Stasi in their mission to 'find something on Dreyman', Captain Wiesler is demoted to the task of steaming open letters in a basement.

One of his similarly demoted colleagues is recognisable as a young career officer who made the mistake of joking about the East German President, Erich Honecker, in a state where joking is subversion.

The Lives of Others ends with the collapse of the Berlin Wall in 1989 and some of its consequences. Two years later, Georg learns from the sleazy former Minister for Culture that he was not considered innocent by the government, as he had thought, but was under 'full surveillance'. He begins to read the files on himself and identifies his secret sharer of those years as HGW XX/7. Cut to two years later. An older Wiesler buys Georg Dreyman's new book *Sonata for a Good Man* in the Karl Marx Bookshop. The book is dedicated to 'HGW XX/7'. The shop assistant asks, 'Do you want it gift-wrapped?' The ex-spy replies, 'No, it's for me.'

A powerful critique of *The Lives of Others* by Timothy Garton Ash in *The New York Review of Books*[11] argues that the film misses what Hannah Arendt called 'the banality of evil': 'Nowhere was evil more banal than in the net-curtained, plastic-wood cabins and caravans of the German Democratic Republic.' Such banality, Ash contends, is very difficult to recreate for a wider audience. More significantly, he criticises as unlikely Wiesler's conversion from a 'driven puritan' at the beginning of the film to a man who would sacrifice his own career for a writer he hardly knew. Yet this redemptive act has a powerful logic in the film's subtext, which reveals occasional glimpses of a human need greater than the repressive socio-political elite of socialist East Germany can satisfy.

Ironically, the deeper a spy can pry into the lives of others, the more convinced he or she may feel that a richer and more fulfilling life is possible. To the outside observer, as Georg temporarily becomes when he identifies Wiesler and watches him from a car, the former spy's solitary existence may seem dingy and desperate. But appearances can be deceptive. When Wiesler sees *Sonata for a Good Man* in the bookshop, and reads that it is dedicated to him, he betrays no obvious emotion. But his words to the bookseller reveal his recognition of a mutual regard between the author and himself across the false barriers of a repressive politics and ideology.

The films and novels considered in this chapter portray a generally grim world of conflict and betrayal. Only Michael Wilding's post-Vietnam satiric narrative *The Prisoner of Mount Warning* approaches Graham Greene's notion of spy stories as 'entertainments'. Like Greene's

Our Man in Havana or le Carré's *The Tailor of Panama*, Wilding's novel portrays a world of paranoia and invention in which 'the game's the thing' – storytelling becomes an end in itself. Aldridge's apparently implacable Cold War opponents, the USSR and Britain, on the other hand, engage in a form of shadow boxing where no knockout punch seems likely and the rumble of distant thunder plays on the nerves of the protagonists. In the murky depths of wartime collaborators and traitorous acts, *Lust, Caution* shows how lust, or love, can overcome caution and blow an undercover operation with fatal consequences. Of these texts, only von Donnersmarck's *The Lives of Others* suggests redemptive possibilities for the spy; but this involves a betrayal of his training and previous outlook and an acceptance of relegation to powerlessness in the state machine.

Three

Secret Agents and the Search for Truth

Introduction

Secrets and lies abound wherever public requirements and private needs come into conflict. Nowhere is this more evident than in the lives of secret agents who work in the service of a government or a cause. Yet while the task of some agents may be to plant disinformation in order to mislead or confuse their enemy, the purported goal of espionage is usually to learn the 'truth' of a situation – the power structure of a regime, for instance, or the battle plans of an opponent. When government or other bureaucracies are directing the activities of spies, and knowledge of operations is restricted to those who 'need to know', the 'whole truth' of a situation may be almost impossible for a single person to know or understand. Hence the appositeness of the phrase from T. S. Eliot's poem 'Gerontion', which was popularised by the CIA's chief of counter-intelligence, James Jesus Angleton, when he described the experience of espionage as being caught 'in a wilderness of mirrors'.[1] (Angleton seems to have been intrigued by Eliot's persona and is even said to have adopted a Thomas Stearns Eliot appearance.[2])

Secret Intelligence and 'Truth'

Although many workers in the burgeoning intelligence services attached to Western governments talk of the boredom and bureaucratic red tape that bedevil their working lives, it is remarkable how many over the past century have also claimed the importance of imagination, both to their work and to their lives more generally. A good example is Michael

Thwaites, the Australian Security Intelligence Organization's former chief of counter-intelligence who supervised the defection to Australia in 1954 of Vladimir and Evdokia Petrov, who were KGB agents posing as diplomats in the embassy of the USSR in Canberra at the time. In his account of these events, *Truth Will Out*, Thwaites mentions the circumstances of his own recruitment to ASIO from a lectureship in English at the University of Melbourne. 'Out of the blue', he says, Colonel Charles Spry, director-general of ASIO, invited him to a meeting. Spry told Thwaites that 'a very effective Soviet spy ring [was] operating in Australia' and Australia's Prime Minister, Robert Menzies, had asked Colonel Spry to upgrade the security services. 'You're a poet aren't you?' Spry said. (Thwaites had won the King's Medal for Poetry when he was a student at Oxford.) 'You have imagination. We want imagination in the organization and people with analytical skills.'[3] Thwaites accepted the invitation and made his contribution to Australian and international history with the defection of the Petrovs followed by Thwaites's ghost-written biography of the Russian spies' lives, *Empire of Fear*.

The exercise of imagination, and the movement of imaginative sympathy, can of course complicate moral dilemmas. In Thwaites's case his imagination seems to have operated within the moral boundaries of his Anglican religious upbringing and the precepts of Moral Rearmament, the anti-Communist movement which he had adopted in post-war years. Thwaites's axis of good and evil was thus quite strictly defined. But in the fictional works of Graham Greene and John le Carré, for example, two acknowledged masters of espionage fiction, these moral boundaries are more blurred as their imaginations engage with the conflicting demands of keeping secrets and telling lies.

The psychological perils of immersing oneself in the secret world are encapsulated in le Carré's *The Spy Who Came in from the Cold* when the author reflects on the role of his protagonist, Alec Leamas, who has been sent by British Intelligence to work undercover in East Germany:

> In itself, the practice of deception is not particularly exacting; it is a matter of experience, of professional *expertise*; it is a facility most of us can acquire. But while a confidence trickster, a play actor or a gambler can return from his performance to the ranks of his admirers, the secret agent enjoys no such relief.[4]

Le Carré expands on this. Deception in such circumstances, he says, is first of all a matter of self-defence. The agent 'must protect himself not only from without but from within, and against the most natural of impulses.' Most difficult of all, 'he must under all circumstances withhold himself from those in whom he should naturally confide', including family, lovers and friends.[5]

Writers of fiction or biography about individuals involved in espionage engage with the psychological effects of sustained deception in a variety of ways, as we shall see. Psychiatrists also have their ways and means of doing this. Psychological profiling of factors in a person's upbringing, background and behaviour which may prefigure an effective career in intelligence is widely used by psychologists in intelligence agencies, but may be of limited value. Case studies or composite descriptions based on a number of case studies can also provide insights. For example, psychiatrist David Charney, who has treated a number of high profile 'caught spies' in the US including Robert Hanssen, has developed a model of stages in the experience of a 'composite spy'.[6] Charney's composite figure typically experiences nine stages as he moves to a decision to spy for a foreign power, is recruited, proceeds with his tasks, retreats, goes into dormancy for a time, then is arrested, when the anger, brooding and remorse set in. Charney rejects easy assumptions about greed – the typical kneejerk reaction from an intelligence agency to 'traitors' in their ranks – that 'the greedy bugger did it for the money'. The 'trained subconscious mind' of the psychiatrist is a more effective tool, he claims, than the rush to judgment. In Charney's view, a core psychological insight can be derived from the cases of the caught spy: he (95 per cent are men) suffers from 'an intolerable sense of personal failure as privately defined by the person'.

Novels and Films: *Our Man in Havana, The Tailor of Panama*

I would argue that the most profound insights into the mental state and behaviour of men and women engaged in espionage are provided by writers of novels and life-stories – autobiography and biography. A central feature of such narratives is often the capacity of individuals to deal with secrets and lies. Films can sometimes complicate and enrich the insights of novelists and biographers.

Two novels which engage closely with these issues are Graham Greene's *Our Man in Havana* (1958) and John le Carré's *The Tailor of Panama* (1996), both of which are set in Latin America. The film of *The Tailor of Panama*, directed by John Boorman and starring Australian actor Geoffrey Rush as Harry Pendel, the tailor, gives another dimension to the presentation of these issues. Le Carré acknowledged the formative influence of Greene's novel on his own when he remarked that, 'After Greene's *Our Man in Havana* the notion of an intelligence fabricator would not leave me alone'.[7] Indeed, Greene's vacuum-cleaner salesman in Havana and le Carré's tailor in Panama both have a gift of the gab which attracts both admiration and scepticism. Their sometimes coruscating sales talk carries both themselves and their listeners away at times; and the slips they make occasionally reveal gaps in their assumed personae, keeping readers on their toes. The imposter-spies are often on the edge of being 'caught out'. But what is remarkable about each of them is that they manage to convince key people, and even at times themselves, that they have secret intelligence of international significance to impart when what they offer are the products of imagination, invention and luck.

The novel and film of *The Tailor of Panama* are closely interlinked. John le Carré was executive producer and author of the screenplay for the film under Boorman's direction. Geoffrey Rush, who plays the film's protagonist, was commuting from Melbourne to Panama for the filming on location, and to Dublin, where studio filming was done. Rush has said that le Carré's novel was a companion-piece and reference work for him to understand the character of Harry Pendel, the half-Irish, half-Jewish London Eastender who learnt his tailoring in prison but transforms himself into a tailor with pedigree in Panama.[8] There was some consideration of filming in Puerto Rico but Boorman insisted that it be done on location in Panama itself,[9] where Noriega had invented a Communist opposition and Harry Pendel in the film invents a 'silent Opposition' for his handlers in British intelligence.

Characters in films come with the cultural baggage of their previous roles. Geoffrey Rush is a brilliant impresario and he has remarked that his previous role as the Marquis de Sade partly informed his playing of Harry Pendel. Similarly, it might be said, he carried *The Tailor of Panama* with him in memory when he subsequently played Peter Sellers in his multiple guises. The role of Andy Osnard, the inexperienced British secret service agent who recruits and runs Harry Pendel as a spy in Panama also carries cinematic cultural baggage. Pierce Brosnan, who plays Osnard in the film, was consciously countering his recent persona of James Bond. Another clever piece of intertextuality in the film is Boorman's absurdist playwright Harold Pinter as Harry Pendel's Uncle Benny, the Jewish Londoner who has set him on his path of crime and redemption and reappears as Harry's unreliable but persuasive inner voice of conscience, with gems such as: 'Try sincerity, that's a virtue'.

Le Carré's character Harry Pendel is the author's most brilliant invention of a con-man since Magnus Pym's father Rick in *A Perfect Spy*. Both characters seem to emerge from le Carré's memories of his con-man father, Ronald Cornwell, who was jailed for fraud during his son's early childhood and went bankrupt twice during his son's early twenties. *The Tailor of Panama*, for all its humorous invention – in the spirit of what Greene called his 'entertainment', *Our Man in Havana,* but far more buoyant than Greene's novel – revolves around the most consequential lie imaginable, the fabrication of intelligence which leads to the invasion of another country. In this, as in other respects, le Carré's novel anticipates the American invasion of Iraq in 2003, with British and Australian support. Le Carré, it should be said, strongly opposed the latter invasion.

Among the most discomforting insights into secrets and lies in *The Tailor of Panama* is how closely allied they are to wit, humour and performativity. Le Carré shows, as Freud has also shown, that while jokes may seem innocuous, they often arise from subconscious anxieties. The chief of these in le Carré's novel is the fear of discovery, a fear that leads Harry to scale the heights of fantasy. As he had learnt to do in prison, Harry becomes a performer: 'A performer is a performer. If your audience isn't with you, it's against you,' he thinks. The author explains: '[W]ith his own fictions in tatters, he needed to enrich the fictions of others.'[10] Harry knows he has 'an excessive dose of fluence'[11] but he can't stop himself. The rationalisation and self-justification take over as Harry ponders his inability to tell his wife Louisa about his past and he tries to persuade himself that '*Everything in the world is true if you invent it hard enough and love the person it's for!*'[12] As he slides across the various accents and registers at his command – Irish, Cockney, Jewish and the professional patter of a tailor who has remade his past – Harry Pendel exposes the human vulnerability which makes him an endearing figure despite the calamities he sets in train.

Harry Pendel is not alone in his manipulation of truth and reality. His handler for British intelligence, Andy Osnard, after failing at several other jobs, seems to find a suitable vocation in MI6. Le Carré writes ironically of Osnard's perception of his career:

> Osnard had found his Grail. Here at last was his true Church of England, his rotten borough with a handsome budget. Here were sceptics, dreamers, zealots and mad abbots. And the cash to make them real.[13]

The metaphoric foundations of secret intelligence in religion, theatre and economics are laid. To these we must add the Imperial theme, for Osnard is told by his bosses that 'The British task is to persuade the Americans to fill the vacuum they've created [in Panama] … We're the last of the Romans. We have the knowledge but they have the power.'[14]

These are the deeply flawed ideological bases from which an anti-heroic James Bond look-alike figure in the movie of *The Tailor of Panama* emerges. When Harry tells Andy Osnard of opposition among some Panamanians to the regime in power, Osnard elevates this to an upper case 'Silent Opposition'. He rewrites the gossip from Harry who has been ironically codenamed BUCHAN (after the author of spy fiction, John Buchan), until the material 'fitted like perfectly turned pegs into analysts' Black Holes'.[15] This new fiction, or hot intelligence, has been made from a tailor's cuttings. The metaphor is comically apt. As Harry tells himself in one of his disconcertingly revealing asides to himself, it is 'All fluence. Loose threads, plucked from the air, woven and cut to measure.'[16] While the odd sceptical voice is raised about the lack of 'substance' or 'collateral' of this intelligence by evaluators back at London Station, such voices are overridden by the perceived urgency of a 'visionary' conclusion which will lead to intervention. We heard all this again recently in the run-up to the Iraq war. A senior American, desperate for a 'smoking gun' or other 'peg' on which to hang the invasion of Panama, says: 'This is a moment for decisive action and having the national conscience adapt retrospectively. The national conscience will do that – we can help it'.[17] But unlike Cuba, where

Castro denied the existence of his Russian rockets, while photographs showed they were there, nothing so decisive can be shown in Panama. Denials of an alleged silent opposition to the Panamanian government seemed to strengthen its likelihood. Whatever basis of evidence the Americans chose to believe, the American invasion of Panama, overseen by President George H. W. Bush and codenamed Operation Safe Passage, occurred. Le Carré's unique contribution, through the fictional means at his disposal, is to show how apparently harmless observations, gossip and storytelling, if mixed in certain ways, can become a lethal cocktail and lead to tragic consequences.

History and Memoir – Points of View

In examining the representations of secrets and lies in works described as fiction or non-fiction, it is important to establish and to recognise the significance of point-of-view. In the Cold War, as in subsequent phases of confrontation between powerful opponents or enemies, the portrayal of truth has varied radically according to the viewpoint of the perceiver. Thus the KGB perceptions of Panamanian Presidents Torrijos and Noriega varied according to their previous value in combating American interests in the region. The Mitrokhin archives, smuggled out of Russia in 1992 by KGB archivist Vladimir Mitrokhin, with the help of the British Secret Intelligence Service, reveal KGB attempts in the mid-1970s to make new 'confidential contacts' among 'progressive' anti-American political leaders, including Torrijos.[18] As Mitrokhin's files show, the KGB attempted to reinforce Torrijos's suspicion of US President Jimmy Carter and his administration by forging a document which purported to show how the US was 'dragging out the Panama Canal negotiations and removing Torrijos himself from power'.[19] Forgery is one obvious way of distorting the truth, of telling lies.

Whatever the truth about Torrijos's involvement in drug trafficking – and President Carter was inclined to believe Torrijos's innocence – American propaganda portrayed his successor, Manuel Noriega, as a would-be Castro and therefore an enemy of the US. Subsequently, Noriega became 'the first foreign head of state to face criminal charges in a US court [and was] sentenced to forty years imprisonment on eight counts of cocaine trafficking, racketeering and money laundering'.[20] The layers of rumour, propaganda, lies and simple truth in these events defies definitive conclusion. In these circumstances, perhaps an informed work of fiction, such as *The Tailor of Panama*, may offer more avenues to a truthful account of these events than chronological histories or legalistic accounts based on sworn testimony.

***

In the past decade, literary studies have followed popular interests in giving greatly increased attention to the genre of 'life-stories', or autobiography and biography. What can such studies offer those of us interested in the nature of secrets and lies and their human consequences? In particular, what might we learn about the search for truth from biographies and autobiographies of secret agents or spies?

From a welter of memoirs by former CIA agents, Duane R. Clarridge's *A Spy for All Seasons* gives promise of throwing light on that question. Clarridge's life in the CIA took him to Nepal, India, Turkey, Italy and Iran, but the critical events in his career took place when he headed the Latin America Caribbean division in the early 1980s. An attractive feature of Clarridge's narrative is its bluff, no-bullshit tone suggesting honesty and directness. He acknowledges he is an 'aggressive personality'.[21] Moreover he displays an aura of masculine self-confidence as he describes the mountains of work to be done and his typical way of relaxing:

> The first thing in the morning, when facing twelve inches or more of incoming and perhaps half as much of outgoing cable traffic to read, I was aided by strong coffee and a nice, heavy-bodied, six-inch Honduran cigar. One of the perks of being in Latin America division was access to a variety of fine cigars from Jamaica, the Dominican Republic, Honduras, Nicaragua, and, once in a while, even Cuba.[22]

Elsewhere, Clarridge describes heavy sessions of Scottish whisky-drinking with a variety of Latin American leaders.

While the US intervention in Grenada and the war against the Sandinistas in Nicaragua devoured large amounts of 'Dewey' Clarridge's time, his memoir also throws some light, or at least colour, on the situation in Panama. As part of the CIA's covert operations in Central

America, Clarridge decided to visit Manuel Noriega 'to explore the possibility of setting up a training camp in Panama'.[23] 'Sometimes in the spy business', he remarks, 'you don't have a choice with whom you deal; unfortunately, it is often the unsavoury individuals who have the critical information'.[24]

Clarridge also indicates that he relishes such occasions.[25] At Noriega's 'modest' home, the two men drink Old Parr Scotch, Noriega's favourite, and he gives Clarridge a box of Cuban cigars. Clarridge notes that Noriega was 'a great collector of frogs, made from a wide variety of materials, including some of semi-precious stones'.[26] He notes that the Spanish word '*sapo*' is a word for a toad or, perhaps in some cases, a frog and is also a colloquialism for 'spy'.[27] Is this an invented James Bond touch in the narrative? Or an indication of Noriega's ambivalent regard for spies – even, or perhaps especially, from the CIA? At any rate, Noriega is receptive to Clarridge's proposal of a training base and offers Snake Island off the west coast of Panama to the CIA – an offer that was later rescinded when Noriega became nervous that it would become an issue in the forthcoming elections. Clarridge adds that he suspects the reason for his change of mind was pressure from Cuba.[28]

Are such episodes in a memoir of any value in establishing broader understanding of the use of secrets and lies in the early 1980s? The British historian of intelligence, Christopher Andrew, taking an overview of Cold War operations in Latin America, observes that 'KGB operations were greatly assisted by the clumsy and sometimes brutal American response to Latin American revolutionary movements'.[29] As head of Latin American operations for the CIA in the early 1980s, Clarridge must take some of the blame for this – especially for the mining of ports, which was evidently his idea.[30] Clarridge's credibility was damaged badly when he was indicted on seven counts of lying to Congress and the Tower Commission during the Iran-contra hearings, only to be pardoned by George Bush senior on the eve of his departure from the presidency in 1992.[31] Even in the crossfire of competing ideologies, in which Latin America has been heavily embroiled, it is surely valuable to observe ways in which certain secrets are kept and lies are told. With such knowledge, our approach to truth-telling may be less naïve in the future. The danger is perhaps cynicism about the value of honesty and truth-telling in human affairs.

Conclusion

I conclude with several books which reassert the significance and value of the never-ending search for truth in human affairs in the twenty-first century. These books are Bernard Williams's *Truth and Truthfulness*, Paul John Eakin's *The Ethics of Life Writing* and Joseph Wilson's *The Politics of Truth*.

Against postmodern assertions of the endless deferral of meaning and the relativity of all versions of 'truth', Bernard Williams argues with philosophical rigour that 'truth has an internal connection with beliefs and assertions …[and that] truth figures in the connection as a value'.[32] Williams makes the following statement:

> Truthfulness implies a respect for the truth. This relates to the two basic virtues of truth, which I shall call Accuracy and Sincerity: you do the best you can to acquire true beliefs, and what you say reveals what you believe. The authority of academics must be rooted in their truthfulness in both these respects: they take care, and they do not lie.[33]

Williams concludes his careful philosophical analysis of what he calls a 'genealogy' of truth and truthfulness on a note of hope:

> The hope can no longer be that the truth, enough truth, the whole truth, will itself set us free…The hope is that [human beings who communicate] will keep going in something like the more courageous, intransigent, and socially effective forms that they have acquired over their history; that some institutions can exist that will both support and express them; that the ways in which future people will come to make sense of things will enable them to see the truth and not be broken by it.[34]

On a somewhat similar note, Paul John Eakin argues that life writing can be a form of moral inquiry in pursuit of something like truth:

> When we tell or write down our lives, our stories establish our identities both as content – I am the person who did these things – and as an act – I am someone with a story to tell. And we do something even more fundamental – we establish ourselves as persons…[35]

However, as Joseph Wilson's autobiographical study, *The Politics of Truth* shows, men and women of conscience can have an uphill battle when the values they espouse conflict with those of an incumbent government. Wilson's book is both an account of his life and career as an American diplomat in Africa, Iraq and elsewhere and of what he calls 'the lies that led to war and betrayed my wife's CIA identity'.[36] Partly as a result of claims made in Wilson's autobiography, US Vice President Dick Cheney's former chief-of-staff, I. Lewis 'Scooter' Libby, was indicted in October 2005 on five counts of perjury, making false statements and obstruction of justice, during investigations by Special Counsel Patrick J. Fitzgerald.[37] He was subsequently imprisoned. Wilson argued that shortly after he had publicly asserted that the Bush administration had twisted intelligence about uranium in Niger to justify war with Iraq, senior officials in the White House had leaked the identity of Wilson's wife, Valerie Plame, who was a CIA undercover operative, in order to discredit Wilson and his exposure of twisted intelligence. Such cover-ups are often the source of new lies, as these events revealed.

What is the impact of such events on secret agents themselves? (The impact on her family is discussed in Chapter 1.) We can discern how a secret service career was 'blown' by the leaks published in newspapers and the electronic media in July 2003. The impact of these disclosures on the once-secret agent is graphically depicted by her husband:

> …Valerie's life was turned upside down. Nobody…could comprehend what it must be like for somebody who has practiced discretion and lived her cover for years – like a character in a stage play where the curtain never comes down – to suddenly find herself a household name. She likened it, aptly, to an out-of-body experience, floating above the new reality, unable to do anything but watch helplessly while people who knew nothing about her speculated about what she did.[38]

Secrets and lies are intertwined here. Valerie Plame had been required to lie to friends and acquaintances about her working life to maintain her cover. She had learnt to play a part. In her husband Joseph Wilson's account, these are the necessary subterfuges of a secret service career. Far more serious are the lies involved when a President orders the invasion of another country on the basis of fabricated 'evidence' that the other country is developing nuclear weapons. A similar scale of values underlies John le Carré's *The Tailor of Panama*. Harry Pendel's little white lies that grow in the telling pale before the arrogance of a government that manipulates intelligence to suit its precarious hold on reality. It is never a foregone conclusion that 'truth will out' in the world of spies and counter-spies. But this should not prevent the exercise of imagination and analytical skills in its perilous pursuit.

Four

Politics and Spying: Representations of Pre- and Early Australia

International men (and occasionally women) of mystery permeate the dreaming about and discovery of the country we now call Australia and its early development as a series of colonies of Britain. Indeed, since the European maritime explorations into the southern hemisphere in the sixteenth and early seventeenth centuries to the early twenty-first century, men and women in the shadows of history have spied in the service of a variety of masters and mistresses as they sought to find the fabled South Land in order to exploit what wealth or advantage it might yield. Only fragments of the lives and thoughts of such men and women can now be recovered because most of their operations were designed in secrecy and sustained for secret ends. But a recognition of some of these secrets and mysteries and the political imbroglios from which they grew are important for twenty-first century Australians who can see themselves being drawn into other imperial ambitions or terrorist plots. Because hard evidence is often lacking, the speculative imagination is necessarily brought into play in our consideration of the spying game in the years before and during Australia's early settlement.

Cartographic Espionage – Portuguese, Dutch, French

Many historians and commentators have been drawn to the question of whether Portuguese mariners in the sixteenth century were the first European discoverers of the continent we now call Australia. K. G.

McIntyre's book *The Secret Discovery of Australia* (revd 1982) argues this case but many historians have disputed it. Yet certain features of McIntyre's argument seem to remain intact: that the master maps of Portuguese cartographers were regarded as secrets and that 'cartographic spies' copied or stole some of these. McIntyre claims that the 'Dieppe Maps' were copied by spies in 1536 and presented to the future Henri II of France.[1] These maps contained 'intriguing outlines of a Great Southern Land' which resembled Australia's northeast and eastern coasts. The attraction of this scenario for some commentators is that it implies that Australia's northeast and eastern coasts had been found and charted by the Portuguese before 1550. But sound, supporting evidence for this claim has been hard to come by. 'Portuguese priority' in the European discovery of Australia remains an intriguing theory. Williams and Frost conclude: 'It is a vexed question. What is certain is that any Portuguese discovery of Australia in the 1520s of the continent now known as Australia had little, if any, bearing on future European contact with it'.[2]

The first *verifiable* record of European mariners sailing into 'Australian' waters occurred in 1606 when William Jansz's ship, the *Duyfken* charted some 300 km of the west coast of what is now Cape York Peninsula in Queensland. Some of Jansz's men went ashore on what was known as *Terra Incognita Australis* (and then New Holland). Between 1606 and 1770, an estimated 54 European ships from a range of nations made contact with this continent of dubious provenance. These voyages were usually connected to the trade in spices to Australia's north in which the Dutch East India Company (the VOC) was the dominant force. This company, like the Portuguese before them, held secret maps of the region.

It is reasonable to assume that the VOC charts were based partly on mapping carried out by Dutch navigators themselves but that some were stolen from the Portuguese by spies for the VOC. Historian Lisa Jardine describes the case of an Italian secret agent named Alberto Cantino who was sent to Lisbon in 1502 under cover of a dealer in purebred horses who bribed a Portuguese cartographer to obtain a map showing the most recent Portuguese discoveries.[3] In 1542, Don Michel Sylva, Bishop of Viseu left Portugal to travel to Italy by way of France and is said to have passed on to Dieppe mapmakers news of an expedition in the Moluccas in 1525 by Gomes de Sequiera and others, who were named by a nineteenth-century French geographer Barbié de Bocage as the probable discoverers of 'Java Le Grande,' the name given to the great Southern Land on the Dieppe maps.[4]

A more notorious case of espionage is that of Cornelis [de] Houtman who, with his brother Frederick, was commissioned in 1592 by a group of nine Amsterdam merchants to obtain classified information about newly opened sea routes to the East Indies. The brothers were arrested and jailed after trying to smuggle the charts back to Holland.[5] Frederick Houtman is the Dutch navigator after whom Houtman's Abrolhos Islands off the coast of what is now called Western Australia are named. These cases are documented examples – the tip of the iceberg, probably – of commercial and industrial espionage in the sixteenth century. Deception operations, propaganda and rumour-mongering were part of the atmosphere. Espionage at this time was deeply enmeshed in trade, commerce, and the rise of capitalism.

The figure of the Dutch spy Cornelis [de] Houtman, mentioned above, is brought to life briefly in Giles Milton's popular history of the spice trade *Nathaniel's Nutmeg* (1999). Houtman's unstable temperament causes problems when he takes charge of a ship. 'As a spy he was in his element,' Giles Milton explains, but 'as a leader of men [as captain of a ship] he was a disaster'.[6] After arriving at Bantam in Java, Milton writes, Houtman is incensed by the price of spices and sets in train 'an orgy of destruction that was to set the pattern for the Dutch presence in the East Indies'.[7]

The name Houtman haunts the history of Australia's west coast. On 4 June 1629 the Dutch ship the *Batavia*, under the command of Francois Pelsaert, was wrecked on a reef off the Houtman Abrolhos islands. This was the prelude to a period of betrayal, massacre and terror. When insufficient drinking water could be found on the islands or on the nearby mainland, Commander Pelsaert set out with crew in the ship's boat for Java and returned some two and a half months later on another ship, the *Sardam*, to rescue some 250 men, women, and children he had left behind. Pelsaert's journals, which are held in the archives of the VOC in the Netherlands, provide the principal basis for subsequent retellings of a melodrama of monstrous proportions.

As a tale of early European encampment on foreign shores, the story of the *Batavia*'s survivors forms a radical contrast to the tale of self-reliance and adaptability in Daniel Defoe's novel *Robinson Crusoe*. While some 20 *Batavia* survivors died from thirst and exposure, a form of primitive authoritarian rule occurred under Jeronimus Cornelisz and the council of advisers he installed, leading to murder, rape, and tyranny. Cornelisz had earlier planned a mutiny against Pelsaert after the *Batavia* had rounded the Cape of Good Hope. He revived these plans when marooned on the shore with the intention of overpowering Pelsaert and his party when they returned from Java and living by piracy on the open seas.

In the meantime, Cornelisz presided over a reign of terror on Houtman's Abrolhos. Historian Philip Tyler has described the way it operated:

> The rule on Beacon Island was based on an authoritarian code devised by Cornelius and enforced through a council of his own nominees. Against an anti-intellectual background where orthodox religious instruction was forbidden and heretical beliefs openly taught, an alien code of life was enforced. Traditional class divisions among the survivors were disregarded and a strict direction of labour was practised. Though property was allegedly held in common by the whole group, in actual practice the possession and distribution of goods was at the whim of Cornelius who acted as though they had been bequeathed to him. In an age when dress was an indication of status, Cornelius's supporters were distinguished by the splendour of their dress and the easy access to a number of women held for common use.[8]

Tyler speculates that religious politics underlies the behaviour of the Dutch on the island: they were an Anabaptist 'fifth column' within seventeenth-century Dutch colonialism.[9] Cornelisz saw himself as the organizer and 'prophet' of an Anabaptist settlement which had broken away from traditional Calvinism.[10] Was Australia's west coast then, for a brief period in the early seventeenth century, a site of transferred European religious and political violence? Did Cornelisz instigate a regimen of strict surveillance, torture, rape, and murder in obedience to his God? Or was he simply a 'tiger animal' out of control? Or a cold-blooded pragmatist who saw a way to improve his chances of survival, escape and freedom for himself and those who associated with him? Tyler prefers a Jonestown scenario. Another writer on these events, Hugh Edwards in his book *Islands of Angry Ghosts*, prefers the image of Cornelisz as a bully and pragmatic survivor.

Because of the spotlight that plays over these events, the significance of their sequel has been relatively neglected. When Pelsaert returned from Java with reinforcements he had Cornelisz and his band arrested. Five leaders of the mutiny, including Cornelisz, were tried, convicted and hanged on the island. Some were punished on the ship returning to Batavia and others were tried and convicted by the Company there. At the time of the hangings just two of the rebels, Wouter Loos and Jan Pelgrom, gained last minute reprieves and became the first foreign agents on Australian shores. Landed on the mainland near the mouth of what is now known as the Murchison River, they were given a sampan, provisions, and instructed by Pelsaert on the kinds of intelligence they were expected to gather. Drawing heavily on a translation of Pelsaert's diary, Henrietta Drake-Brockman, in her historical novel of these events *The Wicked and the Fair*, describes Pelsaert's instructions to his agents:

> So God guards you, you will not suffer any damage from them [the Aboriginal people], but on the contrary, because they have never seen any white men, they will offer you all friendship. Meanwhile, you have to discover with all diligence, what material, be it gold or silver, there happens to be found, and what they esteem as valuable.[11]

By gaining the confidence of the indigenous people, and learning their language, the men might redeem themselves with the Company and with their God. They would be picked up by subsequent Dutch voyagers in several years. Pelsaert's injunction to his agents as they commence this difficult, perhaps suicidal mission is resonant: 'Man's luck is found in strange places.' The fate of Pelgrom and Loos is unknown. They are not the first, or last, agents left on a foreign shore and never heard from again.

British Deception in Europe

Despite evidence that the Dutch called what they knew of the Australian continent New Holland and had made at least fifteen landings since 1606, the South Land is said to have been 'discovered' by James Cook when he documented the location of its east coast in 1770. But British paramountcy in the settlement of the continent did not occur between 1788 and the 1820s and '30s without a number of scares from foreign competitors, especially the French.

Espionage feeds on secrets, plots and conspiracies. In the age of European imperialism, the maritime powers – Portuguese, Dutch, French and British – were awash with military, commercial and geographic secrets. Networks of spies operated in Europe for each of the great powers and these had repercussions for their distant colonies. Perhaps the best documented network in the late eighteenth century is that of a Dutch woman, Mevrow Wouters, based in Rotterdam, who was a spy-handler for Britain. By the early 1780s Wouters was receiving 'weekly reports from Paris, Madrid and Vienna, and regular ones from Dunkirk, Nantes, Brest, Rochefort, Terrol, La Coruña, Cadiz, Cartagena and Toulon: her summaries were being sent across the Channel by packet boat.[12] In a male-dominated profession, Wouters provided high quality intelligence about naval strengths, battle plans and political strategies and was retained by the British Admiralty for over twenty years.[13]

Along with maps and charts, the 'Secret Orders' given to captains of ships, with specific dates or circumstances in which they were to be opened, were of special interest to spies. There is no indication that the secret orders given to Captain James Cook to discover and map the southern continent in 1770 were obtained by a foreign power. However, Cook's secret orders indicate a classic exercise in deception of Britain's perceived enemies. The Admiralty's instructions to Cook, the Commander of the *Endeavour* show that his ostensible reason for the voyage, the observation of the transit of Venus at Tahiti was only a preliminary event, a cover for the real purpose of the voyage which was to discover and annexe valuable posts on the east coast of what was then New Holland. In the event, he annexed the whole of New Zealand and the east coast of New Holland, which he re-named New South Wales.[14] Cook was also instructed to ensure the secrecy of all his discoveries on his return by presenting his log-books and journals of all his officers to the Secretary of the Admiralty, requiring the whole crew not to divulge where they had been.[15]

A Colony's Early Spies

A different kind of spying occurred in the settlement phase of Australian history with the arrival of the First Fleet at Botany Bay in 1788. A shift is evident from international espionage for political or military advantage to internal surveillance in the service of law and order in a convict colony, though occasional skirmishes with the French occurred.

That experience in intelligence was rated highly by British authorities for leadership roles in the colonies is evident in the selection of Arthur Phillip as the first Governor of the projected colony at Botany Bay. Born in 1738, Phillip had been groomed for a life at sea. He attended the Royal Naval Hospital, Greenwich, for the sons of poor seamen, hunted whales off Norway, worked on ships in the Mediterranean and took part in naval battles during the Seven Years War and off South America. After a short-lived marriage failed, Phillip trained as a military engineer in France and it is likely that he commenced his career as a spy in France in the early 1770s.[16] The British Admiralty seconded Phillip to the allied Portuguese navy for which he was expected to return with detailed knowledge of 'coasts, harbours, fortifications and disposition of colonists' in South America.[17] At the end of 1782, Phillip was intended for a secret expedition against Spanish Settlements in South America but this was aborted when his ship was destroyed in a storm. He was employed by the Home Office as a spy in France and Spain.[18] In the period immediately before his appointment as Governor of the Botany Bay settlement, Phillip was employed in spying on naval preparations in French ports. In all, he had spent more than a decade in intelligence work for the British government before he was appointed governor of the convict colony planned for New South Wales.

When he was attached to the Home Office, Phillip's immediate superior to whom he reported was his friend Evan Nepean. Nepean must have been impressed with Phillip's level-headedness, his fortitude under pressure and his personal reticence. Accounts of Phillip's governorship of the convict colony at Botany Bay reinforce his measured judgement and sense of responsibility. As a spy, he had learnt to take his own counsel under general direction from distant places and to face the consequences.

Though Sydney was then very distant from the centre of geopolitical activity, Phillip was kept on his toes by the cat-and-mouse games of the French. The words of singer Sting in 'The Police' are perhaps relevant: 'Every move you make, every breath you take, I'll be watching you'. Tom Keneally's popular history of the Botany Bay experiment *The Commonwealth of Thieves*, gives an engaging account of Phillip's request to one of his officers, King, to spy on 'the illustrious Frenchman La Pérouse' and his men who had sailed into Botany Bay after Phillip had moved the British settlement to Port Jackson:

> The excursion was no doubt partly a spying expedition. Phillip wanted King to fool La Perouse about the scale of the supplies the British possessed by offering him 'whatever he might have occasion for'.
>
> So at three o'clock in the morning of 2 February [1789], King and the astronomer Dawes, set out by longboat with some marines for Botany Bay. King would report that they were received aboard the French flagship by the Comte with the greatest politeness. After King had delivered Phillip's message, La Pérouse sent his thanks to the governor and made the same formal offers of help, La Pérouse playing the game Phillip had set up by saying exaggeratedly that he would be in France in fifteen months time and had three years stores aboard, and so would be happy to oblige Mr Phillip with anything *he* might want.[19]

More potentially momentous intelligence activity concerning French and British interests occurred later and a continent away around Australia's south-west coasts. Working from the intelligence of others, French naval officer Jules Blosseville wrote two reports in 1826 recommending that France establish a penal colony in the south-west corner of Australia.[20] Nicholas Hasluck's novel *The Blosseville File* extrapolates from this scenario to satirically imagine a contemporary French colony called Blosseville in south-western Australia. This was not to happen historically. British authorities were informed of such tentative French designs on south-west Australia: they sent a contingent of British forces to occupy King George Sound, where Blosseville had proposed a capital for the projected French penal colony. Blosseville then turned his attention to New Zealand where, from the French point of view, 'the British appeared to be not so much of a problem'.[21]

A Compulsive Spy, Storyteller and Informer

Despite occasional flurries of fear about external threats, governors and their military staff in Australia's convict colonies were chiefly concerned with their internal security needs. A variety of ways to avoid rebellion and maintain order were employed including torture (especially flogging) and the use of informers to spy on other prisoners and thus gain more lenient treatment for themselves.

In Australia's 'gulag' prisons, as Robert Hughes describes them in *The Fatal Shore*, resistance to authority was common; and at Norfolk Island the prison yard was ruled by 'the Ring' – 'a carceral mafia whose control over the lives of prisoners was both inescapable and minutely enforced'.[22] Suspected informers were denounced as traitors or 'dogs' and either killed or mutilated by their fellow prisoners.[23] Yet a number of prisoners took their chance and turned informer to improve their chances of a reduced sentence. Methods used by authorities and not unknown in modern intelligence services, included the apparently humane approach of infiltrating prisoner ranks and learning their language and way of seeing the world. Commandant John Price on Norfolk Island 'knew' his convicts: he obsessed about 'knowing the convicts: their way of life, the way they thought, their desires.[24] But he used this knowledge in pursuit of a brutal and punitive regime.

I have written elsewhere about two kinds of spy among Australia's early convict population represented by the brutal murderer and informer John Knatchbull and the 'ideological' spy, John Boyle O'Reilly who was a political prisoner in the Swan River Colony.[25]

A different figure from these is the Danish-born Jorgen Jorgensen who had lived in England. Like O'Reilly, Jorgensen was an educated man – and an expressive and persuasive writer. Like Knatchbull, he was a convicted criminal but of less murderous inclinations. Jorgensen's addiction was gambling. He had an impulsive temperament, often seemed 'full of himself' and, as Marcus Clarke remarked of him, he could be 'all things to all men'.[26] His adventurous and romantic temperament appealed to Jorgensen's biographers, Frank Clune and P. R. Stephensen, who compared him to other romantics: 'He, like Napoleon, Byron, Shelley, or even Beau Brummel,' they declare, 'had a reckless indifference to the consequences of impulsive actions'.[27] What chiefly appealed to the romanticists was Jorgensen's Byronic act of bravado in staging a coup in Iceland in 1809, placing himself as the head of government and proclaiming Iceland independent of Denmark. The coup lasted nine weeks before Jorgensen sailed voluntarily to his adoptive homeland England.[28]

Jorgensen's temperament, disposition and weaknesses contributed to his role as a spy for the British government in Europe after the Napoleonic wars and later when he was transported as a convicted thief to Van Diemen's Land. Banished to debtors' prison after one of his gambling sprees, and apparently prevented by an injury from returning to the life of a seafarer, Jorgensen realised he would have to live by his wits. He learnt that an assignment to spy for the British government could be a way to earn his release. He wrote long memoranda on political and military developments in Europe to the Foreign Office which led the Foreign Secretary Lord Castlereagh to describe Jorgensen as 'an ingenious purveyor of significant information.'[29]

Jorgen Jorgensen was a spy in the making. He was smart, linguistically adept, could disguise himself in various roles and write colourful and persuasive accounts of political and military situations based on limited research. A good example of his persuasive literary talent is Jorgensen's letter in 1813 to British MP Samuel Whitbread about a threatened French invasion of Sydney. Sarah Bakewell has described the alleged French plot and its consequences:

> Four heavily armed French frigates were apparently to be sent that November to the Falklands, there to meet an American ship – the United States now being also at war with Great Britain. All five would sail together to Sydney, sneak up the Hawkesbury River and attack the city from the rear, recruiting any convicts who would join them on the way. Once they had seized Sydney and all its subsidiary colonies, they would use New South Wales as a base for further attacks on the Pacific Islands and South America.[30]

This was a sufficiently plausible scenario for British Colonial Secretary, the Earl of Bathurst, to forward Jorgensen's report to Governor Macquarie in Sydney who also took it seriously. Macquarie replied that

'French ambitions in Australia were well known, and that Jorgensen was knowledgeable about Australian ports and sea routes.[31] (Jorgensen had visited Australia in his seafaring days.) The outcome of Jorgensen's report was a heightened awareness of possible French threats to the British in Australia and further pressure for military reinforcements. But because he was in retreat in Europe, Napoleon was increasingly unable to afford ships or men for such expansionist missions.

Jorgensen's task when he was appointed to spy in Europe was a broad one – to 'assess morale and detect new market opportunities for Britain' in a post-Napoleon Europe.[32] These were hardly high-level secret service tasks but they were sufficient to earn him an income. Good as he was at eavesdropping around military establishments and places of recreation, however, Jorgensen was unreliable. Some of his reports were too well laced with fantasy, foreshadowing twentieth-century would-be spies like Our Man in Havana and the Tailor of Panama. Instructed to report on events in Warsaw, Jorgensen found life more congenial in Berlin and concocted reports as if from Warsaw but based on information from Poles he had met in Berlin.[33] By 1820 he was out of favour. He returned to London where a charge of theft landed him in Newgate Prison. After breaking parole, he was re-arrested in 1822 and sentenced to death – a sentence which was commuted to transportation for life.

Jorgensen arrived in Van Diemen's Land in 1826 and led an eventful life there. He became an informer for the Government in Hobart Town by reporting on a major banknote forgery scam.[34] He became a supporter of the tough law-and-order policies of Governor Arthur and was appointed as a convict constable in Oatlands where he was especially proficient at 'spying and detecting'.[35] He later led a triad of 'roving parties,' each of six men, to drive Aborigines out of the settlements which whites had taken over in the Tasmanian midlands. Sarah Bakewell describes Jorgensen as a 'soldier of fortune'.[36] James Dally summarises: 'Gifted with extraordinary high spirits and unbalancing verve, he was ambitious, diversely talented and appreciably amoral'.[37]

Espionage – A Rich Heritage?

Despite a general preference among white Australians for a benign view of their forebears' role in the exploration, discovery, and settlement of the Australian continent, it is clear that the apparently less benign activities of politics and espionage have played a significant role in this history. Historical research and the speculative imagination are necessary partners in an examination of 'the spying game' in pre- and early Australia. Our European connections have ensured a rich (and sometimes murky) heritage of espionage and counter-espionage in the searching for, and finding of, the Great Southern Land.

Once discovered and settled, the infant colonies of Britain on a 'new' continent became breeding grounds for other kinds of spies and spying as the cases of Governor Arthur Phillip and special constable Jorgen Jorgensen show. The uses and abuses of espionage in the early years of Australian settlement can thus be seen in part as fighting old (European) wars in a new zone and partly as a way of dealing with unique situations and security needs.

As different political and social situations emerged, the spying game assumed different forms but it never disappeared entirely from Australian society or from the purview of Australia's keenest social observers and artists. Can they be the precursors of a good and civilised society?

Five

Exploration or Espionage? Flinders and the French

Wars and rumours of war between the British and the French characterise the exploration and settlement of Australia in the early years of the nineteenth century. The British had established their settlement at Port Jackson on the south-east coast and reports varied about its viability. Fired by Napoleonic ambitions, French navigators and scientists were sent to explore what they could of this southern land, both in the interests of 'objective' science and in the political interests of their country. The almost simultaneous voyages of Matthew Flinders and Nicolas Baudin, and their interactions, spying and otherwise, reflect some of the tensions and ironies of these times and highlight the personal tragedies of the two men.

Baudin reached Australia before Flinders in May 1801 but their ships met subsequently at Encounter Bay on 8 April 1802. Flinders's journal records this first encounter both graphically and symbolically from the *Investigator*:

> At half-past five, the land being then five miles distant to the north-eastward, I hove to; and learned, as the stranger passed to leeward with a free wind, that it was the French national ship *Le Géographe*, under the command of Captain Nicolas Baudin. We veered round as *Le Géographe* was passing, so as to keep our broadside to her, lest the flag of truce should be a deception...[1]

Despite the temporary cessation of hostilities between British and French, these nations' representatives were cautious, curious and sometimes overtly hostile towards each other.

It is sometimes argued, in universities and academies especially, that the knowledges associated with the arts and sciences transcend the narrower concerns of politics and nationalism. Such claims for knowledge that transcends personal and national interests seem especially prevalent when imperialist ambitions are high, as they were for both France and Britain in the late eighteenth and early nineteenth century. In these contexts, natural scientists and philosophers were held up as exponents of a 'higher knowledge'; both the natural sciences and *les sciences humaines* gained a high prestige value and were called upon to spread their influence by increasing knowledge and understanding in the wider international sphere. In this spirit of altruistic endeavour, both Britain and France officially approved a number of scientific expeditions. At the same time, participants in these grand knowledge adventures, like the captains of the *Investigator* and *Géographe*, were continually aware of the undercurrents of international rivalry and power play, and of the scope for double-dealing and deception.

While Flinders' focus was on mapping coastlines, Baudin's expedition sought to study 'nature' in Australia – the fauna, flora and indigenous inhabitants of this 'undiscovered' land. The officially expressed ambitions of such voyages were grand, as the Institut National of France reveals in its letter to Sir Joseph Banks, President of the Royal Society of London in May 1800:

> The Institut National of France is desirous that several distant voyages useful to the progress of human knowledge should begin without delay. Its wishes have been endorsed by our Government which has just issued orders for the preparation as soon as possible of expeditions led by skilful navigators as well as enlightened men of science, and will approach the Government of your country for the necessary passports or safe-conducts for our vessels. The Institut National considers that it is precisely at the moment when war still burdens the world that the friends of humanity should work for it, by advancing the limits of science and of useful arts...[2]

Grand intentions are admirable but they can sometimes mask ulterior motives. While there seems little reason to doubt Captain Baudin's sincerity in attempting to fulfil the goals of scientific exploration, it appears that at least two members of his crew, Francois Péron and Louis de Freycinet were engaged in espionage activities in the service of a possible French invasion of British settlements on the south-east coast of Australia.

According to Péron, the high rhetoric of the Institut National de France provided cover for Napoleon's more serious concerns:

> Always vigilant to whatever may humiliate the eternal rival of our nation, the First Consul ... decided upon our expedition. His real object was such that it was indispensable to conceal it from the Governments of Europe, and especially from the Court of St James. We must have their unanimous consent; and that we might obtain this, it was necessary that, strangers in appearance to all political designs, we should occupy ourselves only with natural history collections... It was far from being the case, however, that our true purpose had to be confined to that class of work.[3]

Indeed, Péron was an assiduous gatherer of general and strategic intelligence, as his 1802 report to General Charles Decaen, Governor and Captain-General of Île-de-France (Mauritius) demonstrates. Péron assures the general that he 'neglected no opportunity' of collecting ideas and information of interest to the French government. As a scientist, he asserts, he could ask questions 'which would have been indiscreet on the part of another, especially on military matters'.[4] To Decaen, he asserts that the natural history collections were 'merely a pretext' for the higher duty of providing intelligence on the infant colony to his government with a view to its invasion at some future point by French forces.

Péron's contribution to human intelligence – or 'humint' in present day terms – is arguable. He would not be the first, or last, spy to attempt to ingratiate himself with his superiors by exaggerating his information, insights and achievements, which Péron indicates were corroborated by further materials in a sealed chest. Yet his report to Decaen reveals some of the vulnerabilities of early settlement in Australia to foreign invasion and therefore potential opportunities for the French.

Of special interest is Péron's identification of the Irish prisoners at Port Jackson as potential allies in the event of a French invasion. Péron has no doubt that 'at the mere mention of the French name every Irish arm would be raised' in their support.[5] Péron's identification of the Irish as natural allies is corroborated by other accounts. The case of William Maum, a young Irish teacher of Latin and Greek is instructive. Maum, a political prisoner, was twenty-one when he arrived in the colony in January 1800. After uncovering an Irish conspiracy later that year, Governor King described Maum as a 'depraved character' and an 'incendiary'.[6] After being exiled to Norfolk Island in 1804, Maum wrote to Governor King with details of French attempts to get him to spy for them in 1802. Maum says he complied with the French request up to a point but provided what might today be called 'chicken feed' intelligence. When the French returned and requested more useful military intelligence, according to Maum, they specified what they had in mind:

> the population of the colony – their general opinions – how they endured slavery – how many English – how were their sentiments – the Irishmen's sentiments he was assured of – and particularly whether the English in general were seamen or soldiers, who had been transported for any offence after their discharges, as they were easily worked on.[7]

Maum says he was assured by the French that, as soon as the First Consul learned of 'the great number of persons in this colony who were desirous of Innovation, and change of condition', he would launch an attack – 'first taking Sydney, and procuring all the prisoners to enter the French service'.[8]

Francois Péron's report to General Decaen at French naval headquarters in Mauritius was complemented by an unsigned report by de Freycinet containing the results of his espionage. This latter report was much stronger in the specific detail required for a military invasion than Péron's report. As Péron indicated, Lieutenant de Freycinet had worked in tandem with Péron but occupied himself particularly with 'examining all the points on the coast in the neighbourhood of Port Jackson that are favourable for the debarkation of troops'.[9] Historian Ernest Scott notes how the two French spies worked together: 'Péron, under the guise of a man of science collecting facts about butterflies and grasshoppers, exploited his hosts for information of a political and military nature; whilst Freycinet, ostensibly examining the harbour in the interest of navigation, made plans of places suitable for landing troops'.[10] While absolving Baudin on the available evidence from involvement in the espionage of Péron and Freycinet, Scott steps beyond the historian's traditionally objective demeanour and condemns the pair with almost melodramatic scorn for their 'singular turpitude' in 'pursuing nefarious designs of their own and plotting to rend the breast that fed them'. Their 'ignoble treachery and ungrateful baseness' was all the more despicable, Scott argues, in light of the generous and humane treatment shown to them by Governor King and other British officers.[11]

In 1814, Governor Lachlan Macquarie reflected on these events and their significance:

> It has been generally supposed that the *Geographe* and *Naturalist*, French ships of war under Capt. Baudin … came solely for the purpose of ascertaining how far it might prove expedient for the then ruler of France to establish a Colony on some part of New Holland, to counteract the views of the British Government in this country; and I have no doubt Bonaparte would long since have prosecuted his views in this respect, had his more important Engagements in Europe admitted of his sending out a sufficient Force for the Conquest of this Colony.[12]

But while Macquarie wrote these words on 30 April 1814, Napoleon was bound for his exile on the Isle of Elba. His era of dominance was over; and under Macquarie the Australian colony was developing strongly.

It would be naïve to imagine that the only spies in and around Australia in the early nineteenth century were the French with designs on British possessions. A complementary British readiness to spy on the French and disrupt their activities became evident after the French left Port Jackson in November 1802. Governor King caught wind of a rumour the French officers, while in port, had spoken of a French plan to colonise part of Van Diemen's Land. King promptly sent Captain Charles Robbins in an English schooner, the *Cumberland* – later to become the ill-fated vessel of Flinders' attempted return to England – to intercept the French. When he caught up with the French, Robbins boarded the *Naturaliste* and informed its captain, Charles Hamelin, that they had been sent by Governor King to prepare for the establishment of a British settlement in D'Entrecasteaux Channel. History shows that the English did subsequently form a settlement in 1803. At this stage, however, it was simply a ruse, a deception. King's disinformation was designed to pre-empt any plans the French might have for colonising Van Diemen's Land.

The British officers also boarded Baudin's ship. Baudin records the event:

> I was quite surprised when an officer of the English navy was shown in, accompanied by a geographer whom I had met at Port Jackson ... Mr Robbins handed me a letter from Mr King, the governor of Port Jackson, and soon after, his instructions on what he had to do ... The contents of Mr King's letter provided enough clarification for me to see the reason for his voyage – its sole purpose was to keep watch on us.[13]

A striking feature of these encounters is their air of decorum and urbanity, the iron fist in a velvet glove. King's letter to his friend Baudin is a masterpiece of English formality and restraint:

> You will no doubt be surprised to see a ship follow you so closely. You were aware of my intention to establish a settlement in the south, but this has been brought forward because of the information communicated to me immediately after your departure. This information is that the French wish to set up an establishment in Storm Bay Passage... It is also said that these are your orders from the French republic.[14]

The attempt to mitigate suspicions continued: King went on to assure Baudin, with whom he had established an apparently genuine affinity, that he gave no credence to these rumours and would certainly have mentioned them to him if he had heard about them before Baudin left Port Jackson. Both men had entered the dangerous border zone between personal friendship and international enmity, yet they could still apparently consider each other as friends.

Francois Péron, though a fierce critic of his countryman Baudin, considered Flinders as a far more dangerous foe. Accusing the Englishman of being a spy, Péron suggested that Flinders' rival mission to that of Baudin was one of 'traversing the Pacific looking for strategic points from which the British could launch an attack on Spanish America', France's ally.[15] Moreover, this 'dangerous' man Flinders, according to Péron, could be engaged in extending his country's influence in another direction too, towards Mauritius.

The reports written by Péron and Freycinet for General Charles Decaen, the Governor of Mauritius (then Île-de-France), in 1803 had devastating consequences for Matthew Flinders. Flinders had set sail for his return trip to England on the *Cumberland*, which had been previously used to intercept the French at Van Diemen's Land. The schooner proved unfit for service, needing almost constant pumping to keep her afloat and Flinders decided to seek assistance at Mauritius in accordance with his understanding of his French passport. Unfortunately for him, war with France had broken out again. Hearing of Flinders' arrival on Île-de-France, and in receipt of Péron's damning report on the British in New Holland, and Flinders in particular as a rival, Governor Decaen had the Englishman arrested and imprisoned as a spy.

Not surprisingly, patriotic supporters of the British cause, following Flinders himself, have insisted on his innocence. But what is the truth of the situation? Putting aside Decaen's high-handed assumptions of superiority and Flinders' disrespectful and apparently insolent response to the General – so different from the affable interactions of Governor King and Baudin at Port Jackson – did Flinders have a case to answer?

In the first place, the French passport held by Flinders was for the *Investigator*, the ship on which he had arrived in Australia, and not for the *Cumberland*. In effect he was carrying the wrong licence for the ship he commanded. Second, he had no scientist on board. Third, and most perilously for Flinders, he was carrying secret despatches from Governor King to the British Admiralty. In these despatches King requested more troops in order to, amongst other purposes, defend Port Jackson if attacked by Decaen. In this context, Flinders might be considered a courier of secret documents for the British cause against the French; and that he had thereby broken the terms of his French passport. In Flinders' defence, it is unlikely that his visit under duress of a sinking ship to Île-de-France could be reasonably construed as an attempt to spy on the island for the British by, for example, mapping fortifications or suitable landing points for an invasion force. For his part, though, Decaen seems to have sincerely believed that Flinders was implicated in 'British military designs' on the island for which he was responsible.[16] Moreover, war had started up again while Flinders was at sea and he did not know that Britain and France were again at each other's throats. 'I found myself considered in the light of a spy', wrote Flinders in his journal.[17]

At first, Flinders seethed at his disrespectful treatment as a prisoner of state: at 'the injustice, the haughtiness and the Bastille-like mystery with which I am treated. I am kept from my voyage of discovery, from my country, from my family ... this is indeed some return for the hospitality and assistance which the French ships received at Port Jackson'.[18] 'The sensations raised by this violation of justice, of humanity and of the faith of his own government ... will be readily felt by every Englishman who has been subjected, were it only for a day, to French revolutionary power'.[19] Governor Decaen responded to Flinders' anger by accusing him of 'overstepping all the bounds of civility' and ceased all further correspondence with him.[20]

Could there have been other reasons for Flinders' imprisonment on Mauritius? Flinders wrote to his brother: 'Some odd opinions were started relative to the real cause of my confinement ... in matters of discovery, I should think that he kept me here to give time for Captain Baudin's voyage to be published before mine, and as no probable reason has yet been given for my detainer it may possibly be so'. Flinders here refers to one of the less altruistic uses of scientific and other knowledge – to compete for public recognition and private preferment.[21] Certainly Péron, who took over and completed the history of Baudin's voyage after the latter's death on Mauritius in September 1803 – two months before Flinders arrived there in the *Cumberland* – gained greatly by Flinders' extended imprisonment. Péron's history, published in 1807, gave primacy to the role of French navigators and scientists in discovering 'Terre Napoléon'. As well as beating Flinders and the British to publication, he managed to virtually erase his captain, Nicolas Baudin, from this historical account of his voyages. Péron was a master of the payback; but he remained both a respected scientist and a patriot of revolutionary France.

While Flinders continued to harbour some resentment at the injustice of his treatment on Île-de-France, over time he achieved a degree of equanimity. Over these years, he also became a more skilful and gracious writer. Like Christopher Smart and some twentieth-century poets such as T. S. Eliot and Peter Porter, Flinders found cats a fit subject for his writings. In Flinders' case, his cat Trim had accompanied him on voyages and then in imprisonment on Mauritius until he mysteriously disappeared on the island – perhaps, Flinders conjectured, to be caught and eaten by 'some hungry black slave'. Trim became a literary ornament in Flinders' private journal and an imaginary friend. As Gillian Dooley remarks, Flinders used the journal in part as 'narrative therapy as well as a memorandum to his future, liberated self'.[22] He also found ways to send letters to his wife and friends in England.

The circumstances of Flinders' captivity on Mauritius improved when he was granted parole and he was moved to the countryside in August 1805. His facility in French improved dramatically and his memoir and letters show an interest in the social life, agriculture and commerce of the besieged island. Having arrived in Mauritius when he was twenty-nine and eventually leaving in June 1810 when he was thirty-six, Flinders had spent as much time as a prisoner on Mauritius as he had spent navigating the coasts of Australia. He became friendly with a number of the planters and their families who lent him books and music.[23] Early in his imprisonment, Flinders recorded movements of shipping at Port Louis, including British ships captured by the French. Having imprisoned Flinders as a suspected spy, the French must have known that he would become a repository of valuable information about Île-de-France in the event of a British invasion. Perhaps this was one of General Decaen's reasons for delaying Flinders' release until well after he had received permission from Napoleon in 1806 to do so.

Britain began its blockade of Mauritius in June 1809. A year later, in June 1810, Flinders was released and allowed to leave Mauritius after six and a half years there. The reasons for the timing of Flinders' release are a matter of conjecture. If Flinders were left on Île-de-France, could his presence there provide extra incentive to the British to attack and make a hero of him? In the event of possible British invasion and capture of the island, would Flinders' continued detention there beyond the date when he could have been released be used as grounds for more punitive action by the British? Whatever Decaen's reasons for finally releasing Flinders, he did so in June 1810, placing him 'on parole'. Almost two months later, from 20–7 August 1810, a major naval battle occurred between squadrons of frigates of the British Royal Navy and the French Navy over possession of the harbour of Grand Port. In this battle, the French triumphed and the British navy suffered their worst defeat of the entire war.

Matthew Flinders was fortunate to have left Mauritius before the Battle of Grand Port. By this time, he had embarked on a merchant ship on his way to London via Cape Town. After a voyage of twenty-six days, Flinders arrived at Simon's Bay on 11 July. In conformity with naval regulations, no journal was kept during the voyage but it was resumed for seven weeks at the Cape. The day after Flinders' arrival, Admiral Albermarle Bertie, a chief strategist in British attempts to recapture Mauritius, sent for Flinders and requested him to provide information on the island he was preparing to attack. Flinders had some qualms about doing this as it would be breaking the terms of his parole: after six and a half years on the island, and having made some firm friends there he was evidently reluctant to provide information that could contribute to their demise.

Spying for one's own country is usually (but not always) more straightforward than spying for a designated enemy. Having been accused of being an impostor and spy by General Decaen, a charge which he had vigorously denied, Flinders had no desire to become a spy, even for his own country, so soon after his release. Continued exposure to the 'enemy' on Île-de-France had led to some genuine friendships. However, with Admiral Bertie's insistence and considering his own future when he returned to England, Flinders decided he would contradict the terms of the parole he had given to the French government in Mauritius. In this way, Flinders became a 'reluctant' spy for the British,[24] but a knowledgeable, experienced and useful one. He compiled four quarto pages of answers to questions on Mauritius, put to him by Admiral Bertie. He prepared charts and a plan of Port Napoleon and, using his journal, drew up a list of shipping in the port between January and June 1810. Most significantly, he recommended suitable landing places for a British invasion force.[25]

The value of Flinders' intelligence and the uses to which it was put by the British Navy have never been established. On the one hand, he was not accused of providing false or misleading intelligence. Nor was he singled out for praise for intelligence that may have contributed to the successful British invasion of Mauritius two months later in November 1810. Such are the often invisible contributions of spies and intelligence agents. Flinders had arrived safely back in England on 24 October 1810. In the short period of life left to him, Flinders saw a daughter born and his *A Voyage to Terra Australis* published on 18 July 1814. But he died the next day at the age of forty. While the race to publish first had been lost to the French, Flinders' contribution to the mapping of Australia's coasts would not be forgotten. And the name he proposed for the continent would outlast Péron's Terre Napoléon.

Six

Troubled Waters: Australian Spies in the Pacific – Glimpses from the Early Twentieth Century

Introduction

The national story of Australian spies and spying begins in the Pacific during the political machinations and manoeuvring that led to an Australian Commonwealth in 1901. Although political agitation and unrest in the region were peripheral to the imperial ambitions of Britain, France or Germany, such events seemed more pressing from the Australian continent. From a British imperial (but not yet an American) perspective, Australia offered a vantage point for keeping an eye on British interests in the Pacific and threats to them; and Australia's emergent national interest coincided for a time with this approach.

An Australian perspective on European power-play in the South Pacific, and occasionally on espionage, is offered in the stories and novels of Louis Becke, who sailed these seas from the 1870s to the '90s as an adventurer and trader. Becke's adventures included signing on as supercargo for the legendary American pirate 'Bully' Hayes, but Becke was himself acquitted of piracy charges.[1] The overriding impression left by Becke's *Pacific Tales* and other books is of the primacy of trading – of goods and chattels, of impressions and ideas, information and maps, and sometimes of people. In the background are larger rivalries and enmities between the European empires that vied for authority and control in the Pacific – especially the British, French, German and Dutch. Intelligence gathering and espionage were usually commercially motivated; and although images of a paradisiacal Pacific recur in Becke's writings and prefigure Margaret Mead's popularisation of notions of 'free love' in the South Pacific a generation later (vigorously contested by Australian anthropologist Derek Freeman), Becke's 'trader's eye' is more attuned to the exchanges of beliefs, stories and values that occur in these islands at a time of international unrest.[2] The trader in impressions, information and ideas who is also a writer has much in common with the spy and may be seen as a natural precursor, though the piratical figure of buccaneer Bully Hayes fits more readily than does Becke into a later James Bond stereotype.

While apparently peripheral to European power-plays, Australia by the 1890s was moving towards separate nationhood within broader notions of empire – 'a new Britannia' in these southern seas. In this context of political currents and cross-currents, Australia quietly commenced its history as an international spying nation.

Bridges in the Pacific

William Bridges, Australia's first military spy, was sent in 1898, at the age of thirty-seven, to Samoa to 'assess the situation' in this German possession in the Pacific. Trouble had been developing there and finally erupted into 'open warfare' between factions backed by Germany versus Britain and the US.[3] During his spying assignment, Bridges showed his cross-cultural adaptability with a visit to the rebel King Tamasese.

Several years later, Major Bridges was on another spying mission in the Pacific, this time in New Caledonia. Under cover as 'Mr Bridges', a commercial agent for Dalgetys Ltd, he was tasked with mapping and marking the position of gun batteries around the harbour at Noumea which could provide anchorage for French warships. Between May and July 1902, Bridges obtained valuable information and photographs for Australia's new Director-General of Military Intelligence and Mobilisation in an espionage mission described by General Hutton as 'secret and somewhat dangerous'.[4] Bridges' reports were forwarded to the War Office in London. These early experiences in intelligence-gathering and reporting were influential in Bridges' illustrious career in the Australian Army and later benefited students at Australia's first military college, Duntroon, in Canberra, where General Bridges was the highly praised foundation Commandant.[5]

Australia's early international spying efforts were inevitably small-scale missions carried out by 'lone rangers'. In 1901, the new Australian government sent scholar Wilson Le Couteur as a secret agent to the New Hebrides for three months to gather information on French activity in New Caledonia.[6] Le Couteur's civilian mission fits an imperial pattern of the educated 'gentleman spy' whose knowledge of the history, language and geography of a place or region informs and gives substance to their reportage.[7] Their underlying purpose was the strengthening of empire.

A Changing Focus in Australian Intelligence towards Japan

While much information-gathering and covert surveillance by residents of Australia in the early years of the Commonwealth of Australia concerned Pacific 'areas of darkness' or possible sources of threat such as New Guinea, German Samoa or French possessions in the Pacific, a larger and more persistent threat was perceived in Japan. As Australian Prime Minister Alfred Deakin wrote, 'Japan, or her head-quarters is, so to speak, next door, while the Mother Country is many streets away'.[8] International relations with Japan vacillated during Australia's first decade as a nation but Japan's military victory over Russia in 1905 re-established the island nation as a potential threat to British imperial interests and hence Australia. A change in attitude towards Japan can be discerned during 1907–8 with reports in Queensland newspapers of Japanese 'pseudo-fishermen' making surveys of the Great Barrier Reef and others allegedly mapping stock-routes. Lieutenant-Colonel Bridges, now in charge of the Australian Intelligence Corps, investigated these reports through state police forces and declared them unfounded. Nevertheless, increasing fear and suspicion of Japan became a significant stimulus to activities of the Australian Intelligence Corps.[9]

A. G. Hales

Literary accounts contributed to apprehension, and sometimes a deeper knowledge of international intrigues. A. G. Hales's novel *Little Blue Pigeon: A Story of Japan* (1904), for example, presents Tokyo during the build-up to the Russo–Japanese war as a hotbed of international espionage. The Adelaide-born Hales was a war-correspondent, miner, international adventurer and prolific author. After covering the South African war where he was wounded and captured by the Boers, Hales reported for the London *Daily News* on the Macedonian rebellion against the Turks and was at some of the major Russo–Japanese battles in 1905.[10] He was an acute observer and analyst of British, Chinese and Japanese imperial ambitions, from his independent Australian standpoint.

Hales incorporated these concerns into his entertaining novel about the romance of Clifford, an agent in the service of the British Empire, and Blue Pigeon, a geisha girl of Samurai family background who has learnt English during an unexplained stint of two years in Sydney. Pursued also by Quong Foy, a Chinese-born agent for the Russians, Blue Pigeon is the centrepiece of competing claims by Britain, Russia and China for the heart and soul of Japan. In an interesting twist, some key Russian spies in this novel pose as American missionaries. Fortunately, the seductive but trustworthy Japanese girl Blue Pigeon can tell the difference between Russians and Americans and remains a true asset of the red-bearded Clifford who has won her heart and her loyalty.

From a secret service perspective, Hales's novel is interesting for its depiction of the way agents of Czarist Russia attempt to involve Australia in their attempted destruction of British imperial interests. Their agent in place, Chinese-born Quong Foy, presents a persuasive scenario to fellow Russian agent Boris Metchkin. When the Russo–Japanese war is on, he says, the combined 'yellow races' of Japan and China will demand that the embargo on 'Asiatics' in Australia be removed. This will be a direct blow to Australia and the rest of the Empire, for the Australians 'hate the yellow man worse than the Americans hate the black man'.[11] Quong Foy believes – and so does Boris Metchkin who has worked in Britain – that the rich British aristocrats who run that country will not ultimately defend Australia against Japanese attacks because they have no real interest in supporting the ideals of the democracies. However, the success of this scenario which predicts the dissolution of the British Empire depends on the 'Yellow Bond' of Japan and China – of which Quong Foy believes he has solid evidence through Chinese secret societies. These hypothetical scenarios based on partial evidence and contemporary prejudice contain some shrewd insights and premonitions of arguments later presented to the Paris Peace Conference in 1919 by Australia's Prime Minister Hughes. While not knowing of the secret 'Yellow Bond' (until he is told of it by Blue Pigeon), Clifford agrees with the Russian view that a Japanese attack on Australia would be catastrophic – it would break 'the backbone of the British Empire'.[12]

Another interesting insight provided by Hales's novel is the role that women can play in secret intelligence. Because official reports are usually written by senior (male) officials, the roles of junior or unofficial agents or assets (often female) are diminished or ignored. Yet, as *Blue Pigeon* shows, a whole plot can hinge on the motives, intuitions and intelligence of women. While the melodrama, violence and stereotypes make *Little Blue Pigeon* in some respects 'an archetypal James Bond story',[13] the courage and perseverance of the Japanese geisha girl of Samurai background give her an enhanced symbolic value in the world of international intelligence.

Scholarship, Fiction and Secret Intelligence

A shift in Australian intelligence gathering towards somewhat more sophisticated forms of inquiry was discernible by the end of Australia's first decade as a nation. Lord Kitchener's visit to Australia in January 1910 and his recommendation to strengthen intelligence partly through area officers to be drawn from the military college which he had recommended was a start.[14] The Royal Military College at Duntroon, modelled on West Point, Sandhurst and Kingston, Ontario opened in 1911. Recruitment of well-educated and capable army officers into the Australian Intelligence Corps became more feasible. In 1909, the AIC numbered sixty officers and included Edmund Leolin Piesse from Tasmania who was to figure prominently in intelligence circles during the First World War and the post-war years. While internal surveillance of German interests in Australia necessarily dominated the energies of the Counter Espionage Bureau (forerunner in some respects of ASIO) headed by Major George Steward, Piesse and others also looked further afield and to longer-term international strategic concerns in the Pacific in an Organization foreshadowing certain aspects of the Australian Secret Intelligence Service (ASIS) half a century later.

George Steward served as private secretary of Australia's Governor-General – indeed he served five governors-general – and was ironically dubbed by Munro Ferguson, his fifth, as 'Pickle the Spy' after a popular fictional character,[15] because of the unsavoury individuals who were said to lurk around Government House to meet with Steward.[16] A former boxer and sculler of humble origins from London's East End, Steward was suspicious of intellectuals and critical of Australian censors during the war years; they were, he said, 'for the most part University Professors [and] show a great want of that degree of imagination which is necessary in work of this character'.[17] This apparently damning criticism of university professors raises questions about alliances between academe and intelligence and the uses of imagination in this work. Reliable and efficient in administrative matters, Steward could be brusque in manner but was a reliable guardian and transmitter of secret ciphers between Australia and Britain; and he could be astute in his dealings with men ranging from prime ministers and governors-general to spies and informers. His comments about 'imagination' and its appropriate applications in the spying game have continued to reverberate (but with various interpretations of 'imagination', and its uses and abuses) throughout the history of Australian intelligence.

Scholar Spies and Strategic Intelligence – James Murdoch and Edmund Piesse

Edmund Piesse became friendly with the older James Murdoch – university academic, linguist and historian of Japan – in the early years of the First World War and thus commenced a remarkable collaborative engagement with great potential benefit for Australian intelligence. Such intelligence gathering arose from a deep knowledge base in history, literature, language, religion, the arts and science. When applied to more immediate operational goals such as military tactics or political decision-making, such intelligence could seem complex and sometimes contradictory – as 'real' (as opposed to 'raw') intelligence often does. In such circumstances, the basis for conflict between politicians and their intelligence advisors is ever present.

Piesse first met Murdoch in 1915 when he was thirty-five and Murdoch was fifty-nine. The spymaster Piesse recognised that he could benefit personally and professionally from the older man's knowledge and understanding of Japan, which he soon learnt was far from superficial. The Scottish-born Murdoch had taught in Queensland schools after his arrival in Australia in 1881 with his English wife, Lucy; it was an unhappy marriage that produced one son. Murdoch worked on the radical-nationalist journal the *Boomerang* and visited Southeast and Northeast Asia. He later returned to Japan with his eight-year-old son, taught in schools and entered Tokyo Imperial University in 1889 where for four years he studied and engaged in literary activities, wrote poetry, short stories and a novel and edited a magazine.

A number of Murdoch's stories in *From Australia and Japan* (1892) reveal a young radical socialist of working-class Scottish origins encountering the radically different societies of Australia and Japan. (One of Murdoch's personae in these stories is 'Felix Holt Secundus', a Scottish version of George Eliot's idealistic radical.) As Megumi Kato notes, Murdoch's young narrator differs from many other Western commentators on Japan by participating in what he sees and hears, introducing cultural differences and acting at times as 'a mediator between East and West'.[18] With this kind of outlook, and his inquisitive intelligence, Murdoch was less likely than certain Australian nationalist authors such as Randolph Bedford or C. H. Kirmess to see the Japanese *en masse* in stereotypical terms or to share easily aroused Australian fears of a foreign invader. As he demonstrated in his *History of Japan*, Murdoch's knowledge of Japanese culture became deep and extensive. But Murdoch's imaginative romantic adventurers in *From Australia to Japan* also reveal similarities to characters in fiction by John Buchan, the writer of spy stories; by an interesting coincidence, Buchan was commissioned by Murdoch's publisher the following year.[19] The chief difference between the two writers is that Murdoch's alter ego is that of a working-class hero who asserts himself energetically, but he lacks the aristocratic panache of Buchan's Richard Hannay. Nevertheless, the combination of spy/investigator/writer continued to interact in Murdoch's persona and career.

In further study at the British Museum, Murdoch made translations of sixteenth-century Japanese texts, and returned and taught economic history at the Higher Commercial College (later Hitotsubashi University) in Tokyo, where in 1899 he married Takeko Okada. They bought an orchard near Tokyo. Thanks to Piesse and the Defence Department,

Murdoch returned with his Japanese wife to Australia in 1917 to teach Japanese at the Royal Military College, Duntroon; he was subsequently appointed Professor of Oriental Studies at the University of Sydney.[20]

Despite his relative youthfulness, Piesse was a policy 'wonk' who brought much to the collaboration. A science graduate of the University of Tasmania in 1900, he had studied mathematics at King's College, Cambridge, but was obliged to return home when his father died in 1902; he graduated in law in 1905. Piesse retained a strong interest in the natural sciences thoughout his life and was honorary secretary of the local Royal Society in 1912–14. He was a scientist, humanist and lawyer who became a practical policy maker with a strong belief in evidence-based policy. Having joined the newly established Australian Intelligence Corps in 1909, Piesse produced the first military survey of Tasmania before he transferred to Melbourne in 1916 and was promoted to major and director of military intelligence at the Directorate of Military Operations. Piesse's special talent and his most amenable work was in the collation and analysis of strategic intelligence.[21]

Under Murdoch's guidance, Piesse learnt Japanese. When the Australian government created a Pacific branch of the Prime Minister's Department in 1919 to study 'the affairs of the countries of the Far East and the Pacific' and desirable Australian policy, it did so on Piesse's advice and he was appointed its director.[22] Together, their efforts introduced a small nucleus of Australians to Japanese language and culture with a view to better intelligence in the region.[23] One such beneficiary was Eric Longfield Lloyd who had taken part in the landing at Gallipoli on 25 April 1915; when wounded, he served in the Intelligence Section of the General Staff. He joined Piesse's Pacific Branch and began learning Japanese. Longfield Lloyd held a number of senior roles in intelligence both before and during the Second World War.

A remarkable set of professional conversations opened up between Piesse and Murdoch, and intensified during and after the First World War. These discussions and their ensuing correspondence contained secret and confidential as well as 'public domain' material. They played a strong part in advice given to the Australian Prime Minister and government. Murdoch's regular and often extended visits to Japan provided much useful information and food for thought for Piesse as he grappled with Australian–Asian relations, especially with Japan. Some of Murdoch's observations were provocative challenges to Australian military authorities as when he remarked that, 'The best brains in Japan are in the Army and Navy and often to be found in the Intelligence Service'.[24] At a more general, reflective level, Murdoch had come to reject theories of innate racial differences as 'pestiferous explosive poppy-cock'. As he pointed out to Piesse in 1918, 'If we really want war, all we've got to do is to keep harping upon our pseudo-scientific racial "biology"'.[25]

Murdoch's sources in Tokyo included journalists, academics and high level government officials ranging from the Japanese Head of the Ministry of Foreign Affairs, Shidehara, to the American Ambassador, Roland Morris, whose knowledge and insight impressed Murdoch greatly. When writing to Piesse, Murdoch addressed his correspondence to a codename at Piesse's residential address – 'Mr MacRae'. He knew he had to be careful because, 'the Japanese were watching all correspondence very carefully'.[26]

Information to which Murdoch was given access, or extracted from sources, included Japanese troop movements and numbers. He learnt, for instance, of Japan's 'complete plan for the military annexation of Eastern Siberia'.[27] But he also believed in an older form of intelligence which he described as 'swapping wisdom', as when he distilled the results of a discussion with journalist friends:

> The collapse of Germany has at last had its effect; – German militarism is now being held up as a terrible example and able editors are everywhere preaching to their public the advisability of taking warning and turning over a new leaf ... and on the whole, the country has become reasonable, very reasonable. In short, things are much more hopeful than they have ever been since 1914.[28]

Yet racial discrimination in Australia, as an historical consequence of the White Australia policy, continued to bedevil Australia's relations with Japan and other countries of what was later called the Asia-Pacific region in Australia or the Pacific Rim in the US. Murdoch, who earlier in life had depicted the Chinese in racial terms, became a voice of calm reason as he tried to moderate Australian fears of Japan during and after the First World War. In this process, we can see an interplay of politics, prejudice and international rivalry as different nations vied for advantage at the Paris Peace conference and at the subsequent Washington Conference of 1921–2.

Murdoch's advice to Piesse was presented in reasonable and temperate terms and he also sought to influence Japanese opinion through his contacts there. For example, through Murdoch's connections with Japanese journalists and editors he managed to persuade influential newspapers in Japan to present the view that the 'White Australia' policy was mainly a labour problem and not directed against the Japanese or Chinese as a race.[29] As a result of Murdoch's advice and his own investigations, Piesse became convinced in the early post-First World War years that 'Japan had no designs on Australia and that Australia should remove its discriminatory barriers against Japanese immigration and trade'.[30] Australian Prime Minister Hughes, who was presented with these views in a memo from Piesse, responded with one word, 'Rot'.[31] Piesse would not be the first or last respected senior intelligence advisor to the Australian government to be disparaged and his case summarily dismissed by a Prime Minister determined to defend Australia's borders against real or imagined invaders. (Another senior intelligence advisor in the Howard years to meet this fate was Andrew Wilkie who resigned in March 2003 in protest over Australia's impending entry into the Iraq war.[32]

Prime Minister Hughes's attitudes and approach at the Paris Peace conference were attacked in the Japanese press. The Tokyo *Nichi Nichi* offered a neat admonishment of Australia's Prime Minister while also exposing Japan's continuing southward ambitions in the Pacific:

> If Mr Hughes understands the spirit of the Anglo-Japanese alliance and realises how much Japan contributed militarily and economically to the Allies' victory, he ought to be the first to welcome both the abandonment of racial discrimination, which must precede the formation of the League of Nations, and also the Southward development of Japan, and by falling in with the policy of Japan contributing to the establishment of a permanent peace – the primary motive of the recent war. He on the contrary, in opposition to the policy of the Mother Country, persists in his anti-Japanese attitude, clings to his principles of racial prejudice and, much to our surprise, is entirely devoid of the characteristic magnanimity of a great Empire.

The permanent occupation of the South Sea Islands and the abolition of racial discrimination are to be Japan's chief claims at the Peace Conference. These are not only Japan's reward but are guarantees for the future peace of the world …[33]

Prime Minister Hughes continued to see Japan as a threat and publicly declared that the next war was likely to be in the Pacific.[34] In these circumstances, it is not surprising that Australian foreign policy in the aftermath of the First World War was seen largely as a civilian extension of defence intelligence and that suspicion of Japan was at its heart.[35] Denigrated by his Prime Minister and flying in the face of public opinion, the intelligence expert Piesse and his key advisor Murdoch were hereafter firmly excluded from any influential role in Australian foreign policy. Thus, Piesse's influence on Australian policy towards Japan diminished after the First World War and he was not invited by Hughes to the Imperial Conference in London in 1921. Two years after Murdoch's death in 1921, Piesse resigned from the Pacific Branch and joined a Melbourne law firm. He continued to take an interest in defence and foreign policy issues with special reference to Japan. In the mid-1920s he discounted the dangers from Japan, including espionage, but by the early 1930s he saw renewed danger from that quarter and used his influence to ensure greater public spending on defence in the later 1930s.

Afterthoughts: The Divided Pacific

The Pacific Islands Forum, held in Cairns in 2009 and chaired by Australian Prime Minister Kevin Rudd, was a reminder of the manifold divided interests of inhabitants of those islands. A major topic was climate change underscored by fears of rising seas and – for some islanders – the prospect of obliteration. Politics and power issues, as well as economic concerns were to the fore. Many critical words were spoken about coup-prone Fiji but doors were left open for further negotiation. It is pertinent that the US is not a member of this Forum but an Under Secretary of State was present and Secretary of State Hillary Clinton has expressed a strong and growing interest in Asian and Pacific (or what used to be called Pacific Rim) affairs.

Within these oceanographic limits, Japan and Northeast Asia are of more urgent concern to the great powers than are Australia's neighbouring islands in the Pacific. Because of Australia's strong economy as a middle-ranking power and its continuing strong links with Britain and more especially with the US, Australia's intelligence interests in the region are now more firmly fixed than they were a century ago on Japan, China and Indonesia. This follows the regional argument for an Australian Secret Intelligence Service in 1950 by Prime Minister Menzies who stressed that ASIS would operate in 'South East Asia and in Pacific areas adjacent to Australia'.[36] At that time, under Menzies, the British Commonwealth role remained paramount: the new secret service, it was hoped, 'would in some small measure reduce the onerous world-wide commitments of the United Kingdom ... and enhance the security of the British Commonwealth in the Pacific'.[37] By 1966, however, Australian Prime Minister Harold Holt made the first of many professions of undying love for the US when he charmed President Lyndon Johnson (though not necessarily the Australian public) with his 'All the way with LBJ' statement.

A conservative political culture had lagged behind cultural developments. Even before the Second World War, seasoned observers of the Pacific and its region were raising questions about American–Australian relations. Closer relations would inevitably involve questions of national intelligence and its sharing. Would the intelligence culture change from the scattered kinds of 'lone ranger' exercises described in this essay and carried out in the interests of the British Empire and self defence? One experienced observer, Hartley Grattan, saw these issues in cultural terms. In his article 'An Australian–American Axis?' published eighteen months before Pearl Harbour, Grattan wrote, 'the hard realities of Pacific politics are drawing the Australians into the American sphere'.[38] But this would happen only if 'the spell of Britain was exorcised'.[39] In Grattan's view, only an independent Australia – one which acted 'for itself and apart from Britain' – would be of real use to either country.[40] From these precepts, Grattan praised the development of an independent Australian literature and closer literary and cultural relations between Australia and America.

As Australia–US relations strengthened during the last half of the twentieth and the first decade of the twenty-first century, Australian intelligence involvement in the Pacific and Asian countries has varied widely. From the Cold War to Vietnam and 9/11, new crises have brought different kinds and levels of intelligence interaction between Australia and the US. When I interviewed former CIA chief George Tenet in Washington DC in 2006, he spoke warmly of Australian intelligence officers and his interaction with them and how much he respected especially their knowledge and understanding of Indonesia. The contrast in scale and sophistication of operations and communications technology between the present situation and Australian intelligence operations in Asia and the Pacific a century ago is enormous. Yet we can find points of connection and commonality across this historical span too. From William Bridges' spying on military installations in New Caledonia at the beginning of the century to Edmund Piesse and James Murdoch's investigation and analysis of Japan's strategic intentions during and after the First World War, we can see in embryonic form some of the major concerns of the spying game today. These rapid glimpses emphasise the need for more sustained comparative studies of Australian and US intelligence engagements and their cultural implications in the Asia-Pacific region.

Seven

Under Cover: Projections of British and Australian Secret Intelligence

When did spying begin in or around Australia? Can George Smiley's assertion of an eternal life for spies and spying be held to apply to multi-lingual, pre-European contact Aborigines? What kinds of intelligence were gathered about rival groups, or nations, and what use was it put to?[1] And what of post-contact intelligence, both by Aborigines and whites? These questions deserve further investigation, as do the purposes and modes of spying by European maritime explorers of Australia's shores from the sixteenth to the eighteenth centuries.[2] In this period, the motives were often commercial, with the Dutch East India Company to the fore, and also national, especially between the English and the French during and after the Napoleonic Wars (see Chapters 4 and 5). One thinks of the various mutinies and the British and French explorers, for sixty years after Cook's discovery on the east coast, who visited the western coast in 'pairs' to keep eyes on each other.[3] Then, in colonial times, visits to Australia by officers of the British Raj in India brought some of the values and expertise.

The British convict system in Australia, which the French had planned to emulate if they had settled the southwest corner of the continent,[4] created the conditions in which spying was rife. When Peter Carey's Jack Maggs – his reinvention of Charles Dickens's convict Magwitch from *Great Expectations* – tries to describe the prison conditions in Australia he says: '[E]veryone would be a spy on every other man. It was how they kept us down'.[5]

As these examples suggest, spying has at least two functions – one that operates externally, in foreign waters or lands – and one that operates internally to maintain what is thought of as law and order. This dichotomy has served to define two distinct arms of national intelligence operations in the twentieth and early twenty-first century – the internal function served by MI5, the FBI or ASIO, for example, and the external function served by MI6, the CIA or ASIS. Although a multiplication of agencies and units has complicated this neat arrangement into internal or 'home' affairs – the latter a British rather than an Australian term – and external or foreign affairs, the distinction remains.

Many commentators have remarked Australia's lack of an independent foreign policy following federation and the proclamation of nationhood in 1901. As Alan Renouf noted in his book *The Frightened Country*, a Department of External Affairs had been set up by the federal government in 1901, but 'it was small and unimportant because Australia's foreign policy almost always was that of Britain'.[6] This situation waxed and waned in the inter-war period from 1918 to 1939, but the war in the Pacific and the prolonged Cold War saw the first real stirrings of a cultural diplomacy that reflected a sense of increasing postcolonial independence in Australia.

As outlined in Chapter 6, Australia's first intelligence operation overseas occurred in 1902 when Major William Bridges was sent to French New Caledonia, at the request of the British government, to report on military installations there.[7] Bridges was in charge of 'military intelligence, the formulation of defence schemes and organization of the forces'.[8] Major General Hutton, commander of the Australian forces, ordered Bridges in May 1902 'to collect information on the defences of Noumea, New Caledonia, on behalf of the War office, a task he performed successfully under cover as Mr Bridges, a commercial agent. He was promoted lieutenant-colonel in July'[9] soon after his return from New Caledonia. The theme of promotion, preferment or other forms of British recognition after successful intelligence operations, rather than large monetary payments, recurs in what scarce records are available. In Bridges's case, he rose to brigadier-general and was awarded a CMG. Following his recommendation to the Australian government by Lord Kitchener, Bridges was appointed commandant of the first military college in Australia, which became Duntroon. (The Library there was named after him.) Examples from Britain and America competed for Bridges's attention during the planning of Duntroon, with his preferred model being the US Military Academy at West Point. The Royal Military College at Duntroon opened in 1911 and Bridges remained commandant until 1914, when he left to become inspector general then commander of the Australian Imperial Force, a name he himself chose as a counter to those who would have seen the Australian forces split up.

In Bridges's career, we can see a number of forces at work. First, a tendency to project British imperial needs as Australia's, as in the case of his intelligence assignment in New Caledonia; second, an openness to North America as an alternative source of military authority as in his willingness to explore West Point as a model for Duntroon; and third, an emergent Australian nationalist sentiment as in his insistence on an entity called the *Australian* Imperial Force in the First World War, which however remained deeply embedded in British policies and perspectives. Although conflicting points of view were evident in these positions, Bridges came to stand for a certain Australianness in the manner of his death. Killed by a sniper's bullet a month after the Gallipoli landing in April 1915, Bridges thus became an original ANZAC. He was appointed a KC in London as he lay dying from his wounds and his body was transferred to Canberra and reburied overlooking the Royal Military College. Britishness and Australianness were deeply enmeshed in his living and his dying; and beyond them, the American eagle hovered.

Australia's first major spy, Charles Howard Ellis (known as Dick or Dickie by colleagues) was a more complex and contradictory character than Bridges. Born in Sydney in 1895, Ellis left in his teens to fight on the Western Front in the First World War, where he is said to have acquired 'a healthy scepticism about claims of military infallibility that stayed with him all his life.'[10] After the war, Ellis studied languages at Oxford and the Sorbonne and 'eventually became fluent in several European languages, plus Persian, Russian, Turkish, Urdu and Chinese' as well as becoming an accomplished piccolo player.[11] The first of Ellis's four marriages, to a White Russian, Lilia Zelenski, was one among a number of biographical facts that he later sought to deny.[12] A short while after commencing work in the British Foreign Office, Ellis was recruited into MI6 in 1924 while he was in Berlin. A large part of his task was to recruit agents for Britain's SIS among the White Russian émigré community.

If Ellis had remained a faithful servant of Britain's SIS, we might never have heard about him. But Ellis's apparent brilliance at playing the double game, and achieving results, led him into some tight scrapes and considerable notoriety. Unlike Philby, Ellis was never 'sprung' as an agent of the Soviets, but after several days of interrogation late in his life by Peter Wright, Ellis did confess in 1966 to working for the Germans during the Second World War. In Wright's words, Ellis 'admitted passing over detailed order-of-battle plans for British Intelligence, as well as betraying the Hitler–von Ribbentrop telephone link, even though he knew this material was being passed by von Petrov to the Germans'.[13] Should Wright, or should we, believe this 'confession' any more than we should believe his denial that he worked for the Soviets? And of what significance were the 'secrets' Ellis allegedly sold? There is debate around each of these points. Nevertheless, Wright believed that he and his fellow counterintelligence interrogator, Bunny Pancheff, had 'uncovered a traitor of major proportions', who had passed significant secrets of the allies to both Germany and Russia. Even if only Ellis's German collaboration was true, Wright asserts that had he been caught in 1939–40, Ellis would have been hanged.[14]

The importance of Ellis to the story of Australian intelligence is that though he was trained in Britain and Europe, he played a seminal role in the formation of an Australian secret service. Although, as Toohey and Pinwill point out, it was known to MI5 that 'much of the information he provided to London in the 1930s about the internal secrets of the Nazi Party was false, either faked by his agents or invented by Ellis to please his SIS masters', and he was 'recalled to London and barred from headquarters' for a time, he was duly rehabilitated and posted to New York in 1940 as colonel and deputy head of the British Security Coordination.[15] (His case parallels Philby's in some of its reversals and rehabilitations.) Ellis also 'instructed the newly formed US Office of Strategic Services, the forerunner of the CIA, in the techniques of clandestine communications',[16] where his liaison work between British and US intelligence bureaux was highly praised. As a reward, Ellis was posted in 1946 to Singapore 'to reorganize British intelligence as Chief Controller of the Pacific Area, responsible for SIS activities from India to the Americas'.[17] Alfred Deakin Brookes, later to become the foundation director of ASIS in 1952, took up a diplomatic posting for the Southeast Asian command in Jakarta at this time and it is highly likely that the two Australians met and that Ellis contributed to Brookes's proposal for an Australian SIS in 1946.[18]

Ellis, the multi-lingual British Australian, returned from his Asia-Pacific posting to be given the plum job of chief of all SIS operations in North and South America. By the time he retired in 1953, Ellis, the brilliant Australian, was third in the MI6 hierarchy.[19] He had been caught in the web of British–German–Soviet intelligence rivalries and contributed to the formation of an Australian SIS. Yet doubts persisted about his loyalty (which his family never doubted) to the West and strong opinions were held about his role as an alleged Soviet KGB agent. In the latter role, he is said to have been the channel through whom the KGB 'reactivated' Kim Philby, their most valuable asset in 1954, two years after he had gone into the cold following his dismissal from British SIS.[20] We will return to Philby, without whom any account of British spying in the first half of the twentieth century would be incomplete. In the meantime, let us turn briefly to Nancy Wake, cold-shouldered by Australian authorities until her award, at the age of ninety-one, of the Companion of the Order of Australia medal in London on 3 March 2004.

Complex sets of forces underlie the equivocal unmasking of Dick Ellis as a villain and the promotion of Nancy Wake as a belated heroine in the world of espionage and special operations. Graeme Turner's *Fame Games* illustrates how such forces for fame and infamy operate. Woven through the projections of both Ellis's and Wake's stories is the question of patriotism, especially in time of war. The legend of Nancy Wake – the 'White Mouse' to the Gestapo – is of a woman who worked as a courier in the South of France with the French Resistance movement in 1940–3 and then with the British Special Operations Executive behind the lines in the Auvergne from February 1944 to June 1944, when the allied troops forced the Germans out of France. What kind of patriotism did Nancy Wake display? Her Australian biographer, Peter FitzSimons, seems clear. His book is subtitled 'A Biography of Our Greatest War Heroine'. But who does 'our' heroine belong to? Born in Wellington, New Zealand, in 1912 to a journalist father of English stock and a mother of French Huguenot and Maori background, Nancy and her older sisters and brothers moved with their parents to Sydney when she was a small child. FitzSimons places great weight on her father Charles Wake's desertion of the family when she was young, suggesting a continuing search for father-figures. He also emphasises Nancy's Anglo-Australian brand of patriotism: 'Britain was the mother country, Australia and New Zealand her proud and strapping sons ready to do their bit to defend her…[A]lthough we were from New Zealand and living in Australia', Nancy remarks, 'we were "of" Great Britain, and we were loyal to whoever was on the throne. It was never something you questioned'.[21] As in other spy narratives, Nancy retrospectively examines her capacity to betray friends. Recalling an instance when she had deflected the blame for an indecent poem found in her pocket to a school friend, so that they were both punished, she swore to herself that she would never 'dob anyone in again'.[22] Her school friends recall Nancy's hatred of teasing and bullying 'and her lack of fear of boys or teachers.[23]

Such are the stories that contribute to the legend of Nancy Wake, who is now etched in the national memory bank of Australians. This is not the place to explore the making of Nancy Wake as an Australian icon, but its timing is interesting. When the French awarded Wake their highest bravery award, the Chevalier de la Légion d'Honneur, Australian Prime Minister John Howard reportedly admitted that he didn't know who she was.[24] Given the Prime Minister's interest in war history, this seems extraordinary in view of the fact that Nancy Wake was already a recipient of the George Medal, the Croix de Guerre with Palm and Bar, the Croix de Guerre with Star, the Médaille de la Résistance and the American Medal of Freedom with Bronze Palm. At any rate, these honours and awards suggest that Nancy Wake was 'owned' by the Western Alliance rather than by Australia or New Zealand alone. Though Australian by upbringing, she spied and fought for the British and the French resistance. Olive Stonyer summarises Nancy Wake's most famous assignment:

> [This was her] 500 km marathon bicycle ride to replace the codes destroyed by her wireless operator during a raid. Without re-establishing these codes no new orders of weapon and supply drops could be made. She had to pass through a number of

German checkpoints but still managed to complete the ride in 71 hours, cycling almost non-stop'.[25]

Such was the dangerous role of a wartime spy behind enemy lines in occupied Europe.

If Dick Ellis's adventures and exploits have been kept largely under wraps by British and Australian intelligence and Nancy Wake's achievements as a spy and resistance fighter against the Germans has received belated recognition, the case of Harold Adrian Russel (Kim) Philby (1912–88) has been examined and cross-examined so many times that he seems the paradigmatic and irreplaceable spy of the twentieth century. Hayden Peake's selective bibliography in 2000 lists 157 books and articles that contribute substantially to the Philby story.[26]

The seminal role of Australian writers and researchers in projecting the figure of Kim Philby to the world deserves stronger recognition than it has so far received. Key figures in this story are Murray Sayle, Bruce Page and Phillip Knightley – Australian expatriate journalists in London during the swinging Sixties. In their twenties or early thirties, they worked in *The Sunday Times* Insight team of investigative journalists under north-country Englishman Harold Evans's editorship in an era before another kind of Australian, Rupert Murdoch, took over the paper in 1981 and changed its character in the era aptly called Thatcher's Britain. Stephen Alomes has remarked that 'Page, Sayle and Knightley were central players in Insight's main achievements – exploring dramatic events, exposing secrets, and fusing original writing and good writing'.[27] These three Australians, together with the Englishman David Leitch, who was married to Australian novelist Jill Neville, worked tirelessly towards telling the full story of a man whose life and career had been very professionally hidden from the public gaze. Their work, based on hundreds of interviews with diplomats, politicians, scientists, intelligence officers and others was published in its first iterations in a series of articles in *The Sunday Times* in 1967, some four years after Philby's defection to Moscow in 1963.

At this time, Philby says he had completed a typescript memoir in Moscow which he had no immediate intention to publish.[28] However, when he read the articles in *The Sunday Times* and *The Observer* he admitted that despite 'a number of factual inaccuracies and errors of interpretation', they presented 'a substantially true picture' of his career.[29] These articles completely changed the situation for Philby and, with KGB approval, and an introduction by Graham Greene, he published his memoir *My Silent War* with the aim of 'correcting certain inaccuracies and errors of interpretation, and to present a more fully rounded picture'.[30] Meanwhile, the gadfly Australian journalists were granted short leave from *The Sunday Times* to put their material together in the form of a book. Thus *Philby: The Spy Who Betrayed a Generation*, by Page, Leitch and Knightley, and introduced brilliantly by John le Carré, was published by André Deutsch in London in 1968. The material that had stung Philby, and his KGB minders, into publication, was available in a book by the two Australian writers and Leitch, which could be read side by side with the master spy's own, somewhat disappointingly impersonal memoir. This would not be the first, or last, time that Australian writers 'projected' aspects of British life to the wider world.

Nor should Murray Sayle's seminal interview for *The Sunday Times* with Philby at the Minsk Hotel in Moscow be forgotten. Over a vodka, with armed KGB guards outside, Philby famously denied that he was a traitor: 'To betray you must first belong. I never belonged'.[31] Philby presented himself in the interview with Sayle as having always fought against 'fascism ... and imperialism ... fundamentally the same fight'.[32] The rhetoric was designed to appeal to Sayle and his fellow Australians as well as to a wider public in the West. Page, the leader of the Insight team was described by his editor, Harold Evans, as a 'voracious intellect ... [who] called on Machiavelli, Marx, Coleridge and Keynes with all the vehemence of the autodidact'.[33] As well as being intelligent, these young Australians in London seemed 'classless' to their editor, Harold Evans, and they threw themselves into exposés of Establishment arrogance and misbehaviour with gusto. Le Carré's introduction to *Philby: The Spy Who Betrayed a Generation* brilliantly summarises in its opening paragraph something of the postcolonial appeal of the Philby story to its Australian authors:

> The avenger [Philby] stole upon the citadel and destroyed it from within. Yet both the avenger and the citadel were largely creations of the same historical condition. The avenger was the son of a British Raj; the citadel was dedicated to the preservation of British power; both had been displaced by the

evanescence of Empire. The avenger was an embittered solitary with the arrogance of a man familiar with the terrain of personal philosophies: the Arabian desert. He would root out the old fort with the indifference of the timeless wind, the cunning of the Levantine and the amoral loyalty of Kipling's chosen boy; yet he was still one of them, at war with his own shadow. [34]

Le Carré draws here on biographical facts such as Philby's birth in India, his nickname Kim being drawn from Kipling's boy-hero and his father being a notable Arabist. Le Carré was an early entrant into the legendising of Philby. The Australian investigative journalists whose task was to establish the bare bones of the narrative and to put some meat on them would have been attracted to such mythologising even as they sought to establish 'facts'. They may also have seen Philby in part through Australian mythology as having something of Ned Kelly about him.

There are many reasons for Kim Philby having maintained his appeal across generations and cultures as the paradigmatic figure of the twentieth-century spy.[35] High among these causative factors is the role that a group of energetic and able Australian journalists played, with the active encouragement of their liberal and imaginative editor, in establishing the essential narrative of Philby's career as a spy during his own lifetime. As we have seen, the Insight team's *Sunday Times* reports flushed Philby's memoir *My Silent War* into its published form. When Page, Leitch and later Knightley read the Philby memoir – to which they had had no prior access – they published a revised Penguin edition with a new 25-page preface outlining the points of coincidence and difference with Philby's memoir and explaining why, despite official pressure not to publish, they went ahead.[36]

One of this group of trailblazing journalists, Phillip Knightley, remained tenaciously on the case. Over time, he became the leading authority on Philby from Philby's point of view; and later, a knowledgeable authority on the KGB's point of view. These events occurred because Knightley had struck up a correspondence with Philby in 1968, which continued for twenty years and culminated in the crucial six days of interviews he was finally granted with Philby in Moscow in early 1988, several months before Philby died. Knightley's book *Philby: KGB Masterspy*, based largely on the interviews and correspondence, concludes that Philby 'did it for his ideals' and that he was driven by the need to betray his class rather than his country. Knightley's later introduction to Genrikh Borovik's *The Philby Files*, based on the Russian's extended interviews with Philby in Moscow, juxtaposed with KGB files on him, comments on the book's exposure of the KGB's waxing and waning support for, and belief in Philby, which contrasts with Philby's version in *My Silent War* of 'a seamless web of dedicated service'.[37] In short, the KGB's distrust of Philby (as well as of Burgess and Maclean) – the Soviets' fear that they could be British 'plants' – continued to bedevil these Britons' lives in a Russia which none of them learned to see as 'home'.[38]

In his authoritative survey of spies and spying in the twentieth century, *The Second Oldest Profession*, Phillip Knightley expresses a general scepticism about the utility and value of espionage:

> The trouble is that intelligence agencies have become wellsprings of power in our society, secret clubs for the elite and privileged. And as well as being highly skilled in the use of that power, they have been able to rely on the fascination that intelligence has held for many world leaders, from Winston Churchill to John F. Kennedy, a fascination based in part on the many works of fiction that have made the spy one of the most potent images of our age.[39]

This is not the facile scepticism of a superficial journalist but that of a metropolitan Australian who has investigated contemporary spies and spying in depth and at length from his London base and projected his findings to the world at large. Will spying diminish as a result of such measured scepticism? The answer to that question must be a resounding no. The Cold War has been succeeded almost seamlessly by the War on Terror. American, British and Australian intelligence Organizations are more than doubling the size of their intelligence agencies. There are upsides as well as downsides to this trend: 'Human' intelligence ('Humint' to the CIA), the study of languages and cultural understanding are being emphasised in recruitment to counter the previously unreasonable faith in high-technology communications systems. That is a positive, and it may discourage simplistic, moralistic intelligence about complex individuals and societies. As the major source culture for Australian understandings of espionage in the first half of the twentieth century, Britain has projected a capacity for secret espionage operations that both challenges and intrigues the Australian imagination.

Eight

Traditional Myths and Problematic Heroes: The Case of Harry Freame

Introduction

The figure of Harry Freame, who was born in Japan of an Anglo-Australian father and Japanese mother[1] stands out as an unusually gifted on-the-ground secret agent for Australia whose contributions to military tactics and intelligence in two world wars were cut tragically short in 1940. Freame stands apart from the figure of the 'gentleman spy' who tends to dominate accounts of secret intelligence in Britain and its empire (Fisher). Harry Freame lived his life more physically than such self-styled intellectuals and high-level political intelligence operatives who tend to dominate public perceptions of the spy. He provides the worm's eye view of the spying game and his story reveals the physical as well as mental demands on certain agents involved in clandestine activities.

Gallipoli

Harry Freame enters Australian military history through his heroic conduct as a scout at Gallipoli, the ill-fated landing on 25 April 1915 when the Australian nation and character are said by a number of historians to have been born. Australia's official historian of the war, C. E. W. Bean, described Freame as 'probably the most trusted scout at Anzac'[2] and extolled his courage and ingenuity at the Gallipoli landing for which Freame was awarded the Distinguished Conduct Medal; Bean suggested he deserved the Victoria Cross.[3]

Bean writes graphically of Freame's actions in his Personal Records:

> Harry Freame, a lance-corporal at the landing, was one of the very few who received a decoration for his work in that battle. ... [Freame] and others had held vital positions in that constantly moving and changing fight but none was so ubiquitous as he, now holding a key point on the Nek leading to Baby 700, now finding for his commander scattered parts of the battalion. On the second morning he discovered a group under Jacobs at Quinn's – the embryo of that famous post. Finding them much exhausted and without water, Freame and a New Zealander from the group dashed down the dangerous slope and brought back a supply from the foot of the hill. That finished, he dashed down the hill again carrying his report to his colonel. As he reached the foot his voice was heard calling 'All right!' Afterwards the party learnt that he had been twice hit during the descent.[4]

While these actions led to his recommendation for the DCM, Freame's fellow soldiers at Anzac seem to have been equally struck by his near magical powers as a gatherer of intelligence.

> Possessed of an uncanny sense of direction, Freame was never more in his element than when, at night, he was wriggling his way, like an eel, across the divide of No Man's Land, picking up information, and more information, to satisfy the voracious demands of the intelligence officers...
>
> Silently, but surely, Freame moved about in the darkness, often up to the very brink of the enemy trench, even into it, and it is related of him that, on one occasion, he lay so close to the Turks that he could follow a game of cards in which a number of them were engaged.[5]

But the unseen scout is also a man of action who knows how to defend himself in adversity:

> During one of these nocturnal excursions [Freame] ventured too far, and was caught by the Turks in one of their trenches. There he was held prisoner until the next night, when he was

marched away, under a guard of six men, to Anafarta; but, pulling out a revolver which he had had secreted in his tunic under his armpit, he shot down his captors and escaped to his own lines – keen as ever on further enterprise.[6]

A man of dash and style whose courage bred confidence in others, Freame wore a recognisable black and white spotted bandana in the trenches.

Freame's prominence in historical accounts of Anzac led to mythic tales of his prowess and his inclusion in Roger McDonald's award-winning novel *1915* where he is depicted in colourful terms as 'the scout Freame, steady as a snake ... He was part Japanese and had the silky unruffled look of someone constantly at the centre of important events'.[7] Biographical commentators have remarked how Freame's appearance and speech led to assumptions about him. Freame seems to have encouraged such speculation. Courtney remarks that '(h)is dark complexion and peculiar intonation of speech had led his companions to believe that he was Mexican – an impression which he reinforced at Anzac where, in cowboy fashion, he carried two revolvers in holsters on his belt, another in a holster under his armpit and a Bowie knife in his back pocket'.[8] The hidden holster under his armpit saved the day when he was taken prisoner by the Turks and shot his escort, but he did not escape injury. Later, after being seriously wounded during operations at Lone Pine, Freame was evacuated and discharged as medically unfit on 20 November 1916.

Despite his remarkable exploits and appearance, the courageous and adventurous Harry Freame was yoked in his fellow soldiers' retrospective accounts into the framework of the Anzac legend wherein he 'typifies the spirit of the average Australian soldier'.[9] With this background, it is interesting to observe the historian Bean's apparent hesitation and perhaps ambivalence as he considers whether Freame could achieve his ambition of becoming a commissioned officer with the AIF. In a line which he subsequently crossed through in pencil in his personal records, Bean remarked of Freame's commanding officer, 'though not unsure of Freame, whose character and achievements he well knew, [he] was not sure how Australians would accept him as their officer. In this, I am sure, [he] was for once completely astray – they would have leapt to Freame's skill and daring and the nobility of his leadership'.[10] One senses here Bean's idealism at odds with his assessment of a less inclusive outlook among the rank-and-file Australian troops, and also officers. Bean resists any racist implications of these observations and proposes instead a blander official version of the legend he helped to foster – of undivided courage and mateship under the Australian flag.

Mixed Race Identity

Yet the mixed-raced aspects of Freame's identity in the era of White Australia and empire contributed not only to ambivalence about him among Australian troops but also to his special qualities as a secret agent in the interwar period and the Second World War, as we shall see. Moreover it seems that Freame himself was highly aware of his mixed-race inheritance and its impact on his career. Indeed, this awareness led him to obscure his identity in certain significant respects.

Harry Freame grew up in Japan. To use his full name, Wykeham Henry Koba (or Kobe) Freame is believed to have been born on 28 February 1885 in Osaka, the son of Henry Freame, an Anglo-Australian clergyman/teacher and a Japanese woman, Shizu, née Kitagawa.[11] Other documents however show alternative birth dates in 1880, 1884 and 1888.[12] Little is known of Freame's parents except that his father was an Anglo-Australian Christian missionary and family tradition stressed that his mother Shizu was 'of the Royal house of Kitagawa'.[13] Their son Harry went to sea and travelled widely from his late teens, but his sister Grace became a teacher who remained in Japan and married a Japanese.

Freame's seaman's record shows he made twenty-two voyages between May 1902 and November 1909.[14] On leave in 1906, he married an English woman, Edith May Soppitt, in Middlesborough, but after a two month break was back at sea for extended periods including nine voyages from 1909 to 1912.[15] Edith probably stayed with her parents until after the First World War. Their two children, Henry and Grace, were born in 1921 and 1927 respectively.[16]

Harry Freame's own accounts of his life and career before the First World War are sketchy. His seaman's record is complemented by official documents of various kinds and an interview he gave to the Australian returned servicemen's magazine *Reveille* in 1931.[17] Taken together, these and other sources point to a certain evasiveness about his origins in Freame's life of adventure and intrigue. While some romanticising of events may have occurred in his interview, sixteen years after the Anzac landing, these accounts are largely reinforced by his military colleagues; and deeper sources of identity conflict may be identified along with Freame's recurrent interest and involvement in the world of secret intelligence.

In his marriage certificate in 1906 and his enlistment form for the Australian Imperial Force in 1914, Freame gave his place of birth as Kitscoty, Canada. J. S. Ryan surmises that this small hamlet near Edmonton, Alberta, 'would seem to have been chosen either because of its total isolation, or because of some possibility of its affording credence to a Canadian Indian background rather than a Japanese one ... [These accounts] were concerned to present him as a North American and to disguise his real antecedents'.[18] Why would this have been the case? Were British and Australian racist attitudes towards Japan and the Japanese a reason for Freame's subterfuge? Ryan suggests an earlier source of discomfort with his origins when he lived in Japan. As the son of a Christian missionary in the closing phase of the Meiji era (1896–1912), Freame would have felt the societal pressures in Japan against Christianity and towards national assertiveness and commercial and industrial development; and from his mother's side the pressures towards 'the military and samurai traditions of the house of Kitagawa'.[19] At the same time, he would have experienced the close links as well as rivalries of the Japanese and British naval traditions. His mixed inheritance could have led to complicated reactions.

Intelligence Agent

Harry Freame's trans-national credentials for secret work in military hotspots is evident from his early life. He joined the Japanese navy as a boy and received his early training in scout-craft in Japan, which was followed up later, he says, 'under the scientific teaching of Indians in USA and Mexico'.[20] According to this 1931 interview, Freame's first major intelligence role was in his early twenties in revolutionary Mexico, during the Diaz regime, when he served in Diaz's intelligence department under a German army officer, Major Zeigler. On Zeigler's advice, according to Freame, he took a multi-national assortment of scouts to German East Africa for service against 'a native uprising' (presumably the Hottentots).[21] Thus before he appeared at Gallipoli and carried out his well-attested acts of stealth and bravery, Freame was a seasoned on-the-ground fighter and intelligence agent. It is likely that habits of stealth, secrecy and covering one's tracks became an early and continuing part of his make-up.

In 1911 or 1912 Freame made his way to his father's homeland, Australia, where he worked as a 'horse-breaker' in Glen Innes in the Armidale district of New South Wales. He would later be repatriated to this district when he returned injured from Gallipoli in 1916. At that time, as Colonel F. J. Kindon remarked, 'he was too badly knocked about to serve and was returned to Australia'.[22]

When Harry Freame returned to civilian life in Australia he took up a soldier settlement block of land on the Kentucky estate in New England, New South Wales and became an orchardist. Kentucky was an orcharding community south of Uralla, about twenty-four miles from Armidale. When he stayed in Armidale, we know that Freame sometimes boarded at St John's Hostel.[23] Freame's wife, Edith, whom he had married in England in 1906, and with whom he had had a son and a daughter, died in 1939. Freame married her former nurse and carer, Harriet Brainwood, in 1940.

An apparently successful fruit grower (of apples and pears), Freame enjoyed reminiscing with war-time colleagues, and the walls of his home at Mt Salisbury, Kentucky, displayed sketches and paintings of war-time Anzac and France. According to his former officers, Freame was not only a courageous fighter; he was also a stern disciplinarian and a modest man with strong Christian principles.[24]

Pacific War Secret Agent

The date on which Freame re-entered the world of clandestine intelligence is not clear, though it appears to be some time in the late 1930s. Senior members of Australian intelligence, including Longfield Lloyd, held him in high regard for his exploits at Gallipoli. In particular, Lloyd singled out Freame's 'reconnaissance work': 'His scouting instinct was uncanny; his movements when so engaged usually defied detection and his endurance was as remarkable as his keenness … He combined sincerity with an inflexible determination and a fierce but cool courage'.[25]

When the Second World War broke out, Freame was probably fifty-four years old. He offered his services to the Australian war effort and was appointed to the Eastern Command Censorship staff at the Department of External Affairs. Colonel F. J. Kindon, recalled that when he last saw Freame, he had 'received an appointment on the staff of the Australian Ambassador to Japan, Sir John Latham, and expressed his satisfaction at being again permitted to serve the Empire which he loved.[26] But this appointment was preceded by secret intelligence work in Australia. From 4 December 1939, Freame was engaged in 'defence work of a highly secret nature'.[27] We now know that Australian military intelligence planted Freame as a secret agent among the Japanese community in Sydney[28] and that he left his New England orchard in the hands of his son. Not only was Freame able to report on attitudes, values and suspicious activities of the Japanese community in Australia; according to Freame's second wife, he was also shadowed by the Japanese in Sydney.[29] Spying is seldom a one-way operation and her claim is almost certainly true.

What contacts and enemies Freame made in the Japanese community in Sydney at this time and what he was able to report about suspicious behaviour there are not known. Given his earlier record, it is highly likely that he was an effective informant. What we do know is that on 26 September 1940 Freame was appointed as an interpreter on the first Australian legation to Tokyo. This was to be his cover job. Just as his official role for Defence in New South Wales was as interpreter and translator, so again in his new position he was described as 'interpreter, translator and controller' in Tokyo; but both positions provided cover for his substantive role as a secret agent charged with discovering intelligence about Japanese military intentions, plans and procedures and who was supporting them in Australia and elsewhere.

Unfortunately, Harry Freame's return to intelligence activities in the Pacific War was blighted from the beginning. First, and most seriously, his cover had been blown in an Australian newspaper. On 13 September 1940, the *Sun* published a small article headed 'Interpreter Appointed for Tokio [sic] Legation', which included the following sentences: 'Mr Freame, who was born in Japan, speaks and writes Japanese fluently. He is at present engaged on special defence work'. It appears that this was Freame's death sentence.

Some weeks after taking up his appointment in Tokyo on 21 November 1940, Harry Freame was apparently garrotted – a common form of physical attack in Japan at this time (perpetrators were known as 'garotsuki').[30] Freame was admitted to a Japanese hospital in Tokyo then repatriated to Australia where he died on 27 May 1941. Severe throat injuries impaired his speech but he was able to whisper to members of his family, 'They got me'. Although the official cause of death was given as throat cancer, subsequent investigations established that Freame's throat condition could not be connected with cancer but that it could have been caused by attempted strangulation.[31]

It is difficult to escape the conclusion that a primary cause of Harry Freame's premature death was the leak which led to the article in the *Sun* newspaper. The literature of intelligence and espionage contains many accounts of political and bureaucratic failures which endanger the lives of secret agents; Freame appears to be yet another victim. As he had done at Anzac, Harry Freame put his life on the line in Tokyo for Australian military intelligence but in this instance he was betrayed by his Organization. Following his death, a blame game of accusation and counter-accusation, suitably muffled in bureaucratese, floated between the Department of the Army and the Department of External Affairs. On balance, it seems that the leak emanated from External Affairs and indicates a failure of secure communication on intelligence matters between military and civilian arms of government.[32]

Aftermath and Contexts

The involvement of Australians in the Pacific War against Japan offered unparalleled opportunities for villainy and heroism. High on the list of villains, from an Australian point of view, were collaborators with the Japanese such as Alan Raymond in Shanghai whose radio broadcasts were designed to persuade Australians of the advantages of being under Japanese control.[33] This 'Quisling of Canberra' called on his countrymen and women to 'sever the British connection and withdraw from the war'.[34] On the other hand, the Australian agent as 'good guy' is exemplified in a contrasting figure such as Norman Wootton who quietly went about his political work of reporting on Japanese military plans and helping Australians in trouble.[35] He plays almost no role in the Australian public memory.

The search for final answers in secret intelligence is fraught with puzzles and dead ends. Harry Freame appears to have left no written account of his various roles in 'the spying game'. His discretion, like his courage under fire, seems to be part of his character. Loose talk among senior bureaucrats, journalists and others seems to have been his undoing. Yet no firm conclusion was reached about the cause of the leak that exposed Freame and no independent investigation was held. As with many such cases, despite the personal concerns of participants and their families, a cover-up in the interests of incumbent authorities, justified by the secrecy of undercover operations, is preferred to any searching investigation.

Compared with super-powers, such as the USSR and US during the Cold War, Australia has almost no record of honouring, or even remembering its secret agents. Why then should we remember Harry Freame? First, Freame's occasional engagements in spying activities for Australia in two world wars are reminders that high level strategic intelligence is always dependent on the men and women on the ground listening, watching and reporting; often themselves being shadowed by their opposite numbers. Second, Freame reminds us of the special value of trans-national Australians in intelligence. Freame's dual Japanese–Australian inheritance, and especially his speaking knowledge of Japanese, increased his value as a spy for Australia and his danger to the Japanese on the verge of war. Third, Freame's example shows the problematic nature of intelligence work, balanced between civilian and military needs, in peace and war.

Behind the lines of his public persona, we can also discern some of the complexities in Freame's sense of identity, and how his mixed-race inheritance played into his intelligence work. He learnt early the skills of reconnaissance and scouting techniques in Japan and developed these in military skirmishes in South America and Africa before he transferred to Australia and joined the AIF. Although adept at covering his tracks, Freame came into his own at Anzac and thereafter had no further need to conceal his Japanese origins. To officers and men, he was an Australian with special talents and skills, though never quite perhaps 'one of them'.

Freame's niece in Japan described her uncle in his fifties as a 'lonely' man.[36] Though he retained strong Christian beliefs and principles throughout his life, Freame's mixed inheritance and the external pressures which drove him to disguise his identity when he left Japan suggest an individual well suited for the kinds of secret intelligence work that he was called on to do at several stages in his life.

All spies are part of larger contexts. Before Japan's southward advance and the bombing of Pearl Harbour in December 1941, Australia had a number of 'Japan watchers' who provided useful intelligence to authorities in Defence and External Affairs. These included the academic historian Professor James Murdoch and foreign policy analyst Edmund Piesse, discussed in the previous chapter. In some respects, Murdoch was in the 'gentleman spy' tradition: he wrote and published open source accounts of the history and politics of Japan but was also engaged in secret work in liaison with Piesse and he gave briefings to prime ministers and senior government officials; Piesse was responsible for intelligence in the Pacific during the early interwar years. Together, these men and others attempted to gauge Japanese intentions and strategies in the Pacific in the light of history and changing race relations. But Piesse's conclusion in 1919 that there was 'probably little reason for applying discrimination based purely on race towards the Japanese was summarily dismissed by Australian Prime Minister Hughes, a strong advocate of White Australia policies.

The relatively small-scale Australian intelligence engagements with Asia in the interwar and early Second World War years is thrown into sharp relief by the now well documented accounts of Richard Sorge's spy ring for the Soviets in Tokyo from the mid-1930s to October 1941.[37] From 1929, Sorge spent four years being trained as a professional spy in Moscow. Ideologically committed to revolutionary communism, Sorge used his cover role as a journalist and close contacts at the German embassy to obscure his busy other life as a master spy for Stalin. His major intelligence coup was to give Stalin advance warning of operation Barbarossa, Hitler's impending attack on Russia, which Stalin chose to reject, to Russia's great cost.[38] Sorge also provided well-researched, high-grade intelligence on Japanese intentions in the Pacific.

Like Harry Freame, Richard Sorge was a 'cross-breed' though of a different pedigree – his mother was Russian and his father German – and this was a major component in the cross-cultural adaptability required for many kinds of international intelligence work. But there is no simple formula for success in the spying game; and even for master spies like Sorge or Kim Philby who betray their countries for another, luck plays a major factor in the success or otherwise of their activities. Fortune did not favour Harry Freame, an Australian patriot of Japanese extraction, whose full value to the allies' war effort was never realised when his working life as a spy for Australia was snuffed out in Tokyo in October 1940. Yet the hidden, often heroic lives of men such as Harry Freame, and their talents and skills displayed in perilous situations, deserve due consideration as Australians review their expanding intelligence role in the international community.

A Conclusion and Question

The case of Harry Freame poses some intriguing questions about heroism within different national contexts during and between two world wars.

First, the secret agent or spy is shown to be a problematic figure when it comes to assigning any kind of heroic status in Australia and Japan. For most exponents of 'the second oldest profession', suspicion and distrust are far more prevalent than praise. When deaths occur, 'moral grandeur' is seldom assigned to spies, and the details and circumstances of their work often remain obscure, mysterious.

A second observation is that mixed-race individuals can have a difficult time in ethnically homogeneous, nationalistic fighting forces such as Australia's and Japan's in the first half of the twentieth century. This accounts for Harry Freame's evasiveness about his origins and the myths that developed about him. But his inheritance of both samurai and Western military traditions contributed to his adaptability as a fighting man and secret agent. Never fully accepting himself, or being accepted fully by others, he nevertheless found his home, for a time, in Australia and its mythologies of war, especially the legend of Anzac – even if, at his death, a corresponding loyalty was not shown by his superiors.

Early twenty-first century Australia is a much more diverse, globally connected culture than the one Harry Freame inhabited. A conspicuous aspect of this change is the leading role played by many Asian Australians in Australian public life. One of these is Tim Soutphommasane, an Australian of Lao and Chinese extraction, an Oxford graduate who does not accept the mythology of the global market-place. He calls Australia home and wants to play his part in reformulating our sense of nationhood. His book *Reclaiming Patriotism* (2009) challenges

Australians to restore a proper sense of patriotism in the post-Howard years as 'an inclusive language of shared civic values and as an instrument of progress'.[39] This is the project we now see opening before us.

Nine

Politics, Espionage and Exile: Ian Milner and Ric Throssell

Why are espionage narratives significant at the present time? Two reasons are immediately apparent. First, powerful political pressures are being exerted in Western countries, led by the US, towards homeland security measures which involve increasing numbers of citizens in intelligence gathering and reporting. Newspapers and other media outlets regularly feature stories about spies and spying with varying degrees of 'creative' invention. Second, we are witnessing the emergence of a new enemy of the West to replace the Cold War's Soviet Union. As Clifford Geertz and others have remarked, we are now able to observe the construction of 'an American idea of Islam' as 'an enduring image of an alien phenomenon', which is occurring at a time when 'the American idea of America is the subject of no little doubt and dispute'.[1] When official intelligence agencies are expanding in all affected countries to accommodate the elusive requirements of a 'war on terror', it is perhaps timely to consider some of the human dimensions of the almost universal but essentially covert, sometimes creative activity we call espionage, together with the dilemmas of loyalty, belonging, exile and displacement it generates.

Official intelligence agencies in Australia and New Zealand cannot be considered in isolation from the empires that have largely dictated their fortunes in these countries: their chief source of culture in the twentieth century was Britain, together with the increasing influence of the USA. The institutional histories of Australian intelligence services show close resemblances to the development of MI5 and MI6 in Britain, with CIA influences more evident in the late twentieth and early twenty-first centuries.[2] The tentacles and traditions of British intelligence were especially evident in their influence on Australian politics and social practices following MI5's conclusion that a Soviet spy ring was operating in Australia during and after the Second World War.[3] Desmond Ball and David Horner summarise their conclusions about this period in *Breaking the Codes: Australia's KGB Network*:

> From 1943–49, a group of about ten people, all of whom were members of the Communist Party of Australia or close acquaintances of communists, provided information and documentary material to the Soviet State Security Service, commonly known as the KGB.[4]

While the Australian government had been informed of espionage activity in Australia as early as 1945, a visit by Sir Percy Sillitoe and Roger Hollis from MI5 in 1948 led to the formation of the Australian Security Intelligence Organization (ASIO) in 1949, which Labor Prime Minister, Ben Chifley, referred to as 'the Fourth Arm of Defence'. A 'special operations' unit, the Australian Secret Intelligence Service (ASIS) was established in 1952. The first major test of Australian intelligence was its investigation of Soviet espionage in Australia following the defection of Soviet agents Vladimir and Evdokia Petrov in 1954 and the first Royal Commission into espionage in 1954–5.[5]

This chapter briefly traverses significant moments in the careers of two Australasians – a New Zealander and an Australian – whose lives were engaged to a still uncertain extent in intelligence gathering and reporting. Both were left-liberals in outlook, though some might dispute the 'liberal' tag. Both were considered by some to be traitors to their homelands, though neither was found guilty by a court of law of spying. The names of these two men are Ian Milner and Ric Throssell. In addition to whatever espionage they may have carried out, Milner was a diplomat and literary academic; Throssell was a diplomat, playwright and novelist. They were creative 'men of letters'. Their active-intelligence lives span the period of the Second World War, the Cold War, the Korean and Vietnam wars and the collapse of the Soviet

Union symbolised in the fall of the Berlin Wall in 1989. Milner died in 1991 and Throssell in 1999. Significantly, perhaps, neither of them wrote popular spy fiction, though Throssell features a CIA agent in one of his novels. But the idea of exile, and the experience of it, affected each of them, and each experienced the dislocations, both mental and physical, that espionage entails. The poetics of neither man's experience, as expressed in their writings, could be described as tragic, but a certain pathos attaches to each when we see them, in retrospect, responding to the cross-currents of Cold War ideology. As the notoriety of their alleged espionage activities begins to fade, it is possible to see more clearly how two men of letters, buffeted between East and West, created literary spaces for themselves in their personal writings.

Displacement and Exile: Ian Milner

The autobiography of a spy, or suspected spy, is likely to be self-justificatory, at least in part, but is equally likely to reveal important aspects of motivation, purpose and desire. Ian Milner's memoir *Intersecting Lines* (1993),[6] scrupulously edited by Vincent O'Sullivan and published two years after Milner's death, reveals a mature man behind the 'Iron Curtain' in Prague from the 1950s, who has remained deeply attached to a New Zealand homeland of his memory and imagination. Recalling his return from Oxford University, where he had been a student, to Wellington in the winter of 1939, Milner reminded himself then of a homing pigeon:

> Rhodes Scholars of my generation didn't usually return to New Zealand because they found more inviting prospects in England or elsewhere. I came back because I felt the land – native bush, hills and mountains, sea-scapes and river valleys – was in my blood: I belonged there.[7]

But when war was declared in Europe, New Zealand Prime Minister Michael Savage expressed the nation's loyalty: 'Where Britain goes, we go'.[8] Despite the miles between, perhaps because of them, empire ties still held. Milner had proposed a broader, socialist-inspired world-view which did not hold in New Zealand. By February 1940, Milner was testing his fortunes in Australia. He wrote of the summer heat in

Melbourne after his arrival there and of what was perhaps a fateful early meeting with communist journalist, Rupert Lockwood:

> The summer heat was different in Melbourne. The day after my arrival it was 103°F and the air was scorched; smelt of burning. Melbourne's sirocco, the north wind from 'the desert', was blowing madly, thickening the air with brownish yellow dust ...
> I asked myself why I had come to this barbaric land: millions of acres of Dead Heart and cursed with meteorological horrors.[9]

This is a symbolically realised, retrospective landscape of the fateful city where Milner's reputation would later be scorched by the Royal Commission on Espionage in 1954–5. Milner's memoir, edited by O'Sullivan, enables us to read such fragments as part of a larger personal drama of alienation and belonging.

Another country of Milner's experience and imagination was England, the Mother Country for Anglo-Australians and New Zealanders, where this young man could study Politics, Philosophy and Economics at Oxford University in a syllabus which aimed at nothing less than 'an introduction to modern civilization'.[10] According to his memoir, Oxford in the mid-1930s reinforced Milner's sense of New Zealand-ness but also broadened his world-view by contact with great minds such as Isaiah Berlin, whose 'writings on the history of social and political ideas, especially those of the nineteenth-century liberal and radical reformers', especially impressed him.[11] Oxford was where Milner's socialist convictions were refreshed and stimulated, aided by travels in Russia and Europe. Where would this heady cocktail of ideals and convictions lead Milner? A short distance across country in Cambridge, at this time, four other young men – Burgess, McLean, Philby and Blunt – were commencing their different journeys towards careers as Soviet agents in a period when many intellectuals and students found an outlet for their idealism in socialist or communist movements. Whether Milner covertly joined the Communist Party at Oxford is unknown but his articles for *Tomorrow* in New Zealand and a number of his contributions to the Oxford Union show his sympathy for socialist causes.

After graduating from Oxford, Milner returned briefly to New Zealand before taking up a lectureship in politics at Melbourne

University in 1940 and then, in 1944, the position of First Secretary in Australia's Department of External Affairs in Canberra. Ball and Horner claim, on the basis of their reading of Venona decrypts, that when they were employed by the Department of External Affairs in Canberra (known to Moscow as 'the Nook') in 1945, Milner and his colleague Jim Hill 'worked closely together in providing material to Clayton', the 'spymaster' who passed information on to Moscow Centre through the Russian embassy in Canberra.[12] Frank Cain remains sceptical about these claims in respect of Milner.[13] But if they are true, and if Milner was made aware of Hill's interrogation in London in 1950 by 'Jim' Skardon, MI5's feared interrogator, as seems likely, according to Richard Hall,[14] Milner might well have felt that his time in the West was up. Later, in 1955, Australia's Royal Commission on Espionage found, on the basis of both the testimony of Russian defectors Vladimir and Evdokia Petrov and other material they had seen (presumably Venona material) that Milner (code-named BUR) had given information to the NKGB through the New Zealand-born, Australian-based Soviet agent Walter Seddon Clayton, code-named KLOD.[15] More recently discovered files of the Czech Ministry of the Interior seem to confirm this.[16] Milner responded to the Commission with a personal statement from Prague in 1956,[17] denying the claims that he had passed official information to the Soviets; the claims were never tested in a court of law. Like many others caught in the icy blasts of Cold War rhetoric, Milner's reputation – his 'good name' as John Proctor called it in Arthur Miller's *The Crucible* – suffered. He was called a traitor. He fought back as best he could – quietly, with dignity, from afar. He made another life for himself.

The 1950s was a difficult decade for Milner, as for many others. In his late thirties – that critical moment in many lives – Milner left his UN work in New York in 1950, and his career as a diplomat, to relocate himself in Prague, where he took up a lecturing job at Charles University in 1951. This was not a typical career move and various narrative explanations, or 'cover' stories, depending on whether or not Milner is believed to have been guilty of spying, have been proposed. Special treatment for his New Zealand-born wife Margot's arthritis was Milner's early explanation; later he admitted to having a lover he had met in New York, Jarmila Fruhaufova. Jarmila was a blonde Czech divorcee also working with the UN. It appears that Jarmila – who was

reported (by an FBI watcher) to look like the film actress Kim Novak
– worked indirectly for the Czech secret service when she was in the
UN in New York. She became an official agent of the secret police
after her return to Prague in February 1951.[18] In espionage parlance,
then, as James McNeish suggests, Milner may have been caught in a
'honey trap'.[19] It is difficult to envisage a more complicated scenario of
divided loyalties, feelings and behaviour as Milner tried to contribute
to the making of peace at the UN in the early postwar years, and found
himself compromised both sexually and politically.

Vincent O'Sullivan's and others' researches have shown that Ian
Milner was an idealistic internationalist, who believed in and worked
towards the foundation of an effective United Nations Organization
in the early post-war years. But for most internationalists, there
are one or two countries that really matter. For Milner, these two
countries became Czechoslovakia, where he had moved (or to which
country he 'defected', depending on one's view of his reasons) in 1950
and lived until his death in 1991; and his New Zealand homeland.
Was Czechoslovakia a place of exile? In some ways it must have been,
although it was a place where he also experienced happiness. Cold War
Czechoslovakia under Gottwald in the early 1950s was a communist
police state. Milner, even as a privileged foreigner, must have felt some
of the cold winds of his effective isolation within that society until
at least 1957. During the 1950s and until December 1963, when he
collapsed at a Christmas party at the British Embassy in Prague, and
suffered a nervous breakdown, Milner does seem to have collaborated
with the Czech state police in providing written reports on some 110
staff members of higher education institutions who visited England,
the USA or who lived in those countries during the war. How
important or how damaging these reports were to their subjects is
not clear. With the pseudonym A. Jansky and the musical cover-name
Dvorak, Milner was known to the Czech Ministry of the Interior as
'our collaborator'.[20] What additional authority those documents had
in showing that Milner had also spied for the Russians when he was
in Canberra is also unclear. At any rate, Peter Hruby's research shows
that Milner asked to be relieved of his role as an informer for the
Czech secret police, the St B, at this time, but that he was still working
for Czech intelligence in 1968.[21]

According to Ball and Horner, Milner had commenced his work for the Czech secret service while he was with the UN in New York in 1949: 'Milner had also begun working for the Czech secret service, and once he arrived in Czechoslovakia he was paid 25 000 Czech crowns once a month, compared with the normal university salary of 7 000 crowns'.[22] If these sources are accurate, it seems quite plausible that Jarmila, a young, separated Czech woman with a daughter from a previous relationship, and a graduate of Vassar, provided the means for Milner to cross to the East. To what extent did he use, or was he used by Jarmila? Here too, deep mysteries remain. After his divorce from Margot in 1958, Milner married Jarmila and they lived together in Prague until he died in 1991.

Details of the spying activities of which Milner was suspected (and which he denied) may be of less significance to the student of humanities than the kinds of insight and self-knowledge Milner attained as he laboured under these perceptions of himself. O'Sullivan's edited memoir raises such questions, including those of loyalty and sense of belonging. How far back does a sense of dislocation and exile go? The excavations need to cut deep, perhaps back to children and their parents, especially fathers and sons, as the opening chapter to this volume suggests. Milner's mother and sister both suffered serious nervous breakdowns in his youth, but the key figure in his upbringing was clearly Milner's famous father and headmaster of Waitaki Boys' High School, Frank Milner, whose biography his son returned to Wellington to write in 1980.[23]

The dominant father figure, whose influence had to be sidestepped in some way, recurs surprisingly often in the literature of espionage. Graham Greene's father was also a strong headmaster. Kim Philby's father, St John Philby, was always present in his son's mind, and Philby visited him outside Beirut before his life-changing defection to Russia in 1963. John le Carré's father – a dominating, irresponsible con-man – was the model for Magnus Pym's father in le Carré's most autobiographical novel, *A Perfect Spy* (1986). The dominant motif of Robert De Niro's film of the founding of the CIA, *The Good Shepherd* (2007) is relations between fathers and sons and the secrets they each hold. A tendency towards introspection, deferential behaviour and secretiveness sometimes follow, as these sons of extrovert fathers try to chart their own courses and ambitions beneath the radar screen of public attention. Milner's friend from schooldays, Charles Brasch, noticed that Milner too 'seemed to shun any display, almost to conceal and deprecate himself; even his gaiety was relatively sober and subdued'.[24] If such allusions suggest a kind of guilt by association, with the world of espionage, it might be noted that Milner's studious manner also suggested professorial inclinations.

Like some other sons of prominent fathers, Milner turned to writing as a principal means of expression – in Milner's case, journalism, literary criticism, poetry and translation. Here he could inhabit other worlds that connected with his own. Richard Hall remarks that 'from some time soon after school, Milner had 'another country', the cause of international communism, which knew no boundaries',[25] and this was for him the dominant imaginary world. Whatever batterings Milner's ideological bent took during the Cold War in Czechoslovakia through to the short-lived Prague Spring of 1968, when 'socialism with a human face' briefly revealed itself, it seems to have provided some kind of sanctuary where ideals could be preserved. But the life of a secret agent for increasingly arrogant and discredited Soviet and Czech authorities in the 1950s must have developed the kinds of internal strain that contributed to Milner's breakdown in 1963 and to the fraught, often contradictory emotions he expressed indirectly in his translations, literary essays and endorsement of dissident Czech poets.

Was Ian Milner in exile in Czechoslovakia? To what extent had he chosen this fate, to what extent was he compromised, then pushed? To what extent was he 'at home' there? Perhaps he was able to express something of his ambivalent, outsider status indirectly through his and Jarmila's translations of Miroslav Holub's poems, such as 'We Who Laughed':

> We were expelled
> from the class-room, the square,
> gaming house,
> stock exchange, market-place,
> television screen and
> gilt frame,
> and from any

history,

we

who

laughed.[26]

Published after the short-lived Prague Spring of 1968, Milner's translation expresses the anger and frustration of those opposing a rigidly authoritarian communist regime. Was Milner living out, through Holub and other dissidents, a dream of freedom he could never achieve for himself?

More interesting as a gauge of how Milner coped intellectually, emotionally and creatively with Soviet-style communism in Czechoslovakia are his doctoral thesis and articles that he researched and wrote on his favourite author, the nineteenth-century English novelist, George Eliot. Using a finely modulated Marxist analysis, Milner explores through Eliot's fiction his central concern: how the individual of goodwill (Dorothea and Lydgate in *Middlemarch*, for instance) can achieve a balance between individual desire and the wider social good.[27] Lydgate is compromised by the machinations of Middlemarch (and by his infatuation with the superficial blonde Rosamond – though Milner does not go into this) and it is Dorothea's 'unheroic acts' which give her a low-keyed heroic status in Eliot's world.

In an essay on Eliot's novel *Felix Holt: The Radical*, published in 1963, the year of his breakdown, Milner grapples with the nature of working-class radicalism and finds Eliot 'conservative'.[28] A decade later, in 1973, he explores in greater depth Eliot's story *The Lifted Veil,*[29] set partly in Prague, in which the gloom and introspection of the story's protagonist, Latimer, is seen by Milner as a 'deepening and darkening of his sense of isolation'. The story is a 'record of frustrated passion, anguish and human loneliness'.

It is difficult not to see these essays, and others by Milner on 'Yeats and the Poetry of Violence'[30] or 'Values and Irony in Graham Greene'[31] as part of Milner's submerged autobiography – as illuminating of his mental and emotional condition, perhaps, as his posthumous memoir. Meanwhile, his overt behaviour as a lecturer at Charles University, according to ex-students, seemed reticent and understated. To one such student, Milner seemed 'a Candide moving through the fog of pretence'.[32] But was he? Intellectually, Milner seems to have grasped the value of irony as a way of coping with the clash between belief (or faith) and pragmatism, as his essay on Graham Greene shows. Milner seems to recognise in this essay that ideals, whether Communist or Catholic, are brought to ground by fallible, flawed humans, and that one can become captive to these beliefs and cut off from true 'human fellowship'.

How cut off from 'human fellowship' did Milner feel? The record suggests that he could not experience anywhere the free but purposeful life his imagination had craved – either in New Zealand, Australia or in Czechoslovakia. Holub's poetry expressed something of this need, and may have also carried a specific social protest against the Czech police state which Milner had supported in secret and deceptive ways. Milner's literary essays explored the gaps between belief and practice. Nevertheless, in more mature years Milner was able to achieve a kind of equilibrium. O'Sullivan observes that he achieved something of this balance in late middle-age, when he managed to spend 'some time in New Zealand when he could, and to make Czechoslovakia available to antipodean friends'.[33] But this was never a comfortable, transnational balance and Milner always knew that he was under observation and suspicion in his homeland and in Australia, as indeed he had been under FBI observation in New York. Jarmila and Czechoslovakia, to whom he was captive in other ways, offered an ambiguous sanctuary.

Behind all this, New Zealand remained Milner's stable country of home, memory and imagination – his country of cricket, old friendships, lost loves and landscapes of the mind. His homeland imagined from afar could never be a place of unmixed Edenic blessings however. He recalled that his mother and then his sister had both suffered nervous breakdowns there before he left for Oxford. When he remembers his sister Winsome in the New Zealand landscape south of Oamaru, he does so through a poem by his friend Charles Brasch in which nostalgia is hardened by a sense of pain – a pain which persists:

> Only the thorn
> Alone on the parched rise, the inhuman matakauri
> Dry-green and fibrous, sorrowing,
> The gum trees that offer their flower, their sweet fruit
> Lightly to the dangerous wind.[34]

Exile at Home: Ric Throssell

If most psychological tracks seem to lead back to a famous father in Ian Milner's case, most tracks in the case of Ric Throssell, Australian diplomat and colleague of Milner, creative author and suspected Soviet agent in the 1940s and early '50s, lead back to his famous mother.

Ric Throssell's mother was the well-known Communist author Katharine Susannah Prichard. His father, Hugo Throssell, was a VC winner in the First World War – a war hero, but a less forceful personality than his mother. Hugo Throssell shot himself with his Webley revolver in 1933, when Katharine had left Australia to visit Moscow and London, and Ric was eleven. Thereafter, in an attempt to simplify complexity, Prichard's novels turned more resolutely towards what she saw as the redeeming fires of communist ideology. Despite Hungary, Czechoslovakia and the revelations of Stalinist brutality, Prichard held to her communist beliefs. The official suspicion and prejudice that surrounded Prichard's only son related principally to his linkage to her activities as a communist in the 1930s and '40s. When Ric was eighteen, in 1940, Australian intelligence agents had watched, visited and searched the family home at Greenmount, Western Australia. He later recalled hiding copies of Soviet magazines and the banned Communist newspaper *The Workers' Star* in a trunk in the backyard.[35] Such raids replicated FBI raids on suspected communists in America.

Ric Throssell's close relationship as an only son with his famous mother had many repercussions, perhaps the most indelible of which was his being code-linked with her as 'Academician's son' – 'Academician' being Prichard's Soviet code-name – in intercepted messages from the NKVD at Moscow Centre with their agents in Canberra.[36] Later, he earned his own code-name Ferro – which a perhaps over-educated intelligence officer tried to make sense of by spelling it 'Pharaoh'. A report to Moscow Centre by KLOD (Walter Clayton) about Throssell as a 21-year-old, observed critically that 'his mother dotes on him'.[37]

Ric Throssell did try to differentiate his own values and outlook from those of his mother, but it is difficult to ascertain the success of these endeavours or how deeply they ran. Throssell also claimed not to have become a communist, and I have seen no evidence that would contradict this. His views on many public issues reveal a left-liberal inclination – perhaps not 'straight left', as he described his mother's outlook in a selection of her essays and reviews[38] – but rather 'complex left'. He properly refused to answer questions about his personal beliefs before Australian Security Intelligence officers who questioned him. The tribulations of a thwarted diplomat were compounded from this time, however, and he felt himself cast out into the cold. A leading commentator on ASIO says that Throssell was 'one of the walking dead in terms of his diplomatic career' by 1952.[39]

Remarkably, given the suspicions that surrounded him, Throssell's first appointment as a diplomat was to Moscow in 1945. But he spent less than a year there, because his young wife, Bea, who had followed him to Moscow, sickened and died painfully of a disease they called polyneuritis.[40] Lydia Mertsova, from the Commission of Foreign Writers, and also probably working for the NKVD, spoke 'perfect English' and became friendly with Ric at this time, helping to nurse his dying wife[41] – which led to subsequent suspicions about her influence on the young Throssell. When it was all over, Ric sought leave from the Department and returned to his mother at Greenmount. The Russian adventure had been short-lived and traumatic – a trauma which he would later have to live through again during the Royal Commission on Espionage in 1954–5.

Like Milner, Throssell was a romantic for whom landscapes could evoke feelings of pleasure, belonging or alienation. Recalling his first and only Russian summer with his young wife Bea at a dacha outside Moscow, he describes their brief experience of the countryside:

> We walked for miles, our footsteps silent on the damp carpet of the forest, picking sprays of lily-of-the-valley where its green spears pushed through the blanket of pine needles. Wild strawberries grew among the tangle of lopped pine branches... Beyond the village a river wound its way through the forest's edge. A group of shaven-headed men, white-skinned in the sunlight, splashed naked in the shallows and jumped shouting into the deeper water.[42]

When this Russian idyll was destroyed by his young wife's painful death, Ric returned to Greenmount, in the hills east of Perth, the place of his childhood upbringing and an earlier tragedy, his father's suicide. His mother was still there but the 'wild weeds and windflowers' of this landscape were no longer visible to him. He began lessons in trying to forget.

Throssell returned to Canberra, after his warm summer leave in Western Australia, determined to forget the past by throwing himself into work. He worked in the new UN division, 'convinced that the United Nations could bring peace and security to the world'. Katharine came east to be near her son. At about this time Ric met Dorothy ('Dodie') Jordan, whom he courted and married. Both Ric and Dodie – who had joined the Communist party as a student at Melbourne University – subsequently came under the scrutiny of ASIO and the Royal Commission on Espionage. If Ric Throssell was cast into the role of his mother's protector, he may also have played a similar role for his wife Dorothy, who, along with Milner and Hill, was a source of information for the KGB's spymaster in Australia, Wally Clayton. Dorothy's code-name was initially DZhON, and later PODRUGA.[43] It was alleged at Australia's Royal Commission on Espionage that Jordan was passing official information to Doris Beeby, a Communist Party organiser and *Tribune* correspondent, who also passed information to Clayton.[44] But the evidence from Venona and other sources was not conclusive, either on Dorothy or her husband Ric. For the rest of their lives, however, they were under suspicion.

When I asked David McKnight, author of *Australian Spies and their Secrets*, if he thought Ric Throssell was a spy, he said that this is still an open question.[45] He quoted Alan Renouf, an experienced diplomat: 'The door never closes'. McKnight considers that most of what the Petrovs said has been borne out and that ASIO files, despite their shortcomings, should be read closely and trusted more than some historians have done. Throssell's long-time friend and left-winger, Bill Tully, thought it possible that Throssell dissembled in his evidence to the Royal Commission, but that he would most likely have done so in order to protect others – perhaps his wife.[46] Tully saw a kind of 'nobility' in Throssell and drew a parallel with Alger Hiss protecting his wife, but did not comment on the complications that follow from such marital collusion against social authorities. Tully told me he was honoured to be asked to join Ric and Dorothy for dinner three days before they died, in a joint suicide pact, in April 1999, when Ric was 76. Tully was disappointed by Ric's suicide (Dorothy had cancer but

Ric was physically well.) He still had a lot to give, said his friend – a full and frank autobiography would have been welcome. But the secret pacts of long-term marriage partners such as the Throssells and the Milners were not to be opened up for public inspection. In his case, Throssell could probably have predicted the obituaries that followed his death with headlines such as: '"Spy" and Wife Die as One',[47] 'Key Petrov Identity Dies'[48] or 'Red Stain Pursued Diplomat to his Death'.[49] However sympathetic such obituaries were, they showed Throssell's name to be stained, even in death.

Ric Throssell's personal sense of mental and emotional exile – a sense of being cast out into the cold – was expressed to some extent both in his public protests from his home base in Canberra and in his literary writings. He sought natural justice and stubbornly called for periodic reviews of security rulings which prevented him from gaining promotion in the Department of Foreign Affairs to positions where he would again have access to secret information.[50] This lack of trust, and recognition of his abilities, tortured him. Eventually, he was appointed Secretary of the Commonwealth Foundation in London in 1980. But this was no vindication, and Throssell felt his apparent sidelining very strongly.

If Ian Milner's psychological need was to chart a different course from his father, Ric Throssell's was the more complicated task of extricating himself, like D. H. Lawrence's Paul Morel, from mother-love and its substitutes. When Throssell's mother died in 1969, and was subsequently denigrated by former communists such as Dorothy Hewett in *Overland*, Ric's project of protecting his mother's reputation by writing her biography formed. That biography, *Wild Weeds and Wind Flowers: The Life and Letters of Katharine Susannah Prichard*[51] and the more autobiographical *My Father's Son*, were to be Throssell's greatest legacies to Australian literature, casting into relative insignificance his many plays and four novels. But these too deserve more serious attention than they have received.

The remarkable aspect of Ric Throssell's sense of exile in his own country was the way he projected (and perhaps distanced) himself from events through his acting and writing. Throssell's best-known play *For Valour*,[52] sets a pattern in its depiction of the rise and fall of heroic ideals. Based on his father's fate as a war hero who returns to postwar life in Australia restless and disillusioned, the play shows how the euphoria of patriotism in time of war can decline into a destructive cynicism in its aftermath. Ironically, when he was named as an alleged agent of the Soviet Union by Vladimir Petrov in 1954, Throssell was playing the leading role of Willy Loman in Arthur Miller's play *Death of a Salesman* at the Canberra Repertory Theatre. He remarked in his autobiography *My Father's Son*, that during this traumatic time, 'I could lose myself exploring Willy Loman's bewildered anguish and despair'.[53] For such a man, honour, reputation, 'name', were of fundamental importance. Miller's play is about high hopes and ideals brought low by postwar capitalism and narrowed horizons. As a brave victim of the McCarthy 'witch hunts', Miller seemed another thwarted idealist, with whom Throssell identified.

In the face of Throssell's denial that he had ever 'disclosed ... any official classified information to anyone who was not entitled to have it',[54] the Royal Commissioners found they could not support the Petrovs' hearsay evidence of deliberate spying by Throssell. However, Throssell may have been an 'unwitting' participant in the KLOD group's activities, presumably through information he gave his mother. In *My Father's Son* Throssell writes of 'the impossibility of fighting shadows'.[55] When he explains his situation to a friend, the friend says, 'Either you've been very hard done by, or you are some sort of Philby'.[56]

Three novels by Throssell, published in the 1990s, reflect aspects of the confusing world of secret information and knowledge exchange, as he saw them, and their impact on human lives. They also show the great gaps he perceived between an imagined world of brotherhood and fair play and the realities of contemporary capitalistic societies. The first of these novels, *A Reliable Source* (1990), moves between office politics, journalism and university in a recognisable Canberra to reveal a mixture of idealism, broken promises and treachery. The novel's action revolves around a secret treaty between the Australian PM and the US President to establish a US base in Australia under cover of an environmental program. But the real drama is in the minds of bureaucrats, students, journalists and politicians, in the discrepancy between what they say and what they think and feel. In an important sense, the novelist 'spies' upon the body politic and finds it wanting. Idealistic, anti-war students lack the political skills to win the day against powerful, entrenched forces. Included in this novel is a fine vignette of a harassed Prime Minister, in an early morning lull at Parliament House before the day's stormy events invade his inner sanctum:

> No sound penetrated the room; none of the fever of political negotiation, the contrivances of manoeuvre and counter-manoeuvre, the convenient hypocrisies, the compromises and secret assassinations that permeated the corridors and lobbies of the place, the bargains made and broken, promises and mighty principles – words, words, words. Here in the heart of Parliament House, Anthony Kalman could be alone, briefly. Conscience was his only occasional companion here, and conscience too was often still.[57]

Throssell's novel *A Reliable Source* contrasts this enclosed world of Australia's capital city with a more visionary and protective view of the natural world and an admiration for the proponents of the environment movement (including his own daughter). This new generation espouses the sanctity and beauty of Australian nature. Throssell's memories of the Darling Range in Western Australia, where he had been brought up and the more recently enjoyed coastlines of southern New South Wales, where he and his wife and two children spent holidays by the sea, provide his own counter to negative and destructive cynicism. Such places were threatened, Throssell believed, by American nuclear bases and industrial development. Throssell knew that his compulsion to explore the plots and intrigues of the city exiled him to an extent from his natural surroundings. Nevertheless, his pleasure in the seascapes of Australia's east coast provided occasional relief from troubled thoughts and dreams.

Mixed motives, thwarted ideals: such scenarios are central to Throssell's fiction. The title of Throssell's second novel, *In a Wilderness of Mirrors* (1992), echoes a famous phrase used by James Jesus Angleton, former counter-intelligence chief of the CIA, who trusted Kim Philby implicitly when he met him in America and was stunned when he turned out to be a spy.[58] Soviet spymaster, Oleg Kalugin, remarks in his memoir: 'Angleton was so badly burned [by Philby] that for the rest of his life he saw evidence of far-reaching Soviet plots everywhere …'[59] Throssell's novel employs the figure of a somewhat inept British undercover agent who ingratiates himself in a number of revolutionary hotspots in Asia, Africa, the Indian Ocean and the Caribbean, sites of conflict which Throssell himself visited or heard about while he was director of the Commonwealth Foundation in London in the 1980s. Throssell explicitly distances himself from his protagonist, Selwyn, in an epilogue to the novel, but he shows an uncanny ability to plumb the undercover agent's behaviour and its consequences. Some of the most graphic writing in the novel is reserved for the coup attempts in Grenada and the Seychelles. The novel's protagonist is an almost invisible right-wing secret manipulator pulling strings to America's advantage in these uprisings. Throughout, Throssell shows his awareness of the pleasures and perils of espionage and of lives lived in the shadow of ambiguity and fear.

Throssell's third novel *Tomorrow* (1997) attempts a broader, more ambitious range than its predecessors. It is a courageous, late-in-life attempt to explore, in fictional form, the hopes, dreams and convictions that sustained many communists and socialists of the interwar, war and post-war years of the twentieth century. It is of special interest here that the title, *Tomorrow*, echoes that of the left-wing New Zealand magazine to which Ian Milner contributed numerous articles between 1935 and 1939 which Vincent O'Sullivan described as 'perhaps the most sustained and intelligent assessment of world politics written by any New Zealander in the thirties'.[60] Throssell's research for his novel included conversations and interviews with a number of people about 'how it was for those who believed in tomorrow, giving me their memories of past beliefs and faiths, long-forgotten inspiration, and revelation now unbelievable – or still cherished'.[61] Significantly, the book is about the 'fall' of hopes held by Communists. The events of the 1950s, and their aftermath, seem to have reinforced Throssell's sense of living in a post-heroic age where the little men, like Arthur Miller's Willy Loman, have fallen tragically short of greatness. The poetics of this experience can be summed up as the cadence of the dying fall. The muted pathos that suffuses Throssell's fiction testifies to his sense that previously powerful heroic ideals are no longer sustainable in a fallen world.

Conclusion

If Ric Throssell's and Ian Milner's wings were singed in the Cold War cross-fire between West and East, their retreat to different kinds of exile or displacement – in Canberra and Prague respectively – brought literary and other compensations. Throssell's depictions in his novels of Australian land and seascapes make his love of Australia, if not Australian politics, clear. How ironic then, that when it became clear that Throssell's recurrent appeals for top security clearance in the Department of Foreign Affairs would not be granted, he applied (unsuccessfully) in 1975 for the position of Administrator of Norfolk Island, Australia's iconic convict island.[62] Was this a theatrical gesture by a man steeped in the theatre? Ian Milner, for his part, never lost his affection for his homeland, which grew in the years of his isolation from it. In compensation, Milner and his New Zealand friends built bridges of communication between his two countries, New Zealand and Czechoslovakia, and he wrote and published work that showed an intelligent grasp of politics and a developed literary sensibility, expressed especially through his deep appreciation of Miroslav Holub and George Eliot. The highly developed political sensibility of neither exile would allow him to stand wholly apart from contemporary society, though the ignominy of having been named as spies would prevent both of them from playing any high-profile public role in their societies. Instead, quietly, and indirectly, they wove their dreams, desires and anxieties into their personal writings and through others, after the traumatic events of the Cold War that burnt them both.

Ten

The Secret Lives of Spies and Novelists: Herbert Dyce Murphy and Patrick White

Disguise, subterfuge and deception are features of espionage narratives, ancient and modern. Sun Tzu writes: 'Be subtle! Be subtle and use your spies for every kind of business'.[1] He observes that spying requires 'men of the highest mental caliber'.[2] Without spies an army is 'like a man without eyes or ears'.[3] An iconic example of subterfuge in espionage is the wooden horse of Troy. More recently, Kim Philby presented himself over a working lifetime as an outstanding intelligence officer for Britain while spying for the Soviet Union.

To disguise oneself is typically to alter aspects of the appearance, sound or even smell of oneself to conceal identity; more positively perhaps, to misrepresent or cover up one's actual identity. (Philby's successful ploy was to disguise his communist sympathies by joining right-wing Organizations and adopting conservative causes and manners.) Erving Goffman's sociological investigations in the 1950s and '60s showed that we are all actors when we interact with other humans. If this is so, the concept of acting assumes a more complex and layered form in espionage contexts. To play a part is one thing: to live one's cover identity, often for years, is a difficult and emotionally wearing experience, as John le Carré acknowledges in *The Spy Who Came in from the Cold* when he reflects on the difficult deceptions of his protagonist

Alec Leamas: '[w]hile a confidence trickster, a play actor or a gambler can return from his performance to the ranks of his admirers, the secret agent enjoys no such relief'.[4]

This chapter sets out to briefly explore some of the kinds of disguise adopted, and the insights gained from the lives of spies and to raise some relevant questions about the fixedness or plasticity of human identity. The investigation begins with biography – and proceeds to a novel, demonstrating that fiction and fantasy operate in both these genres. The chief actors are Herbert Dyce Murphy, an Australian-born man of adventure and a teller of tall tales about his exploits; the second is Patrick White, Australia's most decorated novelist. Both men worked for parts of their lives as spies and translated this experience in different ways in their later life and work. The two are linked by White's adaptation of parts of Murphy's reported experience in his novel *The Twyborn Affair*.

Herbert Dyce Murphy's life has been traced by several biographers – notably Stephen Murray-Smith,[5] Moira Watson[6] and Heather Rossiter.[7] Murray-Smith describes Murphy as a 'gentleman adventurer and raconteur' who was born in 1879 and educated in Melbourne but visited Russia with his mother and subsequently attended Tonbridge School in Kent in 1894–5. As a schoolboy, Murphy went on three Arctic voyages with an uncle then made two trips to Australia on a sailing ship. Seafaring remained a lifelong passion. Murphy rejected his parents' wishes for him to work their pastoral properties in New South Wales and Queensland, evidently wanting more adventure than this offered. He studied at Oxford University in 1900 but appears not to have completed a degree there though he later styled himself MA(Oxon). In 1912, Murphy joined Mawson's Antarctic expedition in charge of the dogs and stores and earned a reputation as a teller of tall tales. In Adrian Caesar's *The White*,[8] Murphy appears in the expedition as a reader, storyteller, and sewer – he is good with a needle and thread and reads books – who is contrasted with Mawson, the masculine man of action.

Performing was Murphy's forté. In Oxford, he played the title role of Alcestis in Euripides' play performed without masks. Murray-Smith briskly describes the momentous outcome of Murphy's performance of Alcestis: 'After seeing Murphy perform a female role in a Greek play at Oxford, the director-general of military intelligence recruited him for secret work'.[9] Moira Watson, who was one of the children who listened to Murphy's stories at Mount Martha near Melbourne in his later years, extends the story: '[Sir John] Ardagh [the head of British Military Intelligence] wanted Murphy to act as a spy on the Continent (mainly in France and Belgium) disguised as a woman. His salary was £12 a week and expenses, which he said was a princely sum in those days'.[10]

In the most recent biography of Murphy, Heather Rossiter indicates Murphy's physical suitability at age twenty-one for the role of a 'lady spy':

> Herbert Dyce Murphy was slight, inconspicuous, self-effacing: admirable characteristics for a spy. When he was recruited by British Military Intelligence in late 1900, his pink and white face was still beardless, his hair blond, his eyes bright blue, his voice high-pitched. Herbert's masculine achievements during his four years in the extremely demanding world of sailing and whaling denied the ambiguity suggested by his late-developing physical appearance.[11]

Rossiter adds that cross-dressing was common among men at sea and that the all-male environment at Oxford – women were not admitted until 1920 – encouraged men to play female roles in college.[12] Not all environments were so congenial, as Murphy discovered when he was turned down by Shackleton's 1908 Antarctic expedition for alleged 'effeminacy' – a charge he always vigorously denied.[13]

Murphy's cameo role as a spy became his most celebrated exploit. Accompanied by a retired sea captain with whom he shared a house (and presumably a bed though this is never explicitly stated by his biographer), Murphy spent some two months as Miss Edith Murphy travelling the Belgian National Railways and the French Northern Railway.[14] Posing as a female artist, 'Edith' Murphy collected information for British Military Intelligence. Moira Watson explains:

> [British Intelligence] needed somebody to make sketches of the coastline of France and Belgium, and also to look over both countries' rolling stock in case the railways were needed to transport British troops in time of war. The army spies they sent were soon uncovered and forced to leave immediately, but the beautiful Australian heiress, Miss Edith Murphy, in large

hats and veils, long flowing gowns and parasols, and complete with chaperone [her veteran sea-captain] could travel around freely asking artless questions and poking at machinery with her parasol. She could also conceal a small camera in the folds of her long skirts, or, having an excellent memory and some training in engineering and planning, could retain measurements in her head so that she could draw up plans later.[15]

The main problem with such accounts is that they rely heavily on the retrospective versions by Murphy himself of these times – often adapted to the ears of his young, mainly female listeners. No corroborating records of Herbert Dyce Murphy's intelligence work seem to have been found by his biographers either at the Public Records Office in London or elsewhere.[16] There is no reason however to doubt Murphy's biographers' accounts of his work as a spy: he already held a territorial commission and was therefore highly recruitable for secret work. Moreover, Murphy later served in British military intelligence at the beginning of the First World War before retiring to Australia in 1916. Yet Murphy's stories have a distinctly literary air about them. The male spy in women's clothing recalls Baroness Orczy's *The Scarlet Pimpernel*. It is also interesting to observe that Murphy was acquainted with John Buchan, the most popular spy novelist of the early twentieth century. While Buchan's protagonist, Richard Hannay, is a 'straight' male hero, he shares with Murphy's Edith the fate of an adventurous, buccaneering individual pitting his wits against the encroaching Europeans, especially the Germans.

The practice of disguise and its concomitant, mistaken identity are features both of espionage and of the literary arts from Shakespeare to Oscar Wilde. Critics and hoaxers of various kinds have also practised the art. For example, in July 2006 Patrick White's anagrammatic, would-be writer cousin Wraith Picket suffered the indignity of having his chapter from '*Eye of the Cyclone*' rejected by ten Australian publishers and ignored by two others.[17] In thin disguise, Patrick White's chapter from *The Eye of the Storm* had been as invisible as a spy in the night to these publishers and was consigned by them to the rubbish bin of history. They rejected White's chapter for publication. Perpetrated by the *Australian* newspaper, this hoax revealed among other things the complacent ignorance of a number of leading Australian publishers of the recent literary history of the country they inhabit. They saw neither literary merit nor a reading audience for White's work. From another perspective, one can imagine the ghost of Patrick White – his double or apparition or wraith – warming to the trick played on publishers, if not to the associated news of the dramatic decline of sales of his books in the twenty-first century.[18]

But Patrick White will have his day again as readers recognise his skill in revealing the many-sidedness of men and women. For example, Patrick White's free adaptation of elements of Herbert Dyce Murphy's tale of a 'lady spy' may revive interest for those who currently diminish or ignore White's prodigious creative powers. At the same time, we may see ways in which White's own autobiographical experience in wartime intelligence contributed to his creation of one of his most powerful novels *The Twyborn Affair* (1979). Central to this, and to much of White's work, is the notion of necessary disguise – an essential element of a spy's repertoire.

The transmission of Murphy's story to Patrick White occurred in Melbourne in 1973. After winning the Nobel Prize for Literature in 1973, White was elected Australian of the Year and visited Melbourne where he praised historian Manning Clark and also Barry Humphries, the creator of Edna Everage, whom White described as 'one of the most original, scintillating minds we have produced … if the mirror is sometimes a distorting one, isn't distortion the prerogative of art?'[19] This praise of Humphries could almost be a disguised manifesto for *The Twyborn Affair*. During a visit to the National Gallery of Victoria with the Labor Member of Parliament, Barry Jones, White was told about a painting, a person and a story that would trigger his writing of *The Twyborn Affair*, as David Marr observes:

> [White and Barry Jones] were standing in front of a pretty Edwardian study of figures reading in an arbour when Jones remarked that there was an interesting story behind the painting, for the fragile figure wearing a white dress and carrying a parasol was a man. White was interested. Jones told him something of the history of Herbert Dyce-Murphy, whom he had met as a very old man living out on Mornington Peninsula. White returned to the subject later as they drank at the Duke of Wellington and walked together in the Botanical Gardens. One detail he heard

that day, an exchange he heard between Dyce Murphy and his mother, sowed the seed of *The Twyborn Affair*.

'Are you my son Herbert?' Mrs Murphy had asked this familiar figure in a dress.

'No, I am your daughter, Edith'.

'I'm so glad, I always wanted a daughter'.[20]

Varying accounts preceded this apparently authentic version of how White first encountered the story of Murphy, including the one that he first heard about Murphy from Stephen Murray-Smith rather than Jones; and that Murphy was not the figure represented in E. Phillips Fox's painting *The Arbour* but another one *Al Fresco*.[21] It is clear however that White assimilated aspects of Murphy's story and bent them towards his own personal and artistic obsessions. *The Twyborn Affair*, White conceded, is more explicitly autobiographical than the rest of his novels though there were still 'plenty of disguises'.[22] 'While homosexuals had appeared in many of his books,' Marr explains, 'the closer they come to command the action the more heavily [White] disguised them. In *Twyborn*, a homosexual was to stand centre stage in clear sight for the first time.'[23]

This suggests how 'the spying game', including Patrick White's own involvement in it during the Second World War, can contribute a fresh angle from which to view *The Twyborn Affair*. A neglected aspect of White's experience, from the standpoint of the literary historian, is the period from 1940 to 1945 when he worked in Air Force intelligence in North Africa, the Middle East and Greece. As White's biographer reminds us, 'eavesdropping in the service of the Allies' was one of White's recurrent tasks.[24] Other tasks included the interrogation of prisoners, the interception of messages and in North Africa 'picking over the corpses of enemy dead for maps, letters and diaries'.[25] White also 'compiled reports, collated clippings ... and briefed the press'.[26] In Palestine in 1943, White 'quizzed refugees about bombing targets in the towns they had abandoned in Germany'.[27] 'Probably nothing came out of my interrogations', White later commented in his ironic, self-dismissive manner, 'beyond insights of my own into the characters I came across, and sometimes friendship. But in one instance, the clues provided by one of my craziest and most persistent informants led to such a fruitful bombing raid that we received a letter of thanks and a senior officer in

RAF Intelligence was decorated for his pains.'[28] During the war years, the major emotional impact on White was undoubtedly his relationship with Manoly Lascaris, with its reunions and partings leading to their lifelong partnership after the war. Against this background, it is possible to see *The Twyborn Affair* as a novel triggered by the intriguing image of a 'lady spy' – Herbert Dyce Murphy in drag – which delves more deeply into the writer himself/herself as both novelist and spy than any of his previous works.

The Twyborn Affair begins on the verge of the First World War and ends with a German bombing raid on London in the Second World War in which the protagonist Eddie Twyborn is killed as he crosses the city to meet his estranged mother. If not exactly a series of quests, the novel presents characters setting out on adventures of the flesh or consciousness. White uses a quote from David Malouf as his first epigraph:

> What else should our lives be but a series of beginnings, of painful settings out into the unknown, pushing off from the edges of consciousness into the mystery of what we have not yet become.

Such transitions of consciousness are in this novel expedited by international crises, especially by wars, rumours of war and the deracination of individuals' lives. Suspicion of strangers is rife. In the buildup to the First World War, Joan and Curly Golson, Australian travellers in France, are suspected by local people of being spies. To Joan Golson though, 'They, the servants were the spies'.[29] In these circumstances of heightened fear and suspicion, and instant prejudice, letters and secrets become precious. White recognised this himself when he worked for the Red Cross Postal Message Scheme before he joined the Air Force early in the Second World War: he saw reading other people's letters as a way of keeping his novelist's instincts alive. Marr may overstate the case when he concludes that 'White fought a novelist's war'[30] but many of the techniques of imaginative engagement and analysis required of the intelligence officer and the writer of novels are closely correlated. We see this in the loosely autobiographical figure of Eddie Twyborn. Eddie has earned himself a DSO through his action in the trenches but he remains throughout the novel a person who observes, feels and responds with sensitivity rather than reacting abruptly in the manner of the typical action hero. Afflicted with 'the disease of remembering', Eddie is a secret agent who has learnt to be subtle and indirect, as Sun Tzu advised, and is a master of disguise.

The gender and identity crises that have been observed in *The Twyborn Affair* have their roots in the seething confusions of interwar Europe. The widely publicised adventures of W. H. Auden and Christopher Isherwood offer a window onto this world – in particular, Auden's romanticised images of the spy in Europe as a border crosser in sexual and psychological as well as geographical ways. The notorious Cambridge spies who were recruited by the KGB in the interwar years – especially Blunt, Burgess and Maclean – also lived double lives both as spies and homosexuals.[31] In his novel about the League of Nations, *Grand Days*, Frank Moorhouse too reveals connections between sexual adaptability and spying in the setting of the Molly Club in interwar Geneva. While Patrick White does not embroil Eddie Twyborn in international espionage, as he himself had been, he invests him with some of the characteristics of the secret agent, revealing a remarkable capacity to penetrate surfaces and understand intuitively the secret desires and motives of others. While he may lack training in the tradecraft of spies, Eddie Twyborn in drag seems a highly recruitable figure for the secret service.

Carolyn Bliss has acutely observed that 'Eddie, who once described himself as a 'pseudo-"man-cum-crypto-woman" is neither simply a transvestite nor a homosexual, but rather a fluctuating transsexual who is comfortable as neither male nor female'.[32] Paradoxically, Eddie's failure to resolve these apparent conflicts enables him to recognise the rifts of personality in others and their need for disguises of various kinds. Eddie's x-ray vision of other people occurs in all three parts of *The Twyborn Affair* but is perhaps best illustrated in the concluding section when Eddie has taken control of his life and, as Eadith Trist, runs a high-class brothel in London. Here we see Eddie/Eadith as the spymaster/ spymistress running her agents in the city of London who report their intelligence back to her/him, their controller. Here we also see Herbert Dyce Murphy transformed as Edith Murphy, the 'lady spy' at work in a different milieu. To those who meet her at Lady Ursula Untermayer's stately home 'Wardrobes', Mrs Eadith Trist is an international woman of mystery and they speculate whether this 'accredited brothel-keeper' is not really 'a guardsman, a nun, a German, a Colonial, or the tail end of a dream nobody ever succeeds in arresting'.[33]

Herbert Dyce Murphy's lightly told tale of his deception and disguise in the service of country is taken by White to audacious fictional heights in the third part of *The Twyborn Affair* in a deeply psychological tale of a voyeur: Eadith senses that 'she was fated never to enter the lives of others, except vicariously'.[34] Like his/her creator Patrick White in Air Force Intelligence, she eavesdrops and intercepts others' messages principally in order to understand herself, having recognised that friendship and truth in relationships depend on 'the woman in a man and the man in a woman'.[35] Eadith remains somewhat aloof from the prostitutes who work for her: the 'whore mistress of Beckwith Street' seems 'as somber as a nun'.[36] Like Stephen Ward who employed Christine Keeler and other 'good-time girls' at parties at Cliveden in the 1960s, Eddie/Eadith has access to the aristocrats and powerful politicians of the nervous 1930s. But unlike Ward, or indeed Keeler, Eadith is not caught up in political intrigues nor is pillow talk in her brothel or the country houses she frequents especially attuned to state secrets.[37] However, the aristocratic country house called 'Wardrobes' in *The Twyborn Affair* is replete with gothic secrets and deception, including espionage among a British ruling class in disarray in the first throes of war. Here, secrets are stored so that blackmail may begin. As Dennis Maufey in *The Twyborn Affair* remarks of 'Wardrobes': 'Open any of the cupboards and I'm sure you'll find even the skeletons are catalogued'.[38]

'The spying game' plays a more subdued role in *The Twyborn Affair* than it does in the 'tall tales' of Herbert Dyce Murphy, but it is the more powerful for that. The reader is drawn into a kind of intelligence exercise in White's novel that involves the penetration of the protagonist's disguises and engagement in 'discovering the identity beneath the assumed persona'.[39] Unlike Shirley Hazzard, the Australian novelist who also worked for a time in intelligence (in Hong Kong in 1947–8), White prefers to seek truth or illumination through confusions of identity rather than through romance or international intrigue. The brothel in Beckwith Street exemplifies the kind of setting in which secrets of the soul as well as society may be followed. White wanted to present 'the worm's eye view of events'.[40]

In the fate of Eddie Twyborn, White shows a man under deep cover as a woman who becomes the madam of a brothel in London on the verge of war. From the many selves he enters and the disguises he adopts, Eddie selects one and sets out to reconcile his mother to this person. His culminating moment before his death is when, as Eadith Trist, he presents himself to his mother as her daughter Eadith and she replies, 'I am so glad. I've always wanted a daughter.'[41] This is the line from Herbert Dyce Murphy's story that Patrick White remembered and that inseminated *The Twyborn Affair*: it set on its course a novel that incorporates elements of the spy story genre but extends these into a drama of identity crisis with universal ramifications.

Eleven

A Wilderness of Mirrors: Perspectives on 'The Spying Game' in Australian Literature

Although spying is pervasive throughout Australia's history, it has had fewer examples than Britain or the US – its senior partners in espionage – of spies or spooks who have 'come out', before or even after their retirement, and declared their hand. (A notable exception is Michael Thwaites, who supervised the defection of Vladimir Petrov for ASIO in the early 1950s. Another is Andrew Wilkie who resigned from Australia's senior intelligence agency, the Office of National Assessments, in protest against the impending Iraq war in 2003.) Yet a neglected and growing literature can be discerned that testifies to Australians' continuing involvement in spying, since the earliest explorations of our coasts.[1] This literature offers considerable insights into human behaviour and thought. At a time when intelligence agencies are recruiting at an increasing rate throughout the world, attention is turning to a buried part of Australia's national and international life. Along with this, we see more frequent attention to espionage not only in spy thrillers but also in essays, memoirs and novels in which espionage is an important element.[2]

The principal focus here is on four novels by Australians published from the 1990s which engage significantly with 'the spying game': Ric Throssell's *In a Wilderness of Mirrors* (1992), Frank Moorhouse's *Grand Days* (1993), Christopher Koch's *Highways to a War* (1995) and Janette

Turner Hospital's *Due Preparations for the Plague* (2003). Each of these novels throws light – a shimmering, refractive light – on the profession of espionage and its impact on individuals. A picture emerges of mobile, trans-national individuals engaged in clandestine activity which tests their intelligence, commitment and conscience and brings into question the causes they purport to serve.

A Modern Wilderness – A Fog of War

The cover picture of Throssell's novel *In a Wilderness of Mirrors* shows a recognisable likeness of the author in his middle years wearing mirror sunglasses that reflect the light and prevent any glimpse of the eyes. The temptation is thus placed before the reader to identify the author with the novel's protagonist, the spy Selwyn Joynton, but Throssell warns against any such easy identification in the book's epilogue:

> And Selwyn Joynton – there was a man like that. He is dead now, and I suspect never was my Selwyn, not wholly. Not at all perhaps; but he might have been…Not me. I never was the man he saw in the mirror of his mind.[3]

The syntax, imagery and rhythms here are deliberately elusive and bring to mind the genealogy of the phrase that serves as the novel's title. 'In a wilderness of mirrors' harks back to 'Gerontion', T. S. Eliot's poem of world weariness, confusion and spiritual desiccation. The poem's speaker partially identifies himself in the lines:

> Here I am, an old man in a dry month,
> Being read to by a boy, waiting for rain …

He has lost the ability to make real contact with others, and is left to 'multiply variety/ In a wilderness of mirrors'.[4]

Throssell's novel does not acknowledge T. S. Eliot's poem as his source: in an epigraph he attributes the phrase to James Jesus Angleton, head of counter-espionage in the CIA who used the phrase to refer to the bewildering array of disinformation and lies fomented during the Cold War. Angleton read complex poetry, including Eliot's, cultivated orchids and is one of the 'honourable men' in former CIA director

William Colby's memoir, before Colby sacked Angleton for believing in illogical conspiracy theories about CIA colleagues when there was no evidential basis for them.[5] (A number of commentators have speculated on Angleton's tendency to see conspiracies all around him following his deception by Kim Philby, the British-born spy for the KGB.) At any rate, Angleton felt himself ensnared in what he perceived as a wilderness of mirrors, and is also credited with having popularised this phrase as it applied to the intelligence profession in the Cold War.

Throssell adapts the motif neatly to the world of espionage which his character Selwyn Joynton inhabits. Imagery of mirrors recurs throughout the novel, commencing with Throssell's dedicatory poem at the beginning to his granddaughter in which he purports to address the child while he shaves:

> Child of my child,
>
> In the three faced mirror you gaze
>
> Full of the wonder of living …

Childish wonder and innocence contrast with the man's sense of world-weary experience. In the body of the novel, the author returns recurrently to images of Selwyn Joynton, the deliberately faceless man who makes a living by seeming unremarkable, observing himself in a series of mirrors.

From his orchard in the Dandenongs outside Melbourne, Selwyn lives a cover life as a London-based international journalist with a small import business, while supporting his Italian wife and two children who live there. On one of his return visits to Australia, Selwyn looks at himself in the wing-backed shaving mirror with its multiple reflections:

> His eyes above the top of the hand towel caught the reflection of his image in the mirror: a familiar stranger, every line and plane of his face known, absorbed into the matrix of recognition; but alien nevertheless, different. Selwyn did not see the face in the mirror as himself. It was a mirror image of Selwyn Joynton, no more, like the face that had looked back at him at the Moskva – when was it? That stranger always there, watching.[6]

Throssell's characterisation of Selwyn Joynton does not allow Joynton deep reflections. We are not offered an 'inner life', perhaps because he does not have one. The English-born Joynton seems to have no fixed centre, no philosophy he lives by, no place of belonging – except perhaps in the love of his daughter and her love for him. Both his wife and son seem to dislike and resent Selwyn as an interloper during his sporadic returns from secret adventures overseas. In an outburst before she is hospitalised as a schizophrenic, his wife Marietta accuses her husband of being a liar and a traitor. Both charges seem true. When Marietta dies, possibly by her own hand, Selwyn feels a vague guilt but manages to slough it off. He also feels a residual bitterness that he has failed to reform the world as an earlier youthful self had apparently set out to do. But he has always been compromised. Stated thus, Throssell's spy might seem to have the makings of a Le Carré character, but Selwyn Joynton is no Magnus Pym, or indeed George Smiley. Selwyn's flashbacks are often fleeting and insubstantial as though he himself has relegated them to a tiny corner of his mind. Elizabeth Perkins captures the figure as Throssell presents him. To her, he seems 'a minor devil dispatched from the hell of international power play'.[7] This image is attuned to Throssell's left-liberal inclinations but does not fully account for the author's apparent sympathy with aspects of Selwyn's character.

The roots of Selwyn Joynton's career as a spy are shown in his student days at university in Melbourne where he was an anti-conscription activist during the Vietnam war. But the 'Pom', the fat boy from England, never seems quite 'in step' with his fellow protesters: indeed, he seems to be an informer for ASIO. Later, he is 'run' from London where he is assigned by MI6 to Uganda with cover as a journalist. He refers to himself ironically as 'our man in Kampala', echoing Graham Greene's *Our Man in Havana*.[8] This is the first of three undercover operations in the novel which are associated with attempted coups against socialist governments, the other two being in Grenada and the Seychelles. Throssell had visited each of these places and researched the crises: he inserts his shadowy protagonist into these neo-colonialist adventures while revealing the highly dubious and sometimes absurd nature of the British and American, and in the case of the Seychelles, Rhodesian interventions.

The actual events on which Throssell draws for his accounts were carefully researched. This is evident in the episode of the American airborne invasion of the Caribbean island of Grenada in 1983. In the novel, Selwyn Joynton is the secret emissary to the governor of the island, persuading him on behalf of the British and American governments to invite their intervention following the murder of Prime Minister Maurice Bishop. But the novel presents the American adventure from varying perspectives, with mixed motives and conflicting views on the action. A recent memoir by the actual CIA chief in charge of 'the Grenada episode' has presented the events from an entirely ethnocentric American point of view. The military were keen to intervene, Duane ('Dewey') Clarridge writes: ' No one wanted to be left out of the first military action since Vietnam, but this zeal had virtually nothing to do with Grenada, and everything to do with justifying military budgets on Capitol Hill'.[9] Visiting Grenada after the intervention, Clarridge was given a military bumper sticker which he placed on his own Jeep. It read: 'WE KICKED ASS IN GRENADA!'[10] The 'fog of war' thinking which Robert McNamara retrospectively described in America's involvement in the Vietnam war, had apparently not lifted some eight years later, when a small and relatively harmless target could somehow restore battered military egos in the world's most powerful nation.

Why then, despite Throssell's apparent disapproval of the Grenada intervention and the others in which his protagonist appears does the author give his spy almost sympathetic attention? Is this literary tact? Or is Throssell projecting an understanding of someone deeply involved in an espionage mindset? Throssell had in fact lived most of his adult life under suspicion of having spied for the Soviet Union. He had fought doggedly to clear his name from the slur cast upon it by the evidence of the Soviet defector Vladimir Petrov in 1954. He had made some headway. But when in 1996 the Venona decrypts of KGB cables between Canberra and Moscow were released, it became clear that Petrov was right: his colleagues at Moscow Centre had stated that Throssell (codenamed 'Ferro') had passed valuable information to the Russians.[11] This still did not prove that Throssell had spied but it was sufficient for some Australian newspapers to reiterate the view that Throssell was a Soviet spy.[12]

In Chapter 9 I quoted the view of David McKnight, author of *Australia's Spies and their Secrets*. In arguing it was still an open question whether Ric Throssell was a spy, he quoted Alan Renouf, an experienced diplomat, who said simply 'The door never closes.'[13] The door closed however for Throssell in 1999 when, in good health, he took his own life, in a double suicide with his wife who had also been under suspicion by the Royal Commission on Espionage. Did Throssell regret his life? From the late 1980s and early '90s when communism died and the Soviet Union collapsed, how did he see himself? Had he lived so long with the spectre of being a spy that when the mirror cleared he sometimes saw an image of himself there?

Inter-War Intrigues

Frank Moorhouse's life has not been implicated in the world of espionage to the extent that Throssell's was. But Moorhouse remains one of Australia's most subtle and talented observers of personal and political dilemmas. In *Grand Days* (1993), his novel about an Australian woman Edith Campbell Berry's induction into the complex international politics of the League of Nations, Moorhouse explores several facets of 'the spying game'. The chief site of espionage activity in *Grand Days* is the Molly Club in inter-war Geneva. Here, in this trans-gendered, smoky, international setting, personal and sexual border-hopping seems not so far removed from the trading of secret information.

For Edith, an Australian idealist of her time, a crisis occurs when she discovers that her bisexual lover Ambrose is spying for the British. She reports this to her superior at the League who analyses the implications of Ambrose's spying and finds it less reprehensible than Edith had.[14]

I am indebted to Jane Stenning's excellent PhD thesis on moral pragmatism in Moorhouse and Lawson for pointing out the irony of Edith Berry's situation: that in 'undoing a spy' – as Edith decides to do in Ambrose's case – she must 'become a spy herself'.[15] But Edith's boss at the League, Bartou, is a man of the world who observes that 'To spy on a spy is no crime'.[16] As Stenning remarks, examining one's motives in such circumstances becomes 'a vast tangle of perspectives and actions', and a coordinated response – a decision on how to act – is fraught with complications.[17]

These are Edith Campbell Berry's problems of conscience. When Ambrose's spying is exposed, his situation becomes a good deal worse: he is transferred to 'Siberia' – to a desk job in an unimportant department with little responsibility, where he suffers a nervous breakdown. These are the kinds of mental and emotional pressures, often complicated by sexual pressures, that biographies of the Cambridge spies – have related in varying degrees. Miranda Carter's superb biography of Anthony Blunt, the art historian and spy, and John Banville's novel based on Blunt, *The Untouchable*, demonstrate the scope for revealing this multi-mirrored wilderness in the respective genres of biography and novel.

Vietnam and Cambodia Through a Lens, Darkly

Christopher Koch transports the dilemmas of the trans-national Australian with divided loyalties to Southeast Asia in his novel *Highways to a War*. One of the important puzzles investigated in this novel is whether, in addition to his work as a news cameraman, Mike Langford, the elusive protagonist of this novel, was ever a spy. Langford's own confessional remarks to his journalist friend Harvey Drummond are delayed until the concluding section of the novel, thus drawing the reader in as a co-investigator of the mystery of Langford's life. Mike tells Harvey that at the beginning of the war in Vietnam, as a news cameraman, he had passed on items of 'operational intelligence' to Aubrey Hardwick, a member of the Australian secret service whom Mike had idolised. Hardwick has told Mike that his intelligence was important and had been accepted by the CIA and had even reached the White House.[18] Mike Langford seems to have passed on this information out of youthful patriotic idealism.

Hawkish in his support for the Vietnam War in its early stages, Mike Langford is reported to have said that he later became a supporter of Lon Nol and the Free Khmer movement, believing that they still had a chance against the Khmer Rouge. Mike's love affair with Ly Keang has placed him romantically on the side of the 'ordinary people' of Cambodia.[19] When Ly Keang disappears, Mike sets out to find her, not knowing that she has been secretly recruited by his apparent friend and mentor Aubrey to be a stay-behind spy for the Australian secret service in Phnom Penh when the Khmer Rouge inevitably take control. In this sense, she is 'used' by the Australians. Worse perhaps, she is sacrificed to a lost cause. Mike's obsessive search for Ly Keang is unsuccessful. She has been killed by the Khmer Rouge. Mike himself, we learn at the novel's end, has been crucified by the Khmer Rouge who believe, ironically, that he is a CIA spy. The secrets and betrayals on which *Highways to a War* turns are closely intertwined with the world of espionage.

The charming, ruthless and personally ambitious Aubrey Hardwick is Koch's iconic Anglo-Australian spook in this novel, for whom personal betrayals to obtain often flawed or misguided intelligence are part of the day's work. One of the founding figures of Australian intelligence under MI6's training and guidance, Hardwick seems to newsman Drummond 'a little mad', like all spooks.[20] Harvey observes that as one era gives way to another, reality becomes 'a hall of mirrors: reality emulating some previous legend, and then itself becoming legend…'.[21] Mike's dawning realisation, as he sees through the fog of disinformation and deceit, is that the Americans will not save Vietnam or Cambodia as he had once believed:

> They'll shoot through soon and leave these people for dead: leave them to the Khmer Rouge. And the politicians and the spooks will go and start a new game.[22]

Mike's pessimism is prophetic: he sees no end to secret intrigues and treachery, and it appears there is none.

The 'hall of mirrors image' of intelligence is not denied by Mills, who had been Mike Langford's case officer in Saigon in the 1960s but is rather confirmed by him. When Mills is questioned by Harvey Drummond over the ubiquitous bottle of whisky, Mills admits that personal relationships are early victims of 'the spying game': 'My marriage went years ago', he remarks. '[I]t didn't go with the game. Seldom does. The woman doesn't know who she's married to'.[23] Recalling the fate of Ric Throssell's spy Selwyn Joynton, Mills admits: 'You lose your personality in the end…For as an operative, the day comes when he's not quite sure who he is'.[24] The early ideals, excitement and high hopes are dashed. Personal relationships wither. Confusion and sometimes despair set in. Is this what espionage is all about?

Koch does not offer a universal prescription of 'the spying game': the particular theatre of operations in Vietnam and Cambodia that he evokes has led to the despair of many Western participants and their friends. John Sullivan, a CIA agent who administered lie detector tests on Americans as well as potential Vietnamese and Cambodian recruits to American intelligence, has described himself as Diogenes in Vietnam. He explains: 'Diogenes was a fourth century BC Greek philosopher and cynic who is often depicted carrying a lantern through the streets of Athens looking for an honest man – whom he never found'.[25] Sullivan sees himself as playing that role in Vietnam. In Sullivan's view, the CIA was even more blind to the situation in Cambodia than it was in Vietnam. By the end of February 1975, Sullivan says only one question remained: when would Cambodia fall to the Khmer Rouge?[26] When Sullivan attempted to carry out polygraph tests on two potential 'stay-behind' Cambodian spies for the CIA who would report back after the Khmer Rouge took over, they refused to cooperate. Their example of non-cooperation contrasts radically with that of Ly Keang in Koch's novel who meets her death while setting out to spy for Australia, having been persuaded to do so by an ambitious and self-interested senior spook. In the hall of mirrors, desires, motives and perceptions are very mixed.

The tragic historical irony that lies behind Koch's novel *Highways to a War* is that while America and its allies turned their attention after the calamity of Vietnam to Pinochet's military government in Chile and other trouble spots – cleverly incited in this to some extent by KGB masters of 'hall of mirrors' propaganda – Pol Pot and his Khmer Rouge troops carried out a reign of terror in Cambodia which in three years killed 1.5 million of Cambodia's 7.5 million people.[27]

Middle-East Hijackings and American Complicity

We move now from Australian representations of espionage in interwar Geneva and Grenada in 1983, and Vietnam and Cambodia in the 1960s and '70s to America and the Middle East since the 1980s. Middle Eastern terrorism and aircraft hijackings provide the historical backdrop to Janette Turner Hospital's novel *Due Preparations for the Plague*. The novel draws specifically on the 1987 terrorist hijacking of Air France flight 46 and the calculated killing of its passengers, but was completed in the shadow of events in the USA now known by the shorthand expression '9/11'. Much of the imaginative and emotional appeal of

Due Preparations for the Plague hangs on the impact of such terrorism on those who may survive, especially children. Twenty children were released before Air France 46 (code-named Black Death in the novel) was blown up by Middle Eastern terrorists. Two psychologically maimed survivors living in the United States, Lowell and Samantha, carry out the intelligence work, thirteen years after the event, that reveals CIA complicity in these tragic events.

Like other authors who appreciate the complexities and false trails of espionage and international politics, Turner Hospital employs imagery of fog and mirrors. Early in *Due Preparations for the Plague*, the young woman Samantha tries to imagine the spy code-named Salamander:

> *I spy*
> *With my manifold eye.*
> This is Salamander's morning canticle.
> He leans in close to the bathroom mirror and his words come back lush, fully orchestrated, thick with toothpaste and shower fog. He squints and sees galaxies: bright floating points, moons, multiple planetary rings. He has the eyes of a fly or god. The things that he knows; weighty matters of life and death, or swift death – orbit his consciousness, but he must not speak of them.[28]

This is Samantha's construction of a mysterious figure she imagines from 'undeleted half lines in documents'.[29] Later, this figure becomes more fully known through videotapes and encrypted journals, which the real Salamander leaves for his son Lowell Hawthorne, and the records of a psychoanalyst. Salamander emerges posthumously as an agent who had become embroiled in an elaborate game of double-cross with a Middle Eastern agent codenamed Sirocco and was fatally outwitted in 'the spying game'. The tragedy of Black Death followed. His own death thereafter was assured.

Oddly, Salamander, the CIA agent who was implicated in the fatal hijacking, emerges retrospectively as a relatively sympathetic character. This is surprising given that his wife is killed and his son seriously scarred by events which he helped to set in train. What redeems him morally, to an extent, is his realisation that his son's generation should be spared the lunacy of which he has been a part. Moreover Salamander acts on this recognition, leaving his son a sports bag in a locker filled with the evidence that will expose the plots and counterplots in which he (and his country) have been involved in an attempt to make the world more 'secure'.

Turner Hospital's approach to the creation of her American secret agent becomes apparent in her interview with Peter Birnhaum in 2003:

> *Interviewer:* Why choose such a life?
> *Janette Turner Hospital:* People enter that world because they are highly trained and highly intelligent and go in out of idealism – we have a way of life and a system of government that needs to be preserved. And someone has to be in intelligence work to know who is planning to attack it. So you go in with idealism, but it is the nature of the task that it requires all sorts of decisions of short-term expediency, which can get very murky.[30]

Turner Hospital's first thought, before interviewing any former agents, was that they must be 'cold-blooded'. However, in talking with agents and trying to imagine Salamander more deeply, the novelist thinks of him as 'increasingly tortured and anguished and unravelling, falling apart at the seams, going mad.' Something of this state of mind is revealed in the psychoanalyst's reports to which Lowell Hawthorne and Samantha gain access.

The characterisation of Lowell Hawthorne's father is a remarkable feat and it seems churlish to criticise Turner Hospital for not giving equivalent depth to Sirocco, the spy from the 'other' side – as Brenda Niall claims Le Carré would have done.[31] The moral and emotional complexities of life for children of spies have been captured in a recent biography, *My Father the Spy*, by John H. Richardson which shows the high psychological costs for individuals and their families of this profession.[32] Each experience is no doubt different. But Turner Hospital, like Richardson, shows the deep desire of a son or daughter to know what has previously been secret and to revalue a parent whose life has been lived in the shadows.

***

A typical response of former intelligence operatives to novels and films about 'the spying game' is that they fail to capture the banality and drudgery of much of this work. Yet few would reject the notion that the major challenge in intelligence work is to see a way clearly through the masses of information and multiple perspectives produced by their own institutions and those of their enemies to the 'truth' of a situation.

In this 'wilderness of mirrors' a certain clarity of mind, sense of purpose and above all, perhaps, imagination are required. A perhaps surprising source of this view is the *9/11 Commission Report* which admits that 'Imagination is not a gift usually associated with bureaucracies' and challenges Americans to find 'a way of routinising, even bureaucratising, the exercise of imagination' in the intelligence services.[33] While there may be benefits for the spy agencies in this approach, it would be an unfortunate by-product if the more free-ranging imaginations of novelists, filmmakers and others were restricted to the goals of national security in the US, Australia or elsewhere.

Novels such as those I have discussed by Throssell, Moorhouse, Koch and Turner Hospital offer unique insights from the outside into 'the spying game' as an international phenomenon. They show the moral and intellectual complexities of espionage and the toll that this way of life can have on secret agents and those close to them. They show, too, the prevalence of spectres, screens, shadows and mirrors in a profession where 'spies' and 'lies' rhyme and truth often remains an open question.

Twelve

Memory, Identity and Imagination in Secret Intelligence: Christopher Koch's *The Memory Room*

Introduction

Sometimes a novel emerges from a culture which touches the nerve of its times even though it is set a generation or so earlier. Dickens's *Bleak House* is a novel of this kind. The institutions of law remain forever coloured by Dickens's satiric observations in this novel. Christopher Koch is not a satirist but his novel *Highways to a War* (1995, dealt with in Chapter 11) remains the most memorable of the spate of novels which explored Australians' military involvement in the wars in Vietnam and Cambodia in the 1960s and '70s. Koch's later novel *The Memory Room* (2007), set in China and Australia in the early 1980s, has a similar impact and again recalls events some twenty-five years earlier, with a focus on the profession of secret intelligence.

Origins of the Spying Game in Individual Lives

The Memory Room is a deeply literary, finely etched work which examines the impact of the profession of secret intelligence – the world's second oldest profession as Phillip Knightley reminds us in his book of that title – on the lives of three Australians. In this chapter, I will consider Koch's treatment of the intelligence profession and the secrets, disguises and lies it entails. How do memory, imagination and personal identity interact in the world of spies and international intrigue? How can a novel such as *The Memory Room* increase our knowledge and understanding of this field of human behaviour – and more broadly, the tragedy of lives that become entangled in its webs of intrigue?

One of the literary strengths of *The Memory Room* is its acknowledgment of the spy thriller genre while refusing to adopt the narrow lens of the Bond or Bourne formulae. Instead, Koch chooses to explore how some spies enter their profession and what it makes of them. His novel about three friends from schooldays in Tasmania who become embroiled in international espionage in China and Australia involves the reader in this world and poses difficult dilemmas of identity, loyalty and belonging.

The novel's search begins in a locked room in a Hobart house which Derek Bradley is visiting to read the papers of his old friend Vincent Austin, who has disappeared from his job as an intelligence officer in Canberra, and presumably from Australia. As Vincent's executor and friend, Bradley is the only person given permission to enter the inner sanctum of a house in Hobart owned by Vincent's aunt, Connie Ross, where Vincent had grown up in the 1950s. Bradley's reading of Vincent's diaries and archives and his liberal quotations from them serve to frame and direct the narrative. We encounter the third principal character in this novel, Erika Lange, first through Vincent's diaries and later through Bradley's narrative as he recalls how he became Erika's lover when the three friends coincided in their postings to Peking – Vincent as an Australian Secret Intelligence Service officer, Erika as a press officer and Bradley as a diplomat. Erika's influence on the two men – sexual in the one case and platonic but no less intense in the second – leads them in different directions.

The spying game begins in childhood in this novel; and for Vincent and Erika, their experiences in childhood remain determining factors in their adult lives. Through Derek Bradley's mining of Vincent's diaries and papers, we see the early addiction of Vincent and Erika to reading, acting and spying on others. Like the fabled Bronte family, Vincent and Erika's games stretch their imaginations and they develop a private fantasy world. Both Vincent's parents have died, as has his twin brother. Erika's mother has died and she lives with her problematic German father. Each is a solitary child and they see themselves as orphans and twins. The powerful hold of their secretly forged world on Vincent and Erika will be felt into their adult engagement with real world espionage and their fates thereafter. They both bear the marks of arrested emotional growth.

Koch's novel shows the stretching of imagination through reading and writing. Vincent Austin is a precocious youth who reads Dickens, P. G. Wodehouse (a special favourite), Dostoevsky, Conrad and Graham Greene as well as Ian Fleming and Len Deighton. In their secret room, Vincent writes the text and Erika composes the drawings for an 'adventure strip' called 'Ella of the Secret Service' who works for both MI6 and the Australian Secret Service. Erika identifies with Ella and acts out her role as a femme fatale. When Vincent acquires a camera, the two of them venture out into the suburbs to record and interpret the secret lives of others.

Vincent and Erika seem tailor-made spies. By contrast, Vincent's friend at school and university, Derek Bradley, is presented as a more stable individual – a peace-lover by nature who is nevertheless drawn to excitement and adventure by more volatile personalities. It is the reasonable Bradley who tries to piece together the jigsaw puzzle of his friends' strange lives and the web into which he is drawn by them.

The Memory Room tests a hypothetical statement in Vincent's diary – that some spies are born not made: 'This kind of spy is devoted to secrecy', Vincent writes in the 1950s at the age of eighteen, 'to secrecy in its purest form; *to secrecy for its own sake*'.[1] The latter part of this statement seems an unconscious echo of a traditional justification of the humanities – the pursuit of knowledge 'for its own sake'. The interesting omission from this statement is any acknowledgment of politics or power play, as if the dark arts of espionage were an exercise in aesthetics rather than geo-politics. Koch gives another textual dimension to Vincent's addiction to secrecy when he notes that this is part of his birthright as a Tasmanian. As Koch also shows in earlier novels, the ghosts of convicts of the penal colony still haunt the dreams of Tasmanians.

The psychological analysis of Koch's flawed spy in *The Memory Room* seeks its origins in Vincent's childhood on the farm at Richmond, where his twin brother died when he was eight. Vincent's father was incommunicative and cold, driven in on himself since his wife's death:

only Vincent's aunt Connie, with whom he was sent to live, connected the boy to a wider world. A disturbing incident with an uncle who told Vincent to keep himself 'clean' for the person he will marry contributes to Vincent's repressed, apparently asexual nature. Vincent expresses a strange, premonitory insight when he remarks that the 'ultimate pleasure' of being a spy must be 'the licence to be utterly alone'.[2] This vision of the spy as lone ranger may have seemed feasible in the 1950s but it is far less realistic in the 1980s or the 2000s: ASIS, MI6 or CIA agents are required to work closely with, and to communicate with a range of people in teams, groups or cells. Vincent's 'go it alone' instincts are set to destroy his career as an Australian intelligence operative.

The mind-games which Vincent learns to play are not entirely solipsistic: they include his soulmate Erika. As children, the two of them act out episodes from the comic strip *Flash Gordon*. Erika tells Vincent: 'You and I are good at secrets … We'd be good spies'.[3] While their underground life begins in the secret room at Aunt Connie's house, their fieldwork includes spying on the residents of New Town with Vincent's camera. Erika calls this 'trespassing' and it is like a drug to the pair while seeming useful: they learn the craft they imagine perfecting as adults.

Later, when Vincent is nineteen and at university, he and Erika resume and feed their earlier addiction. They learn 'the techniques of espionage: dead drops, secret writing, the use of hidden cameras'.[4] Their imaginative secret work as children and young adults shapes their self-concepts and prepares them in a curiously limited way for their later surreal adventures in China and elsewhere. Yet imagination has always played a role in 'the spying game': memoirs of prominent CIA men in the 1950s, for example, reflect their view that *Alice in Wonderland* suggestively evokes the world of espionage they had entered.[5] Koch's novel gives due regard to Vincent Austin's university education in conservative political thought during the Cold War, and the influence of Teodor Bobrowski, his Polish Professor of Politics, but Vincent's childhood experiences are fundamental to his being.

Chinese Contexts

When the three Tasmanian friends find themselves together again in the Australian Embassy in China, they are in their early thirties.

Koch calls this second part of his three-part novel 'The Eastern Wall' and draws on his memories of a visit to China in May 1981 with two other Australian writers, Nicholas Hasluck and Hugh Anderson. It is interesting to compare Koch's China in the novel with some of Hasluck's recollections in the latter's published account of the visit.[6] In addition, my own travels in China as a guest of the Chinese Writers' Association several months earlier in February 1981 covered some of the same territory and I met some of the individuals on whom Koch's characters are based. This was a time when China's doors had opened a little and some Westerners were being invited to meet fellow specialists in China in the aftermath of the oddly misnamed Cultural Revolution from 1966 to 1976. In my case, I visited writers, editors, academics and publishers in Peking, Shanghai, Hefei and Canton to enable me to put together a Contemporary China issue of the literary magazine *Westerly* which appeared in September 1981.

The central drama of the Eastern Wall section of Koch's *The Memory Room* concerns a bungled attempt by Vincent Austin to arrange the defection to Australia of an ageing Chinese professor, Liu Meng, and his English-born wife, Dorothy. Koch's characters are based on Professor Yang Xianyi and Gladys Yang, whom I and other Australian writers – including Koch and Hasluck – had met in the early 1980s. Professor Yang and his wife had been guests at the 1980 Adelaide Festival and Professor Yang not only hosted Australian visitors in Peking but was an outspoken critic of China's leaders for the events in 1989 which were widely described as the Tiananmen Square massacre.

In Koch's novel, his Australian secret service agent, Vincent Austin, who shares Professor Liu's enthusiasm for ancient Chinese poetry, hatches a plot to have him and his wife invited to a literary festival in Australia and to defect there. The chief flaw in Vincent's plan is his failure to communicate adequately with his secret service colleagues or to take into account the views of Dorothy Liu, the professor's strong-minded wife. Vincent's plan collapses. He is recalled to Canberra and demoted to a desk job in charge of a registry of secret service files. His friend Derek Bradley is also recalled because of his association with Vincent's plan, through he had opposed and tried to prevent it.

The vital interplay between literature and ideology in China in the early 1980s was evident to visitors such as Hasluck and myself and is taken up in *The Memory Room*. The novel proposes that a good literary memory makes a liberal world-view possible. When Vincent and his friend Bradley visit Professor Liu and his wife at their rooms they take a bottle of Johnnie Walker Black Label whisky. Another guest, introduced as Yang Wenfu, is a Communist party hack and a spook for the Security Bureau whose task is to watch for ideological slip-ups and report on them. Despite proclamations of open-door policies, all Western visitors to China at this time were closely watched, as were their Chinese hosts. Vincent's preference for Scott Fitzgerald over Hemingway seems unsound to the dogmatic spook Yang as does the Australian's view that 'literature is finally about beauty'.

Koch's interest in classical Chinese poetry emerges in a whisky-fuelled discussion in which Vincent's and Bradley's enthusiasms for Tu-Fu and Po Chu-I respectively are expressed. But tension is in the air as old ideological walls rear up. Yang lectures Vincent that his enthusiasm for Tu-Fu is unsustainable because this poet was part of 'a small privileged aristocracy [that] ruled over the starving and suffering masses'.[7] Professor Liu then weighs in with his inclusive view of what it is now possible to say in China:

> Since the fall of the Gang of Four, the Party has declared that we
> are all permitted to respond to writing that expresses the hopes
> and joys and sufferings of individuals – not just didactic works
> that deal only with the problems of society.[8]

In a fit of enthusiasm, Professor Liu proclaims his vicarious love for another poet, Li Po. One cannot help one's nature, the professor and translator says, 'Li Po is my poet – mad, drunken Li Po, the poet of spring and joy …' .[9] Unfortunately, Li Po was the poet who 'tried to embrace the moon's reflection in the river, and fell in and was drowned'.[10] It is perhaps just as well that Koch refrains from giving us Mr Yang's report on these discussions to his superiors in the Security Bureau which would certainly be couched in dogmatic, judgmental prose. Yang and the system he represents are seriously deficient in imagination.

Other revelations emerge from Vincent's attempts to engineer Professor Liu's defection. In the process, he confesses his deep cover intelligence role to his friend Bradley and describes what the 'intelligence game' has done to him:

It's like a dream you can't wake up from. You play a part for so long, that there are times when you begin to wonder what's happened to your inner self. You even begin to be afraid that it's lost. Sometimes I'm not sure who I *am* any more.[11]

The generally level-headed Bradley is amused at first by his friend's 'hushed theatrical tone [that] made him seem like a caricature of a spy'.[12] Though Vincent seems sincere, Bradley rationalises these disclosures by recalling that Vincent 'had lived so long in books and in his head, and had so long been solitary, that he had probably experienced even the most intense emotion at one remove, and a theatrical response to it was the one that he believed to be appropriate'.[13] Yet Vincent's dilemma is real. He knows that his long-desired profession requires its exponents to manipulate other people. 'After a time', he says, 'one desperately needs to be with just one or two people who know who one really is, and with whom one doesn't need to wear a mask'.[14]

The Lives of Spies – Real and Imagined

In an Author's Note to *The Memory Room*, Christopher Koch refers to the 'general help and advice' of a number of officers in Australia's overseas service. One of these was a fellow Tasmanian, Warren Reed, who resigned from ASIS in the mid-1980s after service in Japan and Egypt following a dispute about his cover as a secret intelligence officer allegedly being blown by a senior member of the Australian diplomatic service in Cairo. Reed has spoken and written about both the attraction and the frustrations and difficulties of being a spy for one's country.[15] In his novel *Code Cicada* (2004), Reed gives an insight into the experience of being in psychological and moral 'free fall' with only one's former self to hang on to. Interestingly, Reed gives these insights to a Chinese spy who has developed a rapport with Australia and Australians:

[I]t all depends on what you are *before* you go in. That's your lifeline and your anchor. It's like a safety rope tied to your belt. And if you're not properly harnessed before intelligence grabs you, you can't expect much to cling to. You're in free fall over the cliff.[16]

While the two male protagonists in Koch's novel, Vincent Austin and Derek Bradley, avoid this kind of free-fall into a moral and emotional void, Erika Lange is driven by forces beyond her comprehension to this fate. Unlike Vincent and Bradley, Erika does not proceed to take a university degree but she becomes a journalist in Australia and then in London. When she arrives in Peking in 1980, she is a press officer for Australia's Department of Foreign Affairs. As Derek Bradley pieces together evidence from Vincent's diaries and his own experience, Erika emerges as an intriguing figure of ever-changing colours and moods who attracts and discards lovers and friends, both men and women.

Erika's predecessors in literary mythology may include Mata Hari, and she carries the elusive psycho-sexual power over others of Hardy's Sue Brideshead in *Jude the Obscure*. Erika becomes Bradley's 'addiction' for a time in China. When they start a sexual relationship, Bradley notices that Erika's consent has 'a hint of violence in it …a sort of warning'; and she exhibits 'a baffling blend of mischief and gravity'.[17] Bradley sees in Erika extremes and 'unpredictable possibilities'.[18] While he seeks to bring his lover to ground by proposing marriage to her, he sees something ethereal in Erika: she seems to be 'without roots, without any fixed location', having 'no solid attachment to the real world'.[19] Bradley's addiction to Erika is fed by his fear of losing her – and so it happens.[20]

Journalism is a well-worn cover for both actual and literary spies. Despite her life-long fantasy of spies and spying, though, it is never clear whether Erika is an actual spy, or if so, for whom. She is certainly not ignorant of espionage, and by association she is deeply immersed in the perils and temptations of the spying game. In addition to her intimate relationship with Vincent, we learn that Erika began an affair with a CIA agent, Mike Devlin, when she was in New York in the 1970s – a relationship that led to an aborted pregnancy and a nervous breakdown.[21] Like much in Erika's life, their relationship remains inconclusive and is sporadically renewed when Devlin travels the world. Erika's last, fatal relationship is with a KGB man, Peter Rykov, in Canberra which, like all Erika's relationships with men is intense, exciting and dangerous, for it is driven by power play. Questions remain open: who is playing whom and to what end? There are recurrent hints in the novel that the chief source of Erika's psycho-social problems lies in the deep trauma of childhood abuse by her German father.

Christopher Koch has read widely, spoken with informed sources and reflected on the history of Australia's role in international intelligence from the 1950s to the 1980s. The voluminous literature on the defections of Vladimir and Evdokia Petrov to Australia in 1954 is one such source.[22] The Combe–Ivanov affair in the 1980s when a KGB agent under diplomatic cover sought to cultivate and recruit an Australian associate of the Hawke Labor Government was another incident of significance. The expulsion in 1983 of the KGB spy Valeriy Ivanov led to the second Hope Royal Commission which raised some fundamental questions about the role and function of Australian intelligence.[23]

Another dramatic incident in the 1980s was former MI5 officer Peter Wright's defiance of the Thatcher government in Britain by publishing his book *Spycatcher* in Australia and retiring to live in Tasmania. Vincent Austin's last job as 'master of the registry' of secret intelligence files parallels in some respects Peter Wright's access late in his career to secret intelligence files which enabled him to review the cases of suspected or confessed former spies such as Anthony Blunt and Kim Philby.

Conclusion – Is the Great Game an Illusion?

When Vincent Austin is recalled to Canberra to become 'master of the registry', he is at first keen to redeem himself in the eyes of his secret intelligence colleagues. Thus he agrees to try to bring the KGB man Peter Rykov across to the West. Rykov wants to defect because of his passion for Erika; she in her turn is convinced that she has found her soulmate in Rykov. Vincent tries but fails to bring about Rykov's defection and the Russian decides to return to his homeland. This is Vincent's second great failure in spycraft: it recalls aspects of his earlier failure to achieve Professor Liu Meng's defection from China. Driven by idealism rather than practical politics, and emotionally restricted to his intense but limited relationship with Erika, Vincent is close to breaking point. When Erika is found dead in her house in Canberra – assassination by a Soviet agent is considered possible before her suicide is confirmed – Vincent loses all sense of purpose and self-esteem. A tragedy has run its course. 'For so many years', he writes to his former Politics professor, 'the Game has come first with me. I've given my life to it'.[24] Now he seeks a more personal and spiritual salvation in 'the zone of the innermost spirit'.[25] After a career in espionage of 'constant duality', Vincent now seeks '*a one-dimensional life*'[26] and he 'disappears' to India, with the help of his secret service colleagues, where he hopes to find a more spiritually satisfying life.

When he was recruited to ASIO in the 1950s, the poet and academic Michael Thwaites was told that the work of an intelligence officer required imagination. An experienced and level-headed agent in Koch's novel, Jim Dempsey, concludes that Vincent Austin had 'too much imagination – and that can cause a crack-up'.[27] Reflecting on their shared experience of childhood in Tasmania, Vincent's old friend Derek Bradley thinks they have each been shaped by the 'ephemeral revelations' of their native island, 'states of delight more seductive than anything the real world had to offer'.[28] This explanation of an outsider's naivety recalls in some respects the mid-Westerner Nick Carraway's view of an unexplored, glamorous alternative world in Jay Gatsby and the metropolis. But *The Memory Room* invites readers to look more deeply into the intelligence profession itself, which had promised so much and delivered so little to Vincent Austin.

In an excellent article which draws on Australian and international examples, Wendy Jane Stevenson explores 'the unique psychosocial realities of living as an intelligence professional'.[29] She isolates several work requirements which she claims are unique to the intelligence profession – maintaining cover, keeping secrets and working silently. In Stevenson's view, psychosocial health is threatened by each of these activities.[30] Koch's novel tends to support this view though he seeks root causes further back in childhood relationships and explores their impact on growth and development in adulthood.

Should literary texts be used in this way to explore aspects of the intelligence profession and its influence? A special issue on 'Spying in Film and Fiction' of the Anglo-American journal *Intelligence and National Security* in February 2008 encourages this approach in both media. In his article, 'The Truth of Espionage is Stranger than Fiction', for example, Fred Hitz cites the case of Robert P. Hanssen – the protagonist in the recent film *The Breach* – an FBI officer who spied for the Soviet

Union and then for Russia for two decades while remaining a devout Opus Dei Catholic and disapproving of the Soviet system. When seen beside the entrenched duality of Hanssen, Koch's Vincent Austin may seem positively sane. Yet he and Erika are touched by a certain madness which Christopher Koch has described as 'what's known to psychiatry as *folie à deux*: the madness of two, where a single set of obsessions are shared between two people'.[31]

A multi-faceted novel such as Koch's *The Memory* Room should not be read reductively as a mere guide to a particular profession, for its psychological insights encompass human relationships and the sources of intellectual and emotional growth. Yet the theory and practice of espionage offer great opportunities to the serious novelist, as Koch's novel demonstrates. A major purpose of research in the humanities, and analysis of fiction such as Koch's novel, is to explore questions of identity, memory and imagination. Koch's *The Memory Room* stimulates such exploration in the context of the intelligence profession, and in so doing it expands knowledge of ourselves and others in an increasingly complex international environment.

Thirteen

Spies, Lies and Intelligence: Reconfiguring Asia-Pacific Literatures

Explorers, Poets and Spies

How innocent were the Spanish, Portuguese, Dutch, French and British navigators from the fifteenth to eighteenth centuries who searched for and some of whom ultimately found and settled the Great South Land we now call Australia? The Australian poet James McAuley evokes high idealism and utopian expectations in his long poem 'Captain Quiros'[1] about the fifteenth and early sixteenth century sea voyages of Captain Pedro Fernando Fernandez de Quiros to the South Seas, the Solomon Islands and South America. McAuley's biographer Cassandra Pybus notes why Quiros was such a 'compelling figure' for McAuley: he was 'a brilliant navigator and devout Catholic, obsessed with the idea that he could find the Great South Land and create there an ideal world, the New Jerusalem'.[2]

But idealism and utopian expectations have their darker underside in the lives of navigators and poets. Quiros's expeditions, like those of many other navigators of his time and later were underpinned by imperial ambitions, espionage and chicanery. McAuley's benign view of Spanish imperialism, and his focus on idealistic enterprise in preference to the underside of such voyages is typical of much poetry and social commentary which ignores the rich if problematic underworld of intrigue and espionage.

This chapter argues that the dark side of human behaviour, and the secret negotiations that bring some to power and glory and others to destitution also plays an important role in literature and socio-critical commentary. To understand Iago is to better understand Othello; and Hamlet's turmoils are best understood in the context of a Danish court inhabited by spies such as Polonius, the spymaster, and operatives such as Rosencrantz and Guildenstern. We will understand ourselves better in the context of international relations in the Asia-Pacific if we also explore the place of the 'dark arts' in our national and international lives. We may even find some entertainment and perhaps illumination in these explorations.

The case of James McAuley, the Australian poet, is instructive. During the Second World War, McAuley worked in a research and intelligence unit where he had special responsibility for considering postwar colonial policy. Taking their cue from President Roosevelt, McAuley and his colleagues considered the possibility of Australia and New Zealand taking a radical and expanded postwar colonial policy in the Pacific. McAuley continued to take a special interest in New Guinea after the war and ultimately convinced himself of the necessity for colonial control there. His poem 'Captain Quiros' thus arises in part from McAuley's reflections about the pros and cons of colonialism and his conclusion that the colonial experience is justifiable. At the same time, McAuley strongly rejected Communism and its associated aura (for some people) of idealistic and utopian egalitarianism. He accepted financial support for *Quadrant*, the literary magazine he edited, from the Congress of Cultural Freedom, an offshoot of the CIA, in part to counter the evils of communism.[3]

Few Australians who have worked in intelligence, whether in military or civilian spheres, have had the leisure that McAuley and his poet friend Harold Stewart had in Army intelligence at Victoria Barracks in Melbourne in 1943 to concoct one of the great hoaxes of Australian literary history, the Angry Penguins poems by an invented poet Ern Malley.[4] Hoaxing, propaganda, poetry and spying have their points of connection. As we saw in Chapter 3, when poet Michael Thwaites was interviewed for a position in the Australian Security Intelligence Organization in 1950 he was told that there were people engaged in subversion and espionage (read here the Soviet Union and their supporters) and that a poet could help to counter these activities. Why a poet? Because, said Colonel Spry, the head of ASIO, both 'effort and imagination' were required: 'You write poetry, I know', said Spry. 'Much of the job will just be hard methodical work but imagination is also needed. I believe you could make a valuable contribution'.[5] As it turned out, Thwaites supervised the defection of two important KGB agents, Vladimir and Evdokia Petrov, to Australia in 1954 and subsequently ghost-wrote their biography.[6] In Australia, as elsewhere, poetry, intelligence and espionage are often inextricably linked.

Military Traditions, Critical Thinking and Espionage

While a link between creative writers (and journalists) with intelligence work can be established in a number of cases, the link between intelligence and military experience is even more pronounced. When I invited Singapore poet and academic Edwin Thumboo to a passing-out parade at the Australian Defence Force Academy in Canberra in the 1990s he quickly identified half a dozen fellow Singaporeans on the parade ground (they had been students at ADFA) and remarked: 'Those little fellows with the sun glinting on their glasses and the quick fingers – they will win the Third World War – not your big lumbering Aussie brutes'.

Leo Braudy's monumental study of war and the changing nature of masculinity is a salutary reminder that although stereotypical 'men are y and women x' formulas partially collapsed during the Vietnam War, stereotypes still remain in some quarters.[7] In this context, military intelligence has seemed to attract renegade officers – or perhaps military misfits – who perhaps are better at thinking critically or imagining alternatives than at taking orders and fighting on the battlefield. Although Braudy does not explicitly make the connection, it seems at least plausible that relatively straightforward traditions of war, honour and nationalism in the shaping of personality are complicated when officers switch from military roles to intelligence work.

Australia's First Spymaster

The career of Australia's first spymaster George Steward, raises some of these questions. Born in London's East End in 1865, Steward joined the London Post Office when he was 15 and had the ideal apprenticeship for a future spy: he was night messenger and sorter of foreign parcels at the Post Office.[8] Steward married in London then moved with his family to Tasmania in 1892 but the marriage did not last: his wife and their two sons returned to England in 1894. An ambitious and able administrator, Steward rose rapidly to be town clerk in Hobart before transferring in 1901 to the new Commonwealth Department of External Affairs in Melbourne.

In 1902, George Steward became official secretary to the Governor-General, Lord Tennyson. For the next seventeen years Steward remained as official secretary to five governors-general – a position funded by the Australian government to ensure effective communication and proper financial control of the office. From this official position, in 1916 Steward founded and headed the Counter Espionage Bureau, Australia's first secret service.[9] Frank Cain has described how a bureau that set out to be an intelligence arm that coordinated the information of other bodies and communicated by cipher with London on matters of international security became a domestic political surveillance body giving special attention to Germans in Australia (most of whom were interned), and the sometimes fractious opponents of military conscription in Australia, especially the Industrial Workers of the World (IWW or 'Wobblies'), Sinn Fein and others perceived as leftists.[10] The rejection of conscription to fight in Europe at two referenda in Australia was of course a bitter blow to the British and their representatives in Australia.

Along with other espionage bodies in the Asia-Pacific and elsewhere that attempted to retain British influence in the twentieth century (e.g. in Singapore, as we shall see, and India), Australia's Counter-Espionage Bureau was chiefly concerned with domestic surveillance, though its leaders were ever alert to extend their influence internationally when opportunities arose; and subversive activity in Australia was often linked to international movements. In style and in substance, the military influence on early Australian intelligence Organizations was paramount. George Steward, for example, was a keen citizen-soldier and was a major in the Australian Intelligence Corps before rising to honorary lieutenant-colonel from 1917 until his death in 1920. Fully moustached and upright, Steward appears to have combined military discipline, powers of persuasion and the kind of devious mind that enabled him to understand plots and trace suspected enemies of law and order.

Despite Steward's 'remarkable gifts' as chief spy, he had trouble resolving the conflict between his two jobs. Munro Ferguson, his fifth Governor-General (all of them British to this point), complained to Prime Minister Hughes about the other 'usages' to which Steward's time was put.[11] The Governor-General objected to 'unsavoury characters' who lurked about Government House on secret political business and he dubbed his secretary 'Pickle the Spy'.[12] Since Munro Ferguson was a Scot, he was probably referring to the secret agent code-named Pickle who, in the Scottish writer Andrew Lang's novel *Pickle the Spy* (1897) – and perhaps in real life – spied on Prince Charles Edward after 1750. On the other hand, Munro Ferguson may have thought of Steward as a nuisance whose divided duties had got him into a 'pickle' in the Shakespearean sense noted by Dr Johnson: 'How cam'st thou in this pickle?'[13]

The Singapore Connection

Internal security departments bred intelligence analysts and spies in a number of countries of the Asia-Pacific. In Singapore, for example, a Special Branch was founded in 1916 and operated in British Malaya and Singapore until the Second World War. In his history of Special Branch operations, former National University of Singapore academic Ban Kah Choon notes that the Branch 'never thought of itself as a domestic policing unit concerned only with the immediate problems of native or local origins'.[14] Singapore and Malaya were too involved in international trade for an isolationist stance, and security threats in the region reflected 'the burgeoning unrest in Europe, Northeast Asia and the Eurasian heartland as community ideology, strikes, extremist religious outlooks, Pan-Asianism and nationalism struggled to gain centre stage'.[15]

If a British colonialist standpoint dominated in both Australia and Singapore in the earliest phase of active intelligence in both countries during the First World War, the focus was somewhat different in each country. Whereas the IWW, Sinn Fein and German settlers were a principal focus in Australia, Malayans and Singaporeans heard a wake-up call in Chinese New Year 1915 when there was an attempted mutiny by Muslim Indian troops of the 5th Light Infantry.[16] Ban remarks that the mutiny was considered dangerous because 'it coincided with plans by the Germans with whom the British were at war to undermine the British Empire by fomenting unrest among its native subjects …'.[17]

A significant outcome of these events was the formation of the Special Branch – 'a group of men trained in the arcane arts of internal security such as intelligence gathering, the monitoring of suspects, counter-espionage and the running of agents …'.[18] The most noticeable success of the Special Branch was 'the successful infiltration of its main adversary, the Malayan Communist Party'.[19] Later activities of the Branch included attempts to counter Japanese espionage and the quite successful Japanese propaganda campaign about a pan-Asian vision for the region. The subsequent Japanese occupation of Malaya, in Ban Kah Choon's view, 'signalled the death knell of British colonial power and its prestige throughout Asia'.[20] Japan's military strategies were the result of careful and patient intelligence gathering over a long period aided by a key British air force officer who spied for them.[21]

Spying on allies in the Pacific theatre: Churchill's 'eyes and ears' on MacArthur

The Second World War, and especially the Pacific War, contributed to some bizarre intelligence links in the Asia-Pacific. Some of these involved allies spying on each other. An example that links Australia and the Philippines is the case of Gerald Wilkinson, a British liaison officer with General Douglas MacArthur in Australia who was Winston Churchill's spy reporting on the American General as well as Australian responses to the war. In his book *MacArthur's Undercover War*, the American historian William B. Brewer describes the covert war waged in the Philippines and elsewhere by General MacArthur from Australia (after his strategic retreat from Corregidor in 1942) as the largest undercover operation ever undertaken. But the book carries no mention of Churchill or Wilkinson keeping an eye on MacArthur, the Americans and the Australians. I have read Wilkinson's secret journal of these years in the Churchill College Library in Cambridge and was impressed with the observational and writing skills and the sheer human percipience of the best spies. In Wilkinson's case, his observations range from trade, politics and war strategy to MacArthur's ego and Australian Prime

Minister Curtin's apparently shifting allegiance from Britain to America as pressure in the Pacific grew.

Wilkinson, who was in his early thirties, had been a businessman in the Philippines, as well as a spy for the British. After the Japanese bombing of Pearl Harbor in December 1941 Wilkinson joined MacArthur on Corregidor then made his way to Britain where he saw Churchill, before he returned to Australia. Wilkinson's wife and two children remained in the Philippines and were captured and interned by the Japanese. Hence personal tensions inform Wilkinson's journal. But to a later reader, what stands out is Wilkinson's ability to convey the tensions and changing relations between Britain, Australia and the United States which were in 'a fluid and in some ways critical condition'.[22]

This then is the fascination of reading intelligent intelligence. Becoming engaged with a sensitive, perceptive observer at a time of international crisis has a similar buzz for this reader to a good novel. Ban writes that Special Branch work in Singapore meant that 'it sought and almost always possessed a view of the other side of things, of what the potential adversary thought and believed in'.[23] One of the classic films of our time, *The Lives of Others* set in East Germany, shows this dynamic in operation – and how the intense voyeurism involved in watching other people can sometimes engage one's sympathies and even (as in this film) subvert the spy's mission. Wilkinson was never entirely 'won over' by MacArthur's powerful ego however; he kept his eye on the international historical drama that was being played out during MacArthur's period in Australia when the US became a significant factor in Australian national life and which culminated in 1951 with the ANZUS Pact.

These events also served to form a link between Australia and the Philippines which would grow in the postwar years. Under MacArthur's general direction in the Allied Intelligence Bureau which he had set up, Australians and Filipinos who had escaped the Japanese invasion combined resources. Men like young Filipino Jesus Villamor and Australian Captain Allan Davidson played leading roles in infiltrating spies and Australian radio equipment into the Philippines with the ultimate aim of dislodging the Japanese invader.[24] These were early signs of defence and intelligence cooperation between Australia and the Philippines which have grown and continue to the present day. In May 2007, for example, President Gloria Arroyo witnessed the signing of a defence pact in Canberra which significantly boosted Australia's involvement in combating terrorist cells in Mindanao.[25] Intelligence is a field of frequent exchanges between the defence establishments of both countries. As if to highlight the need for such cooperation, it has been reported that two leading suspects involved in the 2002 Bali bombings were probably hiding in the southern Philippines.[26] The targets change but the work of spies and their agents continues.

The literary dimension: Australia and the Philippines

A small number of eminent Australian and Philippines novelists have explored aspects of 'the spying game' in their work. I do not refer here to the writers of spy-thriller genre novels but chiefly to recognised literary novelists. The writers to be considered here use both historical and contemporary settings; they illustrate some of the different modes available to writers who engage with the largely concealed worlds of espionage and terrorism.

Historical enigmas: Nicholas Hasluck

Historical dimensions of spying are recurrently explored in novels by Australian author Nicholas Hasluck. Hasluck has been a lawyer and a Supreme Court judge in Western Australia. His father Sir Paul Hasluck was an historian who rose to become Minister for External Affairs and Governor-General of Australia. Hasluck's mother was also an historian. Hasluck's first novel *Quarantine* (1978) creates a Kafkaesque atmosphere of impotence in the face of intrigue when a ship from Australia is detained in a quarantine station in the Suez Canal. In Hasluck's fourth novel *The Bellarmine Jug* (1984) an Australian student at the Grotius Institute in Holland discovers a long-lost fragment of the journal of Francois Pelsaert whose ship the *Batavia* was wrecked off the West Australian coast in 1629 with disastrous consequences for the survivors. Through his student's research, Hasluck forensically reconstructs both historical and imagined events, revealing the political intrigue in a Rosicrucian plot to take over the recently discovered Great South Land. Hasluck deftly draws his plot into the novel's present time when his student discoverer is interrogated by a counter-espionage expert about evidence gathered by security agencies in Amsterdam, Indonesia and Australia.

A different tack is taken in Hasluck's ninth novel *Our Man K* (1999) in which he uses other sources and his own research to develop the story of Egon Kisch, a Czech journalist and suspected spy for the Soviets whose visit to Australia in 1934 controversially divided left and right in Australian politics. Hasluck learnt that Kisch and Franz Kafka had been students together at the Altstadter Gymnasium in Prague and the idea of a novel of intrigue and speculation was born.[27] Like his earlier novels of espionage and intrigue, Hasluck's *Our Man K* begins with established fact and develops its themes through the writer's imagination. Hasluck explains: 'My novel about the enigmatic Egon Kisch – *Our Man K* – must be shaped (as all novels are shaped) by serendipity masquerading as research, and by constant speculation'.[28] Nor does the past necessarily remain remote. In Hasluck's words, 'The past is a foreign country. They do things differently there, but what they do may linger in the mind to haunt us'.[29] Hasluck's work prompts these hauntings.

Secrecy and revolution: F. Sionil José's **Mass**

F. Sionil (Frankie) Jose uses the past with a sense of personal urgency in his quintet *The Pretenders* (1962), *My Brother, My Executioner* (1973), *The Tree* (1978), *Mass* (1983) and *Po-on* (1984). Jose's sympathies clearly lie with the rural poor and oppressed in the Philippines over the more than three hundred years of Spanish rule and subsequent American colonisation. The consequences that make for espionage, division and internal conflict in the Philippines are set. As Dudley de Souza explains, the revolutionary, peasant-based Hukbalahap movement which appears in several novels brings on situations ripe for conflict, betrayal and revenge – 'where brother is pitted against brother on two sides of the same fence: the exploiter and the exploited, the landowner and the dispossessed'.[30]

Jose's celebrated novel *Mass* dramatises some of these conflicts and their consequences in 1960s Manila. The strength of this novel lies in its dramatic portrayal of attempts to create a popular movement for democratic change in the *barrios* and universities of this time and in the loyalties, betrayals and moral conflicts that such times of social revolution engender.

One of the features of Jose's work that has always impressed me is its earthy sense of moral purpose. But in *Mass* we also see conflicting senses of loyalty, belonging and identity and the incipient corruption of mass movements as well as of dictatorships. Thus Pepe Samson, as his biblical name might suggest, is a problematic hero – the most interesting kind – as his joining of the Brotherhood movement shows. When Professor Hortenso tries to win Pepe over to the Brotherhood with Marxist rhetoric and ideology Pepe retorts: 'What can we expect from the Brotherhood? Why should I give it loyalty? What can I get in return?'[31] This almost streetwise young man who comes from the backblocks of Cabugawan will not be recruited to a cause by words alone. Psychological factors come into play: Pepe has been rejected by his father and like his orphan friend Toto he might find in the solidarity of the Brotherhood a sanctuary, an alternative family. Helping to set up a cell of the Brotherhood in the Barrio appeals to Pepe despite the sexual and erotic diversions he encounters.

Involvement in an underground movement often depends on respect for a leader. In his search for a leader – and an alternative father figure – Pepe Samson finds he has much to learn from Ka Lucio who had fought for the Huks but has recognised their failure to win over 'the masses'.[32] But Pepe also worries about 'the raucous voice of the mob'[33] which can override rational judgment. He is 'in' the Brotherhood but not yet 'of' them. As he becomes more deeply embroiled in underground activities, Pepe finds himself drawn into cunning, deviousness, conspiracy and the violence he mentally rejects. His older mentor Ka Lucio advises him to 'lead alone … The general idea, you must relay to everyone – but the details, you must keep to yourself'.[34] While these are prudent tactics learnt by the communists, they have uncomfortable echoes of Sun Tzu, Machiavelli and the Bush regime's conduct of the war in Iraq which left the door open for Abu Ghraib and other atrocities to occur. Nor do such tactics lead in the end to popular support for a cause.

For Pepe Samson, ideology cannot overcome his feeling for individuals. Ka Lucio tells him that he must identify his enemy as the rich: '[W]hen you point the gun between their eyes, you must do it without passion – or compassion. Do it as a duty, do it to survive'.[35] But this is too calculated, too ruthless for Pepe, whose feelings are at least partly influenced by the fact that his girlfriend Betsy is rich.

Repelled by this conspiratorial and violent aspect of the Brotherhood, Pepe wants to remain in the shadows but feels himself 'sucked into a whirlpool slowly'.[36] This is a central experience in many studies of conspiracy and spying.

The conflicted Pepe Samson, a student revolutionary who has come to doubt the motives and purposes of the underground movement he has joined might seem ripe for 'turning' into a double agent who would spy on members of the Brotherhood and inform on them to agents of the president. Seeing this, the homosexual intellectual Juan Puneta sets out to 'turn' the heterosexual Pepe into a willing accomplice in undermining and destroying the Brotherhood. This is a fatal mistake. Ka Lucio is murdered – possibly by Puneta. Five student leaders disappear without trace.[37] The President's internal security agents 'trail' and spy on Pepe. When he is arrested, imprisoned, interrogated and tortured, Pepe is questioned about a shipment of guns for the Brotherhood and recruitment methods in the Quezon sector (neither of which he knows about).[38] His captors claim Pepe is 'a member of a conspiracy to overthrow by force a democratically elected government'.[39] Nothing is as it seems. The wilful opponents attack each other: those who question their own side are traitors. Loyalty is all – but loyalty to what or to whom?

The quest motif in *Mass* shows Pepe Samson attempting to thread his way through this confusion. He identifies the enemy in Juan Puneta who believes in 'exploiting the poor'.[40] Typically of Jose's Rosales saga, though, the source of Puneta's evil derives from his family history. We are told that Puneta's grandfather 'sold out the Revolution and went over to the Spaniards. Then, it was the Americans, and the Japanese'. He was a turncoat. Now, says Pepe, as he holds Puneta at gunpoint, 'you will subvert the revolution again and claim it as yours'.[41] In shooting Puneta in his own shooting gallery and presenting it as suicide, Pepe offends against his non-violent principles but rationalises his action as 'justice' for the common people and the nation.

At this point, *Mass* is 'down and dirty': it takes its readers to the depths of the spying game as extreme opponents conspire to obtain power and control. The moral ambivalence which Jose reveals in his protagonist towards the end of the novel is suddenly resolved for Pepe, as we have seen, when he murders (or assassinates) Puneta. Pepe claims to feel no guilt and obtains qualified support from the Church – or rather, from Father Jess who says he believes that social justice can only be achieved by violent means.[42] Pepe's new clarity of purpose, as he prepares to head for the mountains to fight for the revolution there arises from a recognition of where he now belongs – not with the rich people and intellectual elites of the city but with Rosales, the poor village where he started and a wish to serve those people. He leaves behind the spying, lying and compromises of the city where the *ilustrados* – the intellectuals – lose a clear sense of purpose and their revolutionary zeal becomes ripe for compromise and corruption.

'Spotters' and 'Sparrows': Jose Y. Dalisay's Killing Time in a Warm Place

Like *Mass*, Jose Y. Dalisay Jr's novel *Killing Time in a Warm Place* (1992) deals with growing up in the Philippines during the Marcos years. Less elemental than his story *The Island* (1996), *Killing Time* explores the moral and psychological dimensions of opposition to a dictator from the point of view of Noel Ilustre Bulaong, a participant in the demonstrations and other forms of opposition to Marcos. In an Introduction to the 2006 edition of *Killing Time,* Dalisay notes that at the age of nineteen he was himself arrested by military intelligence agents in 1973 and imprisoned during a university year in which he admits to 'studying Mao instead of math'. A recurrent fear in prison was that of 'the dreaded "ajax" – our slang word for "agent", the government's and our jailers' ears'.

Less epic in scope than *Mass*, *Killing Time* explores the Marcos years retrospectively some twenty-five years later from the ironic perspective of a survivor who has gone on to higher education in the US and survived. His memory of the atmosphere in middle-class family homes after martial law in the early 1970s recalls its domination by the fear of spies:

> Now and then we had casual visitors over and who knows how many of them may have been government spies checking out the place – say, the cupboard – for a cache of weapons or Communist Party membership cards, which we were supposed to carry if you believed the papers, but which none of us, to my knowledge, had ever seen. [43]

The fear of government spies has repercussions. Underground or 'safe houses' become necessary: within them, the inhabitants learn to camouflage their political ideologies, stripping their rooms of revolutionary literature and replacing them with *Time, Good Housekeeping* and other anodyne publications and preparing themselves for raids. The narrator, Noel Bulaong, is aware of the destructive power on morale, motivation and personal freedom of government agents: 'no word buzzed more quickly around the HQ than *ahente*, "agent", the secret weaver of our destruction'.[44] In these circumstances, rumours and suspicions multiply and nothing can be more conducive to undermining a clandestine Organization than suspicions of treachery by a 'mole' or a 'plant'.

Stories are swapped in the underground to increase awareness or reduce fears. One such bizarre story is told of a woman in one unit of the New People's Army who is suspected of, and confesses to being a government agent. She is sentenced to death. Her husband asks to carry out the execution. They are allowed to sit on the bank of a river and weep in each other's arms 'for things that were and might have been'.[45] She nods. He shoots her. The narrator's response to hearing this story is instructive: he would never have been able to do the same thing. 'I would have written novels to demonstrate the numbing complexity of truths, decisions, errors, and so on'. He concludes: 'I was the most unreliable comrade I knew'.[46] This is the area of dilemmas, uncertainties, hopes and fears in which the modern novel flourishes and where the spying game and its outcomes can be explored.

Identifying the enemy is a key aspect of most intelligence work, whether in domestic or international conflicts. We have seen Pepe Samson's dilemmas and difficulties before he is able to personalise the enemy in the figure of Juan Puneta. Dalisay's narrator recalls the way 'the [government] informers – "spotters" in police parlance – picked out Sparrows based on tattooed moles on their faces':

> Col. Jesus Garcia, Pasay City police chief, said a mole on the chin means the person is a communist lecturer; on the center forehead, a runner; on the forehead just above the left eyebrow, a Sparrow intelligence agent; two moles on the left cheek, a member of a Sparrow unit; a mole each on the left and right cheeks and one on the forehead, a liquidator; and two moles on the right and one on the left cheeks, a general.[47]

The absurdity of such theories and surveillance techniques is left to the reader's imagination by a narrator in exile from the Manila where he had held a senior government post until he opposed Marcos. Dalisay's protagonist, Noel Bulaong, recalls his detention in prison, the interrogation and torture but also the clash of cultures between uneducated provincial soldiers and their urban intellectual prisoners. The prisoners, like many students and teachers sent to remote communities in China during the so-called Cultural Revolution, often resent their inability to communicate with their captors and violence results.

A witty, ironic tone interspersed with more sombre moments characterises *Killing Time*. The hothouse atmosphere of prison life fertilises dreams, fantasies, rumour, innuendo and (in some) humour. Intelligence agents are prime targets in an unequal tussle of intellects. The narrator recalls one ill-educated major in government intelligence who was promoted on the basis of his theory that communists could be recognised by their composite mask of 'guilt, depravity and outright menace'.[48] However the satiric critique is not all one-way. Unlike Pepe Samson, who takes up arms and heads for the mountains to continue the revolution, Noel Bulaong is left with the classic dilemma of the intellectual: he sees both sides of a problem. When he leaves for America – for 'the distance and the difference and the antithesis', he says, rather too neatly – he has a discomforting sense of guilt for opting out and thereby betraying democratic causes and individuals in the Philippines. 'What next would I betray?' he asks himself[49] and contrasts his fate with that of his former girlfriend Laurie who has gone north to fight with 'the comrades' in 'a liberated zone'.[50]

An Australian in Asia: Robert Drewe

Robert Drewe's second novel *A Cry in the Jungle Bar* (1979) offers some remarkable complementary perspectives to those of Jose and Dalisay on spies, lies and intelligence in the Philippines and Southeast Asia during the Marcos era. Inevitably, Drewe's point of view is different from theirs. His protagonist Richard Cullen works for a UN Agency in Southeast Asia where he has become an expert on *bubalus bubalis,* the indispensable buffalo in Asian agriculture. Drewe adroitly places his fleshy, middle-aged Australian protagonist as a man who engages sympathetically with rural workers in the region. More than once,

Cullen identifies with the working buffaloes that he knows so well. But he is beset by personal demons, a crumbling marriage and a sense that life is passing him by.

Cullen's personal vulnerability together with his frequent communications and visits with rural Islamic communities in the southern Philippines attracts the attention of journalist Ted Orosa who has strong American connections and, Cullen comes to suspect, ties to the CIA. When Orosa makes some none-too-subtle attempts to recruit Cullen as a source, Orosa expresses interest in the Muslims in the south and the highly visible Moros in Mindanao. But other persons of interest to Orosa and his masters include ordinary people of Cebu and Iloilo: 'Less prominent groups in small *barrios* who might [be] more forthcoming to you people', Orosa says to Cullen, 'because of your neutrality. Subversive rather than blatant'.[51] Workers for international agencies are frequently sought out as spies because their cover seems impeccable. But Cullen, despite his problems, is a basically decent Australian, a solid professional and a believer in the work he does. He tells Orosa that as a member of the Organization he is not political. Cullen bluntly asks Orosa if he is CIA, which Orosa denies plausibly, without ever losing interest in Cullen as a possible source in the future.

The principal setting of *A Cry in the Jungle Bar* is a hotel bar in Manila decorated by assorted animal heads (including a pangolin) which give the place, at night, the appearance of a jungle. By day, it looks more like a run-down museum.[52] The human animals who inhabit the jungle bar include an international array of diplomats, journalists, secretaries and spies. In this setting, Richard Cullen is an Australian innocent in a jungle of intrigue. Basically apolitical, he is nevertheless a blunt critic of violence and injustice. When Ted Orosa, still keen to pump Cullen for intelligence, asks him about the situation in the 'boondocks' of the southern Philippines, Cullen replies provocatively (and perhaps recklessly): 'Oh, states of emergency everywhere … martial law, constitutional authoritarianism, the usual thing'.[53] Not one to give up easily, Orosa emphasises to Cullen the threats of terror and instability, the need to strengthen Marcos's presidency from 'the infiltration of subversives' and the threat of revolution. Cullen responds laconically: 'Not much chance of that is there? The President has things pretty well sewn up'.[54]

The truth of Cullen's observation about President Marcos's iron grip through his security forces is reinforced when the journalist Ted Orosa, despite his connections, is sacked for criticising the president's nephew; and further when one of Cullen's colleagues at the Organization, ZM Ali, disappears. Rumours range from the view that ZM was a spy against the government to the one that he is 'a sacrificial lamb to keep foreign critics in line'.[55] The strongest suspicion is that Marcos's men have decided that ZM was mixed up with the MLNF in Mindanao. ZM Ali's papers include reports on buffalo diseases in Mindanao that seem to link him with Cullen. Will the Australian himself be a target of the President's secret police?

The deeply ironic concluding section of *A Cry in the Jungle Bar* presents Cullen and his Australian colleague Gallash in Mindanao where they have been sent by the Organization to report further on the material for which ZM Ali has apparently been expelled. The novel's denouement occurs in the strife-torn southern Philippines. While the events that surround Cullen's likely death – the novel leaves him facing three Moro soldiers who mistake him for an American and have their guns trained on him – can be seen more as the result of a 'cock-up' than a conspiracy. Having followed a *barrio* prostitute to her primitive dwelling, Cullen leaves without having sex with her when he sees her small child and miserable circumstances. Under martial law curfew, he is confronted by a pimp, who stabs him and he staggers on to be confronted by the jeep and three young men dressed in MNLF commando uniforms. Drewe's sardonic conclusion to this novel shows his iconic Australian again out of his depth in Asia, pleading for his life.

Conclusion

This chapter suggests the need for closer attention to clandestine intelligence activities in the fortunes of individuals, nations and international relations in the Asia-Pacific through a combination of literary, historical and political studies.

The persistence of spying through history has been indicated by evidence of 'cartographic spies' among European maritime explorers in the regions and searchers for a 'Great South Land'. The practice of spying, both within nations and internationally, has persisted through war and peace and is currently in a new growth spurt in response to an

American-designated 'war on terror'. Throughout history – and especially in the twentieth and early twenty-first centuries – literary authors have contributed enormously to the profession of spying and its representation in literature.

While much intelligence work is closely linked to military Organizations and the attitudes, habits and values that flow from engagement with the military, I contend that a more flexible, critical and imaginative mindset is required in 'the second oldest profession'.

The career of George Steward, Australia's first spymaster in the early twentieth century shows Australia still closely allied with British institutions and interests but establishing some areas of difference. The Special Branch in Singapore demonstrates an extension of this influence in British Malaya and Singapore from 1916 to the Second World War. In both Australia and Singapore, however, moves towards independence were fostered by local needs and conditions. British influence declined dramatically after the Japanese invasion and occupation of Malaya and Singapore.

The ubiquity of secret agents and spying in wartime is exemplified in journals and diaries from the Second World War which show even the allies spying on each other. For example, we have seen Gerald Wilkinson, a British agent in General Douglas MacArthur's office in Australia spying on the American general for British Prime Minister Winston Churchill (who himself was an intelligence junkie). This is an example of 'close to the source' intelligence involving the fortunes of Britain, America, Australia and the Philippines and it reveals a significant literary dimension in the portrayal of people and events. More broadly, the Pacific War brought Australia and the Philippines into each other's intelligence orbits.

A small sampling of novels since the 1970s in Australia and the Philippines has revealed some illuminating literary dimensions of spying. From the historical enigmas of Nicholas Hasluck to F. Sionil José's novel *Mass* and Jose Y. Dalisay Jr's *Killing Time in a Warm Place,* we witness an oscillation between theory and practice: spying exercises both these perspectives. *Mass* and *Killing Time* reveal moral and psychological dilemmas behind the facades of the Marcos years in the Philippines. Robert Drewe's *A Cry in the Jungle Bar* explores the Marcos period from an Australian and international perspective. In all of these novels, spies, lies and intelligence contribute to a world of distorted perspectives and power relations, lightened from time to time by a corrective irony and humour which reveals another, perhaps superior, kind of humane intelligence at work.

Fourteen

Of Spies and Terrorists: Australian Fiction after 9/11

Introduction

Wherever we were located in the world, we saw the images and heard the rhetoric of 11 September 2001: the United States of America had been attacked on home soil, the world would never be the same again, and a new paradigm now prevailed in international affairs. A defensive posture by the world's sole superpower was seen by its leaders as insufficient: the best form of defence was attack, though it also included reductions to freedom of movement, belief and association.

The American-led wars in Afghanistan and Iraq, supported by Britain, Australia and some European countries were contradictorily described as both pre-emptive and retaliatory and were bolstered by a rhetoric of freedom and democracy that has sounded increasingly hollow in the world at large. In no sense could either war be considered 'clean', though the conflict in Afghanistan had been supported in the UN and other international bodies. These new conditions of international conflict have produced massive increases in secret intelligence and covert operations in the Middle East and China as well as in the US and allied nations. In this post-Cold War epoch, the figure of the spy in literature has morphed into that of the terrorist and adopted protean shapes and forms.

This chapter will consider some of these forms in recent Australian fiction but will pause a moment longer on the rhetoric and realpolitik of 11 September 2001.

Despite its now well documented difficulties and problems, the report of the 9/11 Commission (2001) provided a remarkably substantial and balanced analysis of the events in New York, Washington and Pennsylvania on 11 September 2001 and what it calls 'the new terrorism' from an American point of view. The report's theme is counter-terrorism and the 'global strategy' that is required to combat the threat of further terrorist attacks. Implicit throughout the report is the necessity to secure the freedom of the American people to live without the fear of further attacks.

The report's focus is on the improvement of intelligence and counter-terrorism initiatives with special emphasis on al-Qaeda and Afghanistan. *New York Times* reporter Philip Shenon's history of the 9/11 investigation (published in 2008) vividly documents the personalities and problems behind the appointment of officers and the researching and writing of this report – including White House attempts to prevent access to relevant parts of the Presidential Daily Briefings. Some evidence was suppressed, including evidence of Saudi involvement in the terrorist attacks. But the overall success of the bipartisan Commission in establishing its independence and retaining its focus despite the many pressures applied to it deserves credit. *The 9/11 Commission Report* deserves a place in the literature of our times along with the more imaginative forms of poetry, drama, film and fiction that have responded to these changes in international affairs in the early twenty-first century. But what kinds of literary responses have occurred in other countries? In Australia, for instance? And what literary genres are employed – and adapted to their authors' purposes?

Espionage and Terrorism in Literature

A largely unnoticed history of literary espionage and terrorism in books by Australian writers in the nineteenth and twentieth centuries has been brought to new prominence by these violent events in the early twenty-first century. Not surprisingly, Japan, China, Germany and Russia have figured prominently in such narratives through the twentieth century. From a long way back, Australians have been watching others closely, reporting on them and trading in secret information, sometimes in exotic situations and locales.

A more general question about genre is raised by such work. Are the serious literary novel and the espionage thriller Siamese twins or forever set apart? Conrad's *The Secret Agent*, Greene's *Our Man in Havana* and le Carré's *The Spy Who Came in from the Cold* are considered literary 'classics' but it is interesting that Greene called his novel an 'entertainment' and both Conrad and le Carré were hyper-aware of their popular audiences and commercial success. From the 'thriller' side of this fence, we can sometimes see a complementary interest in features of 'serious' literary espionage such as psychological complexity, interiority, questions of identity and dilemmas of conscience. But in Grisham, Forsyth and Furst, for instance, action, suspense, intrigues and puzzles are strongly laced with violent thrills and spills. The truth is that for writers who deal with characters playing both sides of the fence (that is, secret agents, spies and some terrorists), the temptation to write both serious literature *and* popular fiction is ever-present.

Australian Insurgents in the Terror Wars: *Underground, The Unknown Terrorist, Orpheus Lost.*

Australian journalist David Marr recently accused Australian novelists of giving too little attention to 'the urgent present' and failing to address 'in worldly, adult ways the country and the time in which we live'.[1] While this criticism fails to acknowledge the real insights into the present that can be made in novels set further back in history – such as Christopher Koch's novels that deal with secret intelligence in Indonesia, Vietnam, Cambodia and China – Marr's charge has drawn attention to the work of a number of younger writers who are shaping the contemporary Australian imagination. Such writers include Andrew McGahan, Richard Flanagan, Janette Turner Hospital and Adib Khan, together with contributors to the 'thriller' genre such as Adrian d'Hage.

Kerryn Goldsworthy has rightly described Andrew McGahan's novel *Underground* (2006) as fulfilling David Marr's wish for a novel that goes 'straight for the throat' of contemporary Australia. McGahan's novel is set a few years in the future in about 2011. The novel's narrator is Leo James who writes his memoirs in the last few days of his life as he faces death by firing squad. Leo is the twin brother of Bernard James, the prime minister of Australia who takes over as the second prime minister after the recently departed John Howard and bears an uncanny resemblance to Australia's former prime minister. In his last days, Leo addresses his captors in a narrative which switches backwards and forwards across key events such as 9/11, the American president's visit to Australia in 2003, and events such as a televised mushroom cloud over Canberra and an especially powerful Queensland cyclone which enabled Leo's temporary escape from his brother's anti-terrorist forces.

An especially clever aspect of this satiric novel is Leo's adventure with Aisha, a twenty-four year old member of the Great Southern Jihad who turns out to be Nancy Campbell, a University of Queensland Law graduate and daughter of an English professor: Nancy has been recruited to an al-Qaeda-related sleeper cell in Australia. She adheres to the 'new Islam', which pays no attention to the Koran – which she hasn't read (like many Australian Marxists who had never read *Das Kapital*). The re-named Aisha believes that she and her fellow jihadists have destroyed Canberra but they are deceived by an elaborate hoax whereby Australia's capital has become a centre of world government run by the Americans; and she learns to her chagrin that her Great Southern Jihad has been created by American and Australian double agents.

An important member of the new world government in Canberra is Osama bin Laden who needs the Americans as much as they need him. The novel's final irony is Leo's imprisonment in the empty House of Representatives of Australia's parliament which his jailer, Australia's prime minister, has always felt to be a place of imprisonment – 'hemmed in by laws, constrained by the necessity for votes and debates and compromise'.[2]

Underground combines narrative drive with satiric bite and, as a reviewer has noted, 'the feral quality of good political cartooning'.[3] In a succession of sharp scenes, McGahan shows a nation nuking itself – by allowing its government to use the terrorist crisis to imprison refugees, ban books and other forms of dissent and to introduce absurd tests of patriotism. The Bush White House offers a model of reckless adventurism and suppression of rights in the pursuit of freedom, and Australia seems destined to follow, drawn on by 'grey, corporate money ... nervous and greedy for more'. Like the Roman empire, the American empire will assuredly collapse. But when the barbarians enter, will the institutions of civilisation already be dead?

Like McGahan's *Underground*, Richard Flanagan's novel *The Unknown Terrorist* also attacks the jugular with satiric barbs. Flanagan's protagonist, Gina Davies, is a pole dancer in a King's Cross nightclub who is swept into the public eye as 'the unknown terrorist' after a series of accidents including a sexual encounter with a man called Tariq who is (wrongly) suspected of planting bombs at the Homebush Olympic Stadium in Sydney. Flanagan's principal target (as we shall see when the novel is dealt with at more length in Chapter 15) is the Australian media whose journalists and their employers fall too readily for government propaganda and make their ratings-based reputations on vastly exaggerated projections of violent threats to people and property.

Strangely, perhaps, Flanagan's book has been praised more highly by American than Australian critics. In Texas, for example, the book was described as 'a primer on the paranoia that is sweeping the world' (*The Austin Chronicle*) while the reviewer for the *New York Review of Books* remarks that '(Flanagan's) methods name a callousness at loose in the world today, a luridness, and a widespread helplessness before them both. If only they were a product of his imagination.' *The Washington Post* compared Flanagan's 'tightly crafted narrative' to Kafka and Capote and described *The Unknown Terrorist* as a 'disturbing gaze at the social and psychological mechanisms of terror'.[4] In writing back so strongly to the imperial hubris that has shaped recent American foreign policy, Flanagan seems ironically to have enhanced his reputation in that country. *The Unknown Terrorist* appealed to a reading public which is largely opposed to the war in Iraq and reductions in human rights at home; it also exemplifies a growing interest by Australian publishers in gaining a slice of the large American reading public for their works.

Janette Turner Hospital's novel *Orpheus Lost* (2007), as discussed in Chapter 15, exhibits a deeply informed understanding of American military culture and its regional roots. Having lived and worked in South Carolina since 1999, Turner Hospital explores in this novel a regional culture that is both deeply religious and militaristic. A post-Civil War separatist sentiment and a heavy commitment to the

National Guard is one of many paradoxes in the American South and in American culture more broadly.

We turn now more directly to Australian interactions with Asia in the spying game.

Straddling Cultures: Adib Khan's *Spiral Road*

Like his protagonist Masud Alam in *Spiral Road* (2007), the novelist Adib Khan was born and grew up in Bangladesh. He has lived and worked in Australia for more than thirty years. From the time of Adib Khan's principal character Masud's arrival at Dhakar airport to his fraught attempts to depart after spending some weeks with his family there after a long absence, Masud is haunted by the impact and influence of 9/11 on the subcontinent. Masud is shadowed during his return visit to Bangladesh by an Australian Secret Intelligence officer, Steven Mills, who suspects Masud of association with terrorists.

Yet Masud is also regarded with suspicion by Bangladeshi immigration officials, one of whom grills him about Australia and Australians: 'Are Australians prejudiced against Muslims?' he is asked. 'I'm an Australian. I'm not prejudiced against myself,' Masud replies. But the official persists: 'There's a difference between someone like you and the descendents of the British.' Masud retorts: 'There are people from all over the world living there.' When he is asked, 'Do Muslims feel threatened in Australia?' he replies, 'You need to ask a practising Muslim'.[5]

Masud's choice not to name any religion on his immigration form, though he was brought up Muslim, epitomises his problem in trying to straddle two countries in his mind and heart. For various reasons, he has learnt to distance himself from people in Australia and in his native Bangladesh for whose independence he had fought in 1971. Adib Khan presents his protagonist as a cool, somewhat remote individual afraid or unable to commit himself to a single person, country or cause. His reflections trace the lineaments of fear and desire of a sensitive and intelligent Asian-Australian immigrant.

The literal and metaphoric Spiral Road which Masud Alam travels during his return to family and friends in Manikpur, now part of Dhakar, takes him through the dangerous territory of secret wars that have flared up around the world since 11 September 2001.

When Masud re-enters the family home, now much diminished since his childhood, his mother holds up the Koran in both hands muttering *surahs*, and he experiences a strong sense of 'instant purgation'.[6] Yet he tells the family that he is not a practising Muslim any more. His main concern is for the global environment and he has joined the Greens in Australia.[7] Masud's extended family have different responses to 9/11 and its consequences. His Uncle Rafiq, for instance, argues that flying the two planes into the towers was 'a symbol, a gesture of rage, frustration, attention-seeking ... A statement to say that if you continue to humiliate us, we will find devastating ways to retaliate'.[8] Masud angrily retorts that innocent people were killed, this is not symbolism but murder.[9] But the uncle is not so easily dismissed: 'Aren't innocent lives lost in Palestine? Isn't that murder? ... A moral stand is not the sole right of white nations'.[10]

Spiral Road explores with considerable finesse the ways in which the iconic figure of Masud is torn by competing claims on his mind and feelings. He is most deeply affected by the sight of his admired father reduced to a state of puerile dependency by Alzheimer's and his loyal mother struggling to cope. But hero-worship is stripped away in this novel. When Masud discovers his father's hidden diaries they reveal his secret affair with another woman and the existence of their love-child. From this emerges a truer picture of Masud's father whom he now recognises as 'deceitful, cunning ... impulsive. But my father nonetheless'.[11]

The struggle for personal freedom in Adib Khan's novel, as in much of Naipaul's work, involves a process of disenchantment – a stripping of illusions. Yet the necessity of ideals is also revealed in the lives of Masud himself as a young man in the 1970s and in his favourite nephew Omar who, Masud discovers, is involved in a secret cell operating a training camp for Islamic 'freedom fighters' in the remote borderlands of Bangladesh. Masud gets caught up in his nephew's new version of fighting for 'freedom' – in small, secret, mobile cells training Bangladeshis and Arabs in acts of sabotage and murder on Western targets. There are continuities here with the motives and methods of those, like Masud, who fought the Pakistani forces to ensure the independence of Bangladesh. Stealth and secrecy are still the modus operandi. But when Omar and his cell try to recruit Masud to their cause they find he is unrecruitable – and therefore dangerous to them. His previous experiences in raids and killings during the independence struggles together with his time in Australia have rendered him incapable of supporting the cause of these young men. Although he looks like promising material to both the Australian secret service and to al-Qaeda, his conscience tells him he can serve neither cause. Masud's refusal to cooperate with his nephew and his cell has fatal consequences for Omar whose hero-worship has distorted his view of his uncle.

The psychological complications of *Spiral Road* are finely tuned and the reader is drawn into the reasons for Masud's emotional disengagement. Both Jane Austen and the Koran are part of his inheritance. Can they be integrated in any satisfying way? Is Australia a lifeline? Having resisted recruitment to the Australian government's cause in the 'war on terror', Masud is accused by religious zealots in the streets of Dhakar of spying on a mullah who was giving a speech at the bazaar. Masud narrowly escapes a beating or worse and reflects ironically that similar scenes of prejudice and violence could be experienced at any airport in America:

> Seeing my Muslim name, immigration officials would want to know the motives for my visit, although the Australian passport would probably lessen suspicion. Here (in Bangladesh) it's my name that suppresses hostility, but being an Australian isn't an advantage. I am a resident of a Christian country, they remind me, mostly inhabited by whites. Cousins of the Americans and the British. They invaded Islamic countries. They all speak English.[12]

Spiral Road explores complex issues of patriotism, loyalty and identity. In his most revealing discussion with the Australian spy, Steven Mills, Masud is puzzled at the Australian's apparent inability to understand 'cultural divides and the lives of those who are compelled to defy them'.[13] At this stage, Masud thinks his family is his first (and perhaps only) priority – a position which modifies somewhat later. As for loyalty to country, he observes that he is 'neither a traitor nor a blind patriot', which draws from the Australian the ironic comment that 'a safe occupation of the middle ground is so common to migrants'.[14] The ripostes continue. Masud asks if Steven would be happier if he broke out regularly into a heartfelt rendition of 'Advance Australia Fair'. Mills says he'd prefer 'Waltzing Matilda', before the discussion moves to more strategic issues.

Of the many moral and emotional issues facing Masud Alam, the most difficult one is whether to betray his nephew Omar for whom he is now prepared to drop all euphemisms and call a terrorist. Which is more reprehensible, he asks, silence or betrayal?[15] Should Masud tell his brother, Omar's father, in the first instance, that his son is a terrorist? While thinking he should not, he effectively does this. Unfortunately, the truth does not make everyone free when loyalties become so tangled; and Omar meets his violent end protecting Masud, the uncle he wrongly believed would support the new generation's violent struggle for what they perceive as freedom.

A 'higher thriller': The Beijing Conspiracy

In contrast to *Spiral Road*, Adrian d'Hage's novel *The Beijing Conspiracy* (2007) foregrounds direct action, conspiracy and violent conflict. The novel's plot concerns the planning and execution of a series of warning attacks against Western and Chinese targets by al-Qaeda-related cells culminating in the 'final solution' – a new version of the Holocaust – to be achieved at the Beijing Olympic Games. The novel earns the accolade of a 'higher thriller' because of its astute incorporation of scientific, political, military and religious knowledge into its plot.

The author's experience is brought to bear on this novel. Adrian d'Hage is a highly educated, well-informed former member of the Australian Army who served in Intelligence before being transferred to Infantry where he earned a Military Cross for action in Vietnam. He was later head of Defence Planning for security of the Sydney Olympics including chemical, biological and nuclear threats. Unusually, he is a student of religion who says he commenced his honours degree in theology as a committed Christian and graduated 'of no fixed religion'.

While *The Beijing Conspiracy* exhibits less interest in the psychological adjustments of individuals involved in the secret wars of our times than Adib Khan's *Spiral Road*, *The Beijing Conspiracy* creates some horrific scenarios of where these wars may lead. The novel's plausibility is enhanced by the author's knowledge of military intelligence, contemporary politics, religion and the media.

The villains and heroes in *The Beijing Conspiracy* are neatly counter-pointed. The chief villains are Amon al-Falid, an American-educated Egyptian whose vision splendid is of the US, Britain, Australia and all Western countries being defeated and operating under strict Sharia law.[16] He is matched for villainy by an American evangelical Christian, Richard Halliwell, who uses his massive pharmaceutical company and his influence with an American president uncannily like George W. Bush to develop biological weapons to use in the desperate 'last days' that Halliwell and his Christian right evangelical friends see as their times.[17] On the side of the angels are a feisty Australian microbiologist, Dr Kath Braithwaite, her boss Professor Imran Sayed – an outstanding scientist and moderate Muslim – and a tough, independent and charming CIA officer, Curtis O'Connor. Together, these three prevent 'the final solution' in Beijing but only after a 'first warning' attack of devastating proportions on Sydney – presented in graphic chapters which show the fruits of the author's actual pre-planning for defence of the Sydney Olympics against terrorist attacks.

Excessive religious zeal underlies much of the evil portrayed in *The Beijing Conspiracy*. Even Kath Braithwaite's ex-husband was an Australian Christian neo-con. But Kath has had the courage and good fortune to leave him behind. A far more lethal influence is the Christian right in North America epitomised in the loathsome Richard Halliwell. On the other side, the suicide bombers of Sydney are Islamic zealots as are their leaders in Islamic China and the Middle East. D'Hage seems not to accept the Huntington thesis of an inevitable clash between Christian and Islamic civilizations. Rather, he recognises that highly motivated political forces are conspiring to defeat the moderates and liberals across the world.

One of the secrets of d'Hage's popular appeal is his ability to make apparently far-fetched scenarios read like extensions of yesterday's news. When the American president is shot down by missiles over Canberra while visiting Australia after al-Qaeda's 'first warning' attacks on Sydney, he is succeeded by a Vice-President with many of the unfortunate hallmarks of Dick Cheney. The corrupt links between the White House and the pharmaceutical industry in this novel echo charges of similar corrupt links between government in the US and the armaments and private security industries. The novel is a reminder that many of the horrors of the past five years in Iraq and elsewhere exceed what might have been imagined – Abu Ghraib, Guantanamo Bay and rendition to name just a few. In this context, the excesses of *The Beijing Conspiracy* may seem merely truthful to today's readers.

Conclusion

This chapter began with *The 9/11 Commission Report* which famously charged American intelligence analysts with deficient imagination when they failed to 'connect the dots' that would have led to prediction and pre-emption of the attacks on New York and Washington in September 2001. Attempts to bureaucratise the imagination, as proposed by the Commission, may not however be the best way to freely imagine what could, might or probably will happen in the next decade as a result of those events and the forces unleashed in response to them. Intelligence analysts, as well as a broader public, should be urged to read what we call fiction as well as traditional forms of reporting.

Brief consideration of five novels by Australian writers – all published in 2006 and 2007 – show a range of imaginative responses and literary techniques revealing these writers grappling with the implications of their country's involvement in the oddly misnamed, apparently never-ending 'war on terror'. If that is an actual war, these novels suggest that it is being lost.

McGahan, Flanagan, Turner Hospital, Khan and d'Hage all demonstrate a close and welcome engagement with a period of major upheaval in world affairs. All five reveal critical perspectives and imagine vivid scenes, characters and situations. Significantly, while indicating political weakness and lack of leadership and independent judgment, they together reveal Australia as a country of increasingly complex trans-national individuals and stories. Because stealth and secrecy are hallmarks of the burgeoning activity in espionage and terrorism, it behoves us to read and discuss this new fiction with a view to better imagining and interpreting the clandestine conflicts of our time. The final chapter will therefore return to other novels that engage significantly with the spying game in our times.

Fifteen

Australian Literature's War on Terror

It would be difficult to overstate the significance and influence of the terrorist attacks on New York and Washington DC on 11 September 2001 on Australia, the Asia-Pacific region and indeed the world. Yet we in Australia, as close allies who share, among other things, a Free Trade Agreement with the US have a role in questioning the hubris of the world's most powerful empire and checking its sometimes rash behaviour. An Australian Broadcasting Commission television program *The Chaser's War on Everything* attempted to play this role in May 2007 when they took their cameras to New York City and interviewed Americans on the streets about the meaning of '9/11'.[1] Most interviewees did not know what the date was or what had happened on that day. So iconic had the expression 9/11 become, so shrouded in myth and confused by spin, that the actual historical basis for the wars in Afghanistan and Iraq and consequential bombings in Bali, Madrid, London and elsewhere had been forgotten.

Other attempts to put 9/11 into ironic perspective have occurred in fiction and in Australian public life. In Robert Drewe's novel *Grace* an Australian woman tourist from a southern city seeks an exotic change when she visits a crocodile farm in Australia's northwest and exclaims that she is sick of New York and Bali: 'I'm Nine-Elevened Out', she says in unconscious mimicry of the Americans from whom she seeks to distance herself: 'I'm so over it'.[2]

More ambitiously, and seriously, Australian High Court judge Michael Kirby observed that Americans have become 'obsessed' with

11 September.[3] 'That is not an event that occurred in this country, and I think we have to keep our eye on the threat to Australia.' Moreover, Kirby added, more people died every day from the disease AIDS than died on 11 September in New York and Washington.[4]

A burgeoning international literature expressing anti-American sentiments among America's allies in the early twenty-first century is complemented by popular television series such as British television's *Spooks*. In one episode, senior members of MI5 bemoan an American tendency to see everyone as a terrorist. Warming to this theme, MI5's Harry complains ironically that the Americans will soon 'run out of countries to invade'.[5] Meanwhile, a CIA helicopter is landing on the roof of MI5 headquarters at Thames House with the purpose of extraditing a dangerous British-Iranian terrorist. Harry prevents them: 'You are not kidnapping British citizens'. The CIA agent responds: 'We have the right to kidnap anyone who threatens America.' In the short term, the Brits prevail but the suspect escapes, murders and causes mayhem. Were the Americans right? MI5's bosses think so – they sack Harry. In such episodes we see an unequal rivalry between allies in their war on terror and, behind it, the fracturing of international law in the 'rendition' of prisoners to secret locations for interrogation. The British may lose such contests but in this television series they retain the moral superiority of standing up (for a time at least) for individual human rights.

Australia's relations with its near neighbours in the Asia-Pacific which in the 1980s and '90s were tentatively moving towards a deeper engagement across independent nations in culture as well as trade have been reoriented in various ways towards America since 2001. Australia's then Prime Minister, John Howard, who was in the US on 11 September 2001, was viewed by some opinion-makers in the Asia-Pacific as the US's 'deputy sheriff' in the region. While this may have strengthened Australia's position in defence negotiations with some Asia-Pacific nations it may also have come at a cost to the kinds of literary and cultural, people-to-people exchanges which were developing between universities and communities of writers in the region.

Yet espionage and planned acts of terror have been real enough in Australia and should not be diminished. Two examples will suffice. The first has Indonesian connections. British-born Australian citizen Jack Roche was released on parole from prison in Perth in 2007 after serving four and a half years of a nine-year sentence for plotting with al-Qaeda to bomb the Israeli embassy in Canberra.[6] Guadeloupe-born Frenchman Willie Brigitte was convicted by a French court in 2007 of conspiring to carry out large-scale terrorist attacks in Australia including the bombing of a nuclear reactor at Lucas Heights near Sydney. Brigitte's handler while he was under cover in Australia was from the Lashkar-e-Taiba group.[7] Both Brigitte and Roche were converts to Islam. Behind such events a propaganda war proceeds for 'hearts and minds' – a phrase coined for a previous war in Vietnam.

Australian Spy Genre Novelists

Sandy McCutcheon

Novels by Australians about spies, spying and the terrorist threat can be expected to provide insights and perspectives beyond those of the propaganda wars. While they may challenge the imagination and stretch sympathies such works can also be expected to raise fundamental questions about humanity. Biographical information about authors will help to place their particular emphases in perspective. This literary genre may have special relevance for our times.

Recent Australian exponents of the spy novel have been attracted to the genre for some interesting reasons. In his autobiography *The Magician's Son*[8] Sandy McCutcheon describes how his anxieties and feelings of betrayal as an adopted child in New Zealand, from whom the secrets of his birth were withheld, affected him. These feelings were transferred in part to the experience of McCutcheon's protagonist in his first novel *In Wolf's Clothing*.[9] The dedication to this book is intriguing: 'For Brian David Parry [the author's late-discovered birth name] who has been working undercover in Australia and New Zealand since 1949. And for all those who have attempted, unsuccessfully, to track him down'. The autobiographical subject's searches for his true identity and his rebellions against social mores parallel the psychological action in McCutcheon's spy novels written before and after the autobiography. In *The Cobbler's Apprentice*,[10] McCutcheon's more recent spy novel, for example, his protagonist is a young Palestinian, Samir al-Hassani (Sami), captured in Iraq who escapes from Guantanamo Bay and gets involved in a series of terrorist and counter-terrorist plots. The CIA, Mossad and the Palestinians all court Sami for their own purposes. (Australians and New Zealanders play smaller parts in the plot.)

McCutcheon's novel shows how these conflicts foment the motive of revenge on all sides. For example, the ex-CIA agent now Senator Andrew Mortimer wants to avenge his wife killed by a Hizbollah car bomb; and Mossad agent Ari Sapir is motivated by the death of his parents and brother in the Six-Day War and a bus bomb. The novel also reveals a fascination with the creation of new identities and legends which can never replace deeper-seated sources of identification. Revenge takes bizarre forms. Sami comes to see honour in becoming a biological WMD in the USA and starts a plague which kills nine thousand people. When captured, he aims to re-infect at Guantanamo, though the US has now discovered vaccines which will prevent a further outbreak.

Warren Reed

While McCutcheon's novel emerges in part from the author's deeply personal experience of adoption and not belonging, Warren Reed's novel *Code Cicada*[11] arises directly from his professional experience in Australian intelligence. The main characters in *Code Cicada* are officers of the Australian Secret Intelligence Service (ASIS) and the diplomats and overseas intelligence officers with whom they have dealings. The bugging of the Chinese embassy in Canberra triggers serious confrontations between Australian and Chinese agencies and leads deeper into secret negotiations between Australian, Chinese, Japanese and Indonesian spies. The plot is a conventional one in counter-espionage narratives since Greene and le Carré: the search for a mole. In the process some astute, well-informed remarks are made – for example when a Chinese spy under diplomatic cover tries to recruit an ASIS officer the Chinese character says: 'Let's be frank, the games Washington plays aren't going to help Australia be accepted as part of the region'.[12] The novel is especially convincing in its exposition of commercial and industrial espionage, in particular the rivalry between China and Japan for Australian minerals and energy.

Code Cicada can be criticised from a literary point of view. Characters are insufficiently differentiated, dialogue is repetitious and there is more telling than showing of events and their psychological consequences. Yet the business of human intelligence, or HUMINT, in this world of acronyms, is often convincingly rendered. The perceptive and likeable Chinese spy Zhang reflects that 'a spy's personality had to be tailored to suit each occasion'.[13] Playing both sides of the fence can be wearing, though, as the Australian 'singing cicada', as the Chinese call him, finds out. But Clarke, the Australian villain who finally 'sings' and whom the Chinese try to exfiltrate from Jakarta has another card up his sleeve: he is actually working for the Indonesians. His motive for betraying his home country, Australia, and his friends is not thoroughly explored but seems to derive chiefly from frustrated ambition in his job and rivalry with colleagues – a frequent motive for 'turning' in the lives of actual spies. What moral centre the novel offers is given by the Chinese diplomat/spy Zhang who has told Clarke that 'it all depends what you are *before* you go in. That's your lifeline and your anchor. Once in intelligence you are in free-fall over the cliff'.[14] At the novel's close it is not surprising to find some of the more balanced officers from CIA and ASIS preparing to quit the spying game, as the biographical author has himself done.

Literary novels and terrorism

The powerful appeal of spy novels in early twenty-first century Australia is also highlighted by work by major literary novelists Richard Flanagan and Janette Turner Hospital. Flanagan's novel is set in Sydney, Turner Hospital's in North Queensland, South Carolina and Iraq.

The Unknown Terrorist – *Richard Flanagan*

Richard Flanagan's novel *The Unknown Terrorist*[15] is not so much about home-grown terrorists in Australia as about the instigation of fear in the public mind. A prominent villain in Flanagan's novel is a commercial TV host, Richard Cody, whose ratings are slipping: in order to raise them and prevent his sacking he invents a narrative from his brief experience of (including his rejection by) a young woman who is a pole dancer at a night club in Kings Cross. Gina Davies, the novel's protagonist, is swept unwittingly into the public eye by a series of accidents, the desperation of a television journalist and the zeitgeist of unease about terrorism. Gina has met a man called Tariq in the street during Mardi Gras and had sex with him that night. She later discovers that he has been murdered. The dead man may be a terrorist who has planted bombs at the Homebush Olympic stadium in Sydney. Images of Gina with Tariq have been caught on camera.

How to foster and 'grow' the terrorism tale? The novel's account of Richard Cody's thought-processes have the markings of an uncomfortably plausible absurdist drama:

> The man was obvious – a Middle Eastern name and a no doubt predictable past – and, from what the news reports were saying, a known terrorist. But the pole dancer was different: an Aussie turning on their own – an unknown terrorist ... And the more he thought about it, the more it all made sense, and what at first seemed ludicrous – a pole dancer and an Islamic terrorist! – now seemed insidious and disturbing. What better cover? After all, hadn't Christine Keeler slept with both the Russians and Profumo? ... And what a story it would be! It had everything – sex, politics, even bombs![16]

Rumour, innuendo and the fabrication of evidence are at the heart of both the spy novel and real intelligence – think of Greene's *Our Man in Havana*, le Carré's *Tailor of Panama* and the actual agent codenamed Curveball in Iraq who fed the Americans cooked-up evidence of WMDs. But Gina Davies, known as the Doll, is an innocent bystander drawn into a plot that grows in the minds of journalists and Australian Security Intelligence Organization officers who have vested interests in its propagation. Sydney's illustrious red-light district, Kings Cross, provides the surreal, steamy, summer atmosphere in which such stories can grow. The Tasmanian author of this novel, Richard Flanagan, who is a public advocate of environmental values[17] and thrives in the outdoors seems to watch with a horrified fascination just held in check by irony as he writes of the violent and intrusive victimisation of innocent people in a drama not of their own making. An authorial anger at the trampling on human rights, privacy and dignity periodically erupts in this text.

What checks do we have in our apparently open society on rampant demonisation of those who live outside the pale? An interesting aspect of *The Unknown Terrorist* is Flanagan's choice of Gina Davies as his protagonist. Although she is no intellectual, Gina is clearly aware of how the media have turned her into 'a murderous porn star'.[18] But as with Kafka's protagonists she is unable to control her circumstances. Flanagan has said that his treatment by journalists and political leaders when he publicly criticised the destructive clearfelling of Tasmanian forests[19] gave him some insight into Gina Davies' predicament.[20] What hurt Flanagan most was the Premier of his state calling him 'a traitor to Tasmania'.[21] Gina Davies, the Doll, is also demonised as a traitor. An ASIO operative influences weak media figures such as Cody to imply that Gina has murdered her lover when it appears that another ASIO agent was actually Tariq's assassin and the Homebush bombs were planted.

The socio-political critique at work in Flanagan's novel rejects increased policing powers for Australian secret services to arrest, interrogate and detain suspects without charge.[22] Beyond the tragedy of individual lives ruined, the novel explicitly criticises media, politicians, the secret agencies and police who combine to whip up a dangerous hysteria about Australian vulnerability to the 'disease' of terrorism.[23] The 'big picture' endorsed by the Australian government and officials including those in the secret services is that of American President George W. Bush (although his name is not mentioned in the novel) of a 'war between good and evil'.[24] By a leap of logic that may recall the domino theory propagated during the Vietnam war, Flanagan's ASIO operative declares that the 'truth' of the Bali bombings is that 'the terrorists want to turn all our cities into Baghdad', that 'people need to be frightened' and that this is also part of ASIO's job.[25]

Richard Flanagan's dedication of his novel to David Hicks – the Australian who served five and a half years without charge at Guantanamo Bay before he was convicted by an American military tribunal of supporting terrorism – indicates the author's wish for this novel to be part of public debate about human rights in the new age of terrorism. Hicks was still in prison at Guantanamo Bay when Flanagan's novel was published in 2006. Whether Hicks's subsequent conviction and return to serve a further term of imprisonment in Australia will diminish the novel's longer-term impact on public debate remains to be seen. Early indications suggest less hysteria and a more critical perspective.

A Perfect Post-September 11 Novel? – Janette Turner Hospital

Janette Turner Hospital's novel *Orpheus Lost*[26] has serious claims to be the most successful work of fiction about terrorism and spying in the twenty-first century. It is the most aesthetically satisfying such work by an Australian. *Orpheus Lost* switches location between the US, Australia and the Middle East. Like Flanagan's *The Unknown Terrorist*, Turner Hospital's novel adapts incidents and details from publicly reported events in the Iraq war and challenges official accounts from the Bush White House about its progress. Iconic locations such as Abu Ghraib and Guantanamo Bay and incidents such as the mistaken return of the wrong body parts of an Australian Private Jake Kovco are woven into a novel which seeks redemptive moments in the horrors of war, torture and imprisonment.

If tropical North Queensland is where her taproots lie, Janette Turner Hospital's experience of living and working in South Carolina since 1999 has contributed to her engagement with another regional culture which is both deeply literary and militaristic. A post-Civil War separatist sentiment combined with a heavy commitment to the National Guard is only one of many paradoxes which an observant newcomer notices. Turner Hospital has remarked:

> It's inescapable, the presence of war in this state. It's part of the life here. Partly because a disproportionate part of the regular army is from the black and poor people of America … The South Carolina National Guard – which includes students and colleagues [at the University of South Carolina] – is about to be deployed to Afghanistan. So I've never known so many people intimately connected with the army, the National Guard, Iraq and Afghanistan in an ongoing way.[27]

The novel's glimpses of Promised Land – the name of an actual town in South Carolina fictionalised and relocated by the author – epitomise the paradoxes of Turner Hospital's new/old Deep South. The clammy climate, swings on porches, the laconic talk among neighbours and deep, dark secrets are reminiscent of Southern regional writers including Faulkner, Tennessee Williams and Flannery O'Connor. In Turner Hospital's novel, Promised Land incorporates a dramatic contrast between old mad religion and the new mad wars. The disposition of plot and character reinforce this opposition: Leela, the novel's protagonist, is the daughter of Gideon Moore, a visionary Pentecostalist who disapproves of his daughter's academic ambitions in mathematics; and Leela's first boyfriend, Cobb Slaughter, is the son of a psychologically damaged Vietnam veteran who follows his father's example by entering the wars of his time in Afghanistan and Iraq before joining a private security agency. He becomes the stalking nemesis of his former girlfriend when Leela is suspected of associating with a subway bomber in Boston.

The novel contains several variations on the Orpheus and Eurydice story – of figures who follow or are followed as they advance towards or retreat from their underworlds of torture and suffering. Spying on people, as a voyeur or intelligence operative or novelist is a recurring theme. Interrogation of suspected terrorists on the home front or abroad can be brutal beyond all Geneva Convention constraints. Leela's intelligence and her relentless curiosity make her a different kind of interrogator – a proxy novelist who retains the milk of human kindness as she questions the motives of Cobb Slaughter and what he knows of her lost lover Mishka Bartok. When Leela is picked up off the street, on suspicion of associating with a terrorist, and is herself abducted and interrogated in a secret location she reflects that '*secret* knowledge ... illicitly gained and kept private – was absolute power'.[28] Such power-plays permeate the novel.

But what really distinguishes *Orpheus Lost* is its music – not just the musical expressions of Orpheus such as Gluck's and Monteverdi's but the musicality of the prose. Virginia Woolf and Conrad are conscious influences on Turner Hospital's writing;[29] and reviewers have noticed the 'formal bravura' of *Orpheus Lost*[30] and an apparently effortless 'sense of drama that bridges the gap between highbrow and popular fiction'.[31] One commentator acutely observes that Turner Hospital 'seems to be doing for fiction in a post-September 11 world something akin to what Graham Greene did for the dramatisation of moral ambivalence during the Cold War'.[32] But Turner Hospital evokes no sympathy for terrorists in *Orpheus Lost*: to the jihadist Jamil Haddad 'music is licentious' and this shows his deafness to the longing, desire and hope that make us human.

The life of sentiment in Turner Hospital's novel is not represented by the militaristic American Cobb Slaughter or by his jihadist foe Jamil Haddad but by Mishka Bartok, the Australian of Hungarian Jewish and Lebanese extraction who plays both the violin and the oud in the subway in Boston and who entrances the heroine of this novel, Leela, to follow him into the underworld. 'For loss, we have music', a music teacher tells Mishka. 'And that is why we have music. For love and for devotion and sorrow'.[33] The novel's combination of an intense literariness and engagement with the causes of contemporary terror make this book both provocative and resonant.

Memory, Imagination, Literary Studies

If literary studies can make a difference in international relations, perhaps it is at the level represented by music in Turner Hospital's novel – in drawing people across the borders and boundaries of nations through imagination and sympathetic understanding.

But novels, poetry and drama can also change ideas and attitudes through engagement of the intellect. Thus there is value in trans-disciplinary studies, which cross from literary works to politics, biography and history. For example, the novels I have discussed in this chapter intersect with notions of patriotism in the modern world. One thinks also of the flouting of human rights in the Patriot Act in post-September 11 America. From an Australian perspective, historian Mark McKenna has argued that Australian history and culture have been militarised exponentially in the past decade[34] and that this is epitomised in the strengthening of Anzac Day – Australia's remembrance day for those killed in war – into 'a sacred parable we dare not question'.[35] He cites another historian Robert Manne's statement that 'the sentimentalised version of the new Australian militarism' has aided Australia's 'faithful service alongside the Americans in the war on terror'.[36]

Should literary studies hold themselves aloof from such debates, arguments and research in the disciplines of history and politics (and even security studies)? The novels I have discussed are only a small sample of works which intersect with, and could enrich, transdisciplinary studies. In Canberra recently I attended a seminar in an emerging field called 'Terrorism History'. A political scientist described the rapidly expanding literature on terrorism as 'the dismal science'.[37] The seminar hardly entertained the thought that literary imagination and cultural knowledge were perhaps more crucial to understanding terrorism than trying to create a new science. Yet when a poet and literary scholar was recruited into the Australian Security Intelligence Organization in an earlier era he was told that as well as hard methodical work, imagination was needed.[38] And the *9/11 Report* itself has stressed more recently that the failure of imagination as well as analytical skills was an important factor in the events leading to that problematic catastrophe.[39]

Without detriment to their core mission in the humanities, it seems to me that literary studies can give richness and depth to a range of transdisciplinary fields that include International Relations, Terrorism History and Cross-Cultural Studies. The study of literature can build bridges of understanding into foreign territory. Hearts and minds tire quickly of propaganda and seek richer imaginative fare. Literature can thus properly be enlisted to fight terror with the 'soft weapons' of words and ideas.

Notes

Introduction

1 Bernard Cookson, *Sun*, 29 April 1987.
2 *Australian*, 22–3 May 2010.
3 Christopher Andrew, *The Defence of the Realm* (London: Allen Lane, 2009) p. 430.
4 Nicholas Hasluck, *Dismissal* (Sydney: Fourth Estate/Harper/Collins, 2011).
5 Frank Moorhouse, *Cold Light* (Sydney: Vintage/Random House, 2011), p. 658.
6 Ibid., p. 659.

One Points of Departure: Spies and Families

1 Norman Sherry, *The Life of Graham Greene*, vol. 1 (New York: Penguin, 1989).
2 Charlie Higson, *Silverfin* (London: Puffin Books, 2005); Anthony Horowitz, *Stormbreaker* (London: Walker Books, 2000).
3 See Julie Wheelwright, *The Fatal Love: Mata Hari and the Myth of Women in Espionage* (London: Collins & Brown, 1992).
4 Lauren Kessler, *Clever Girl: Elizabeth Bentley, the Spy Who Ushered in the McCarthy Era* (New York: HarperCollins, 2003), pp. 296–7.
5 Stella Rimington, *Open Secret: The Autobiography of the Former Director-General of MI5* (London: Hutchinson, 2001), p. 184.
6 Ibid., p. 151.
7 Joseph Wilson, *The Politics of Truth: Inside the Lies that Led to War and Betrayed My Wife's CIA Identity* (New York: Carroll and Graf, 2004), p. 242.
8 Valerie Plame, *Fair Game: My Life as a Spy, My Betrayal by the White House* (New York: Simon & Schuster, 2007), pp. 93–9.
9 Ibid., pp. 4–5.
10 Kirk Honeycutt, 'Fair Game – Film Review', 20 May 2010 www.hollywoodreporter. com/hr/film-reviews/fair-game-film-review-10040928/31/5/2010.
11 Plame, p. 161.
12 Ewen MacAskill, 'Jailed spy recruited son as accomplice', *Canberra Times*, 1 February 2009, p 18.
13 Jimmy Burns, *Papa Spy: Love, Faith and Betrayal in Wartime Spain* (London: Bloomsbury, 2009).
14 See Peter Stanford, 'Papa Spy, by Jimmy Burns', *Independent*, 16 October 2009.
15 Vin Arthey, *Like Father Like Son: A Dynasty of Spies* (London: St Ermin's Press, 2004).
16 Ibid., p. 72.
17 Hayden Peake, 'The Philby Literature' in Rufina Philby, Mikhail Lyubimov and Hayden Peake, *The Private Life of Kim Philby: The Moscow Years* (New York: Fromm International, 2000), p. 324.

18 Anthony Cave Brown, *Treason in the Blood: H. St John Philby, Kim Philby and the Spy Case of the Century* (London: Robert Hale, 1995), p. 76.
19 Ibid., p. 76.
20 Ibid., p. 78.
21 Phillip Knightley, *Philby: KGB Masterspy* (London: Andre Deutsch, 1988; 2003), p. 21.
22 See Philby, Lyubimov and Peake, p. 418.
23 Brown, p. 481.
24 Eleanor Philby, *The Spy I Loved* (London: Pan, 1968), pp. 28–9.
25 Brown, p. 379.
26 Rufina Philby, p. 98.
27 Ibid., p. 98.
28 'John Philby', Obituary, *Daily Telegraph*, 23 August 2009.
29 See Jack Kneece, *Family Treason: The Walker Spy Case* (Briarcliff Manor, NY: Stein and Day, 1986).
30 Philip Shenon, 'The John A. Walker Spy Ring', *New York Times*, 4 January 1987.
31 See Pete Earley, *Family of Spies: Inside the John Walker Spy Ring* (Toronto: Bantam, 1988), pp. 286–7.
32 Kneece, pp. 17, 23.
33 Ibid., p. 167.
34 Haay J. Kolb, *Overworld: Confessions of a Reluctant Spy* (London: Bantam/Corgi, 2005), p. 13.
35 Ibid., p. 25.
36 Ibid., p. 44.
37 Ibid., p. 51.
38 Ibid., p. 58.
39 Ibid., p. 59.
40 Ibid., p. 139.
41 Ibid., p. 142.
42 John H. Richardson, *My Father the Spy: An Investigative Memoir* (New York: HarperCollins, 2005), cover blurb.
43 Ibid., p. 10.
44 Ibid., p. 201.
45 Ibid., p. 205.
46 Ibid., p. 278.
47 Ibid., p. 278.
48 Ibid., p. 24.
49 Scodly, *Catholic Standard*, cited in *My Father the Spy*, p. 212.
50 Evan Thomas, *The Very Best Men: Four Who Dared: The Early Years of the CIA* (New York: Simon & Schuster, c.1995), p. 327.

Two Loyalty Tests: Spies Under Review

1 Haiyan Lee, 'Enemy Under My Skin: Eileen Chang's *Lust, Caution* and the Politics of Transcendence', *PMLA* 125 (2010), 640–56.
2 Ibid., p. 646.
3 Ibid., p. 646.
4 James Aldridge, *A Captive in the Land* (London: Hamish Hamilton, 1962), p. 280.
5 Evan Thomas, *The Very Best Men: Four Who Dared: The Early Years of the CIA* (New York: Simon and Schuster, 1995).
6 Michael Wilding, *The Prisoner of Mount Warning* (North Melbourne: Arcadia/Australian Scholarly Publishing, 2010).
7 Ibid., p. 79.
8 Ibid., pp. 95–6.

9   Ibid., p. 234.
10   *The Lives of Others* (*Das Leben der Anderen*), director Florian Henckel von Donnersmarck, 21ˢᵗ Century Pictures, 2007.
11   Timothy Garton Ash, 'The Stasi on Our Minds', *New York Review of Books*, vol. 54, no. 9, 31 May 2007. Online at http://www.nybooks.com/articles 2010.

Three Secret Agents and the Search for Truth

1   According to Hayden Peake, Angleton characterized Soviet disinformation and intelligence operations as a 'wilderness of mirrors' in a TV interview. When author David C. Martin used the phrase as the title of his book, it became 'a popular epithet for counter-intelligence' (*The Private Life of Kim Philby*, p. 343).
2   Richard Helms, *A Look Over My Shoulder* (New York: Random, 2003), p. 153.
3   John Farquharson, 'The improbable spook with a lasting legacy', *Canberra Times*, 9 November 2005, p. 25.
4   John le Carré, *The Spy Who Came in from the Cold* (New York: Coward-McCann, 1964), p. 149.
5   Ibid.
6   David Charney, 'The Psychology of Insider Spies', lecture at the Center for Peace and Security Studies, Georgetown University, 23 February 2006. The quotes which follow are from this lecture.
7   Le Carré, Acknowledgements, *The Tailor of Panama* (New York: Alfred A. Knopf, 1956).
8   *The Tailor of Panama*, directed by John Boorman (2001). Interview on DVD.
9   Ibid.
10   Le Carré, p. 64.
11   Ibid., p. 67.
12   Ibid., p. 77.
13   Ibid., p. 165.
14   Ibid., p. 169.
15   Ibid., p. 195.
16   Ibid., p. 200.
17   Ibid., p. 247.
18   Christopher Andrew, with Vasili Mitrokhin, *The World Was Going Our Way: The KGV and the Battle for the Third World* (New York: Basic Books, 2005), p. 107.
19   Ibid., p. 110.
20   Ibid., p. 111.
21   Duane R. Clarridge, with Digby Diehl, *A Spy for All Seasons: My Life in the CIA* (New York: Scribner, 1997), p. 300.
22   Ibid., p. 226.
23   Ibid., p. 235.
24   Ibid., p. 237.
25   Ibid.
26   Ibid.
27   Ibid., p. 238.
28   Ibid.
29   Andrew and Mitrokhin, p. 30.
30   Clarridge, p. 269.
31   Ibid., pp. 394, 397.
32   Bernard Williams, *Truth and Truthfulness: An Essay in Genealogy* (Princeton University Press, 2004), p. 84.
33   Ibid., p. 11.
34   Ibid., pp. 268–9.

35 Paul John Eakin, ed., *The Ethics of Life Writing* (Ithaca, NY: Cornell University Press, 2004), p. 5.

36 Joseph Wilson, *The Politics of Truth: Inside the Lies that Led to War and Betrayed My Wife's CIA Identity* (NY: Carroll and Graf, 2004).

37 Carol D. Leonnig, 'Libby's Lawyers Seek Papers on Plame's CIA Employment', *Washington Post*, 1 February 2006, p. A5.

38 Wilson, p. 388. See also Valerie Plame, *Fair Game* (New York: Simon & Schuster, 2007).

Four Politics and Spying: Representations of Pre- and Early Australia

1   Kenneth Gordon McIntyre, *The Secret Discovery of Australia* ([1977] Sydney: Pan/Picador). Abridged and revised edition, 1982.

2   Glyndwr Williams and Alan Frost, 'Terra Australis: Theory and Speculation' in Glyndwr Williams and Alan Frost, eds. *Terra Australis to Australia* (Melbourne: Oxford University Press, 1988), pp. 1–37.

3   Lisa Jardine, *Worldly Goods* (London: McMillan, 1996), pp. 107–8.

4   Helen Wallis, 'Java Le Grande: The Enigma of the Dieppe Maps' in Glyndwr Williams and Alan Frost, eds. *Terra Australis to Australia*, pp. 39–81.

5   Miles Harvey, *The Island of Lost Maps: A True Story of Cartographic Crime* (New York: Random House, 2000), pp. xi–xvii.

6   Giles Milton, *Nathaniel's Nutmeg or; The True and Incredible Adventures of the Spice Trader Who Changed the Course of History* (Harmondsworth: Penguin, 1999), p. 59.

7   Ibid., p. 7.

8   Philip Tyler, 'The Batavia Mutineers', *Westerly*, 4 December 1970, pp. 33–45.

9   Ibid., pp. 33–43.

10 Ibid., pp. 38.

11 H. Drake-Brockman, *The Wicked and the Fair* (Sydney: Angus and Robertson, 1957), p. 367.

12 Alan Frost, *Arthur Phillip 1738–1814: His Voyaging* (Melbourne: Oxford University Press, 1987), p. 130.

13 Ibid., p. 130.

14 J. Holland Rose, 'Captain Cook and the Founding of British Power in the Pacific', *Geographical Journal*, 73.2 (1929), 102–9.

15 Ibid., p. 106.

16 Alan Frost, 'Phillip, Arthur', *Oxford Dictionary of National Biography* (Oxford: Oxford University Press 2004–2007) [online version].

17 Ibid.

18 Alan Frost, *Arthur Phillip 1738–1814: His Voyaging* (Melbourne: Oxford University Press, 1987), pp. 130–1.

19 Tom Keneally, *The Commonwealth of Thieves* (Sydney: Random House Australia, 2005), pp. 118–19.

20 Leslie R. Marchant, *France Australe* (Perth: Artlook, 1982), pp. 230–1.

21 Ibid., p. 232.

22 Robert Hughes, *The Fatal Shore* (London: Collins Harvill, 1987), p. 539.

23 Ibid., 539.

24 Ibid., 545.

25 Bruce Bennett, 'In the Shadows: The Spy in Australian Literary and Cultural History', *Antipodes*, 20.1 (2006), 28–37.

26 Marcus Clarke, *Old Tales of a Young Country* (Melbourne: Mason, Firth, & McCutcheon, 1871), p. 82.

27 Frank Clune and P. R. Stephensen, *The Viking of Van Diemen's Land: The Stormy Life of Jorgen Jorgensen* (Sydney: Angus & Roberston, 1954), p. 278.

28 James Dally, 'Jorgen Jorgensen', *Australian Dictionary of Biography*, vol. 2 (Carlton:

Melbourne University Press, 1967) p. 27.

29 Clune & Stephensen, p. 282.

30 Sarah Bakewell, *The English Dane: A Life of Jorgen Jorgensen* (London: Chatto & Windus, 2005), p. 142.

31 Ibid., p. 143.

32 Ibid., p. 145.

33 Clarke, pp. 84–5.

34 Bakewell, pp. 173.

35 Ibid., p. 195.

36 Ibid., p. 216.

37 James Dally, p. 27.

Five Exploration or Espionage? Flinders and the French

1   Matthew Flinders, *A Voyage to Terra Australis* (London: G. and W. Nicol, 1814), vol 1, p. 188.

2   Gavin De Beer, *The Sciences Were Never at War* (London, New York: Nelson, 1960), p. 238.

3   Francois Péron, 'Péron's Report on Port Jackson' in Ernest Scott, *The Life of Captain Matthew Flinders, RN*, Appendix B, pp. 437–8; see also Leslie Marchant, *France Australe* (Perth: Artlook, 1982), who disputes Péron's contention that Napoleon sent the mission.

4   Anthony J. Brown, *Ill-Starred Captains: Flinders and Baudin* (N. Fremantle: Fremantle Press, 2004).

5   Péron, pp. 454–6.

6   G.W. Rusden, *Curiosities of Colonization* (London: W. Clowes & Sons, 1874), pp. 86–9.

7   Rusden, cited in Brown, p. 277.

8   Brown, p. 277.

9   Péron, p. 464.

10 Ernest Scott, *The Life of Captain Matthew Flinders, RN* (Sydney: Angus & Robertson, 1914), p. 259.

11 Ibid., p. 262.

12 *Historical Records of Australia*, series 1, vol. 8 (Library Committee of the Commonwealth Parliament, 1916), p. 241.

13 Cited in Jean Fornaserio, Jean, Peter Monteath and John West-Sooby, *Encountering Terra Australis: The Australian Voyages of Nicolas Baudin and Matthew Flinders* (Kent Town: Wakefield Press, 2004), p. 220.

14 Ibid., pp. 221–2.

15 Klaus Toft, *The Navigators: The Great Race Between Matthew Flinders and Nicolas Baudin for the North-South Passage Through Australia* (Sydney: Pan Macmillan, 2002), p. 267.

16 Fornasiero, p. 279.

17 Matthew Flinders, *A Voyage to Terra Australis* (London: G. and W. Nicol, 1814), vol. 2, p. 367.

18 Cited in Toft, p. 269.

19 Flinders, vol. 2, p. 368.

20 Ibid., p. 374.

21 Private Journal, 9 February 1803.

22 Gillian Dooley, 'Matthew Flinders as Writer', *Australian Book Review*, no. 239, March 2002, pp. 25–48.

23 Witgar Hitchcock, 'Matthew Flinders in Mauritius 1803–1810' (manuscript).

24 See Fornasiero et al, p. 382.

25 Edward Duyker, *Francois Péron: An Impetuous Life* (Melbourne University Press, 2006), p. 306.

Six Troubled Waters: Australian Spies in the Pacific
– Glimpses from the Early Twentieth Century

1   A. Grove Day, *Louis Becke* (Melbourne: Hill of Content, 1966), p. 112.
2   See Bruce Bennett, 'The Traveller's Eye: Louis Becke's South Pacific' in *Homing In: Essays on Australian Literature and Selfhood* (Perth: Network, 2006), pp. 147–55.
3   C. D. Coulthard-Clark, *A Heritage of Spirit: A Biography of Major-General Sir William Throsby Bridges* (Carlton: Melbourne University Press, 1979), p. 27.
4   Ibid., p. 43.
5   Ibid., p. 112.
6   C. D. Coulthard-Clark, *The Citizen General Staff: The Australian Intelligence Corps 1907–1914* (Canberra: Military Historical Society of Australia, 1976), p. 7; R. C. Thompson, 'Australian Imperialism and the New Hebrides, 1862–1922'. PhD thesis, Australian National University, 1970.
7   John Fisher, *Gentleman Spies: Intelligence Agents in the British Empire and Beyond* (Stroud, UK: Sutton, 2002).
8   N. Meaney, *Towards a New Vision: Australia and Japan Across Time* (Sydney: UNSW Press, 2006), p. 4.
9   Coulthard-Clark, 1976, p. 26; see also D. C. S. Sissons, 'Australia's Attitudes to Japan and Defence 1890–1923'. MA thesis, University of Melbourne, 1956.
10 Donald Grant, 'Hales, Alfred Arthur Greenwood (1860–1936)', *Australian Dictionary of Biography*, vol. 9 (Carlton: Melbourne University Press, 1983), pp. 159–60.
11 A. G. Hales, *Little Blue Pigeon: A Story of Japan* (London: Hutchinson, 1905), p. 173.
12 Ibid., p. 12.
13 Megumi Kato, *Narrating the Other: Australian Literary Perceptions of Japan* (Clayton: Monash University Press, 2008), p. 23.
14 Coulthard-Clark, p. 76.
15 See Andrew Lang, *Pickle the Spy; Or, the Incognito of Prince Charles* (London: Longman Greens, 1897).
16 Chris Cunneen, 'Steward, Sir George Charles Thomas (1965–1920)', *Australian Dictionary of Biography*, vol. 12 (Carlton: Melbourne University Press, 1990), pp. 81–2.
17 Ibid., pp. 81–2; see also Coulthard-Clark, 1976, p. 56.
18 Kato, p. 26.
19 D.C.S. Sissons, 'James Murdoch (1856–1921): Historian, Teacher and Much Else Besides', *Transactions of the Asiatic Society of Japan*, 2 (1987), pp. 1–57.
20 D. C. S. Sissons, 'Murdoch, James (1856–1921)', *Australian Dictionary of Biography*, vol. 10 (Carlton: Melbourne University Press, 1986), p. 619.
21 N. K. Meaney, 'Piesse, Edmund Leolin (1880–1947)', *Australian Dictionary of Biography*, vol. 11 (Carlton: Melbourne University Press, 1988), p. 228.
22 Ibid.
23 Sissons, 1987, pp. 46–8.
24 Royal Military College of Australia, *Annual Report*, 1918.
25 Murdoch to Piesse. E. L. Piesse, Papers and manuscripts. National Library of Australia MS 882/5/16.
26 Ibid., 14/3/1919, NLA MS 882/5/7.
27 Ibid.
28 Ibid., 25/1/1919, NLA MS 882/5/7.
29 D. C. S. Sissons, Papers and Manuscripts, NLA MS 3092: 1956–2006, pp. 79–80.
30 Meaney, 1988, p. 228.
31 Australian Archives, Canberra Office, CP 447/2, item SC, 42; cited Sissons, NLA MS 3092, 87.
32 See Andrew Wilkie, *Axis of Deceit* (Melbourne: Black Inc Agenda, 2004).

33 *Nichi Nichi Shimbun* (Tokyo) 27/1/19, cited in Sissons NLA MS 3092, 81.

34 N. Meaney, *Towards a New Vision: Australia and Japan Across Time* (Sydney: UNSW Press, 2006), p. 117.

35 P. G. Edwards, *Prime Ministers and Diplomats: The Making of Australian Foreign Policy 1901–1949* (Melbourne: Oxford University Press, 1983), pp. 53–4.

36 Brian Toohey and William Pinwill, *Oyster: The Story of the Australian Secret Intelligence Service* (Port Melbourne: Heinemann, 1989), p. 27.

37 Ibid., p. 29.

38 See Laurie Hergenhan, *No Casual Traveller: Hartley Grattan and Australia* (St Lucia: University of Queensland Press, 1995), pp. 147–8.

39 Ibid., p. 135.

40 Ibid., p. 148.

Seven Under Cover: Projections of British and Australian Secret Intelligence

1   The wide-ranging *World of the First Aborigines* (1981) by Ronald and Catherine Berndt, for example, discusses 'intelligence' only in terms of mental capacity; and the methods of gathering information or evidence before inter-clan warfare receive only passing mention.

2   The Portuguese, Spanish, Dutch and others plotted to obtain each others 'secret maps'. See K. G. McIntyre, *The Secret Discovery of Australia* (Medindie, SA: Souvenir Press, 1977).

3   See R. T. Appleyard and Toby Manford, *The Beginning: European Discovery and Early Settlement of Swan River of Western Australia* (Nedlands: University of Western Australia Press, 1979), p. 23.

4   See Leslie Marchant, *France Australe*, Chapter 8. Marchant discusses Blosseville's plan for a penal colony in south western Australia from 1819 to 1826. Nicholas Hasluck's novel *The Blosseville File* draws on some of this material.

5   Peter Carey, *Jack Maggs* (St Lucia, Qld: University of Queensland Press, 1997).

6   Alan Renouf, *The Frightened Country* (Melbourne: Macmillan, 1979), p. 499.

7   See C. D. Coulthard-Clark, *A Heritage of Spirit: A Biography of Major-General Sir William Throsby Bridges* cited in Desmond Ball and David Horner, *Breaking the Codes: Australia's KGB Network, 1944–1950* (St Leonards, NSW: Allen & Unwin, 1998), p. 12.

8   *Australian Dictionary of Biography*, entry by C. D. Coulthard-Clark, pp. 408–11. The biographical details which follow are taken from this source and from *A Heritage of Spirit* (Carlton, Vic: Melbourne University Press, 1979).

9   Ibid., p. 409.

10 Brian Toohey and William Pinwill, *Oyster: The Story of the Australian Secret Intelligence Service* (Port Melbourne: Mandarin, 1990). Toohey here draws on accounts in William Stevenson, *Intrepid's Last Case*.

11 Ibid.

12 Toohey points out that Ellis tried to cover up this marriage in his *Who's Who* entry (21).

13 Wright, *Spycatcher* (Port Melbourne: Mandarin, 1989), p. 329.

14 Ibid., p. 330.

15 *Oyster*, p. 21.

16 Ibid., p. 22. See also Anthony Cave Brown, *'C': The Secret Life of Sir Stewart Graham Menzies* (London: Sphere, 1989), p. 366.

17 Ibid.

18 Ibid.

19 Ibid.

20 Ibid., p. 23.

21   Olive Stonyer, 'Nancy Wake, the White Mouse', http.www.live_and_learn.com.au.

22   FitzSimons, p. 14.

23   Ibid.

24   Olive Stonyer, op cit.

25   Ibid.

26   See Hayden Peake, 'The Philby Literature', in Rufina Philby, Mikhail Lyubimov and Hayden Peake, *The Private Life of Kim Philby: The Moscow Years* (London: St Ermin's, 1999), pp. 299–400.

27   Alomes, *When London Calls* (Cambridge: Cambridge University Press, 1999).

28   Philby, *My Silent War* (New York: Grove Press, [1968]), p. xii.

29   Ibid.

30   Ibid.

31   Quoted in Alomes, *When London Calls*, p. 192.

32   Ibid.

33   Ibid., p. 190.

34   Bruce Page, David Leitch and Philip Knightley, *Philby: The Spy Who Betrayed a Generation* (London: Deutsch, 1968). Introduction by John le Carré, p. 9.

35   One important reason, not discussed in the text, is the expectations, assumptions and values of the British reading audience. John le Carré touches on this in his comparison of Philby with George Blake: 'Like a great novel … the story of Kim Philby lives on in us … Hardly a tear was shed for George Blake: Blake was half a foreigner and half a Jew … But Philby, an aggressive, upper-class enemy, was of our blood and hunted with our pack; to the very end, he expected and received the indulgence owing to his moderation, good breeding and boyish, flirtatious charm' (Ibid., pp. 28–9).

36   The book was published in the US by Signet in 1969 and Ballantine in 1981 under the title *The Philby Conspiracy*. Neither of these titles contained the new preface but the Sphere issue of the book in 1977 did include it.

37   *Philby*, 1968, p. xi.

38   Donald Maclean may have been the exception. He brought his children up in Russia and found suitable work there, despite marital and other difficulties.

39   Knightley, *The Second Oldest Profession* (London: A. Deutsch, 1986), p. 6.

Eight Traditional Myths and Problematic Heroes: The Case of Harry Freame

1   J. S. Ryan, 'The Earlier Life of Wykeham Henry Freame', *Armidale and District Historical Society Journal and Proceedings*, no. 27, March 1984, underlines the uncertainty of Freame's date of birth: '[T]he actual date of birth in four places of record – the Army enlistment, his own passport, his son's birth record and his own marriage certificate, show, respectively, 1885, 1888, 1884 and 1880, pp. 58–9. See N. Meaney, *Fears and Phobias: E. L. Piesse and the Problem of Japan 1909–39* (Canberra: National Library of Japan Occasional Papers no. 1, 1996), pp. 29–30.

2   C. E. W. Bean, *The Story of Anzac* (Sydney: Angus and Robertson, 1921), p. 309, n. 2.

3   C. E. W. Bean, 'Personal Records in respect of Dr Charles Bean: Manuscript: Harry Freame, DCM', Australian War Memorial file 38, 893, 47/14.

4   Ibid.

5   'Assembly' / 'AIF Celebrities (14): Sgt. H. Freame, DCM', *Reveille*, 30 September 1931, p. 29.

6   Ibid., p. 29.

7   Roger McDonald, *1915* (St Lucia: University of Queensland Press, 1979), pp. 397–8.

8   James W. Courtney, 'Freame, Wykeham Henry Koba (1885? – 1941)', *Australian Dictionary of Biography*, vol. 8 (Carlton: Melbourne University Press, 1981), p. 581.

9   'Assembly', p. 29.

10 Bean, 'Personal Records'.

11 Courtney, p. 581.

12 Ryan, pp. 58–9.

13 Ibid., p. 60.

14 Ibid., p. 62.

15 Ibid., p. 64.

16 Ibid., p. 66.

17 See 'Assembly'.

18 Ryan, p. 59.

19 Ibid., p. 61.

20 'Assembly', p. 30.

21 Ibid., p. 30.

22 F. J. Kindon, 'Sgt. W. H. Freame, DCM', *Reveille*, 1 July 1941.

23 Jim Belshaw, http://belshaw: blogspot.com/2008/09. Posted 11/9/08. Accessed 3/2/09.

24 *Reveille*, p. 29.

25 Ibid., p. 31.

26 See Kindon.

27 McBride to McEwan 30 Sept 1940.

28 See Courtney.

29 R. Rowe, Private Secretary, Minister for External Affairs to Colonel Hodgson. Canberra, 24 June 1941. National Archives of Australia A981, AUS 186.

30 The Director of the Australian Security Service commented that 'there has long existed there (in Japan) a category of persons who bear the cognomen 'Garotsuki' – and the dying man's own reported words were strongly suggestive of injury received perhaps in that way' (Longfield Lloyd).

31 See Rowe.

32 Major W. R. Scott, Minute Paper, Department of the Army, 9 October 1940. National Archives of Australia MP 729/6, 15/403/16 (August 1940–May 1941).

33 Bernard Wasserstein, *Secret War in Shanghai* (New York: Houghton Mifflin, 1999).

34 Ibid., p. 180.

35 Colin Fraser, 'The Friendly Spy Who Died Alone', *Quadrant*, December 2008, pp. 86–8.

36 Ryan, p. 60.

37 See Robert Whymant, *Stalin's Spy: Richard Sorge and the Tokyo Espionage Ring* (London: Tauris, 2006).

38 Ibid., p. 123.

39 Tim Soutphommasane, *Reclaiming Patriotism: Nation-Building for Australian Progressives* (Port Melbourne: Cambridge UP, 2009), p. 138.

Nine Politics, Espionage and Exile: Ian Milner and Ric Throssell

1   Clifford Geertz, 'Which Way to Mecca?' *The New York Review of Books*, 12 June 2003, pp. 27–30.

2   See David McKnight, *Australia's Spies and their Secrets* (Sydney: Allen and Unwin, 1994), Ch. 1; Frank Cain, *The Origins of Political Surveillance in Australia* (Sydney: Angus & Robertson, 1983); Harvey Barnett, *Tale of the Scorpion* (Sydney: Allen & Unwin, 1988).

3   McKnight, p. 13.

4   Desmond Ball and David Horner, *Breaking the Codes: Australia's KGB Network* (St Leonards, NSW: Allen and Unwin, 1998), p. xiv.

5   See Robert Manne, *The Petrov Affair* (Melbourne: Text, rev. ed. 2004).

6   Vincent O'Sullivan, ed. *Intersecting Lines: The Memoirs of Ian Milner* (Wellington: Victoria University Press, 1993).

7   Ibid., p. 156.

8   Ibid., p. 160.

9   Ibid., 168. Lockwood remained a friend and confidant of Milner.

10   Ibid., p. 137.

11   Ibid., p. 139.

12   Ball and Horner, p. 253.

13   Frank Cain, 'Venona in Australia and its Long-term Ramifications', *Journal of Contemporary History*, 35.2 (2000), 231–48.

14   Richard Hall, *The Rhodes Scholar Spy* (Sydney: Random House Australia, 1991), p. 165.

15   Ball and Horner, p. 253. This crucial claim has been disputed by a number of New Zealanders, including Vincent O'Sullivan, James McNeish and Aaron Fox.

16   Peter Hruby, 'Ian Milner – Soviet and Czech Agent on Four Continents (1944–1968) and His Family', unpublished paper, Prague, p. 5.

17   See Vincent O'Sullivan, *Intersecting Lines*, Appendix: Personal Statement, pp. 188–96.

18   James McNeish, *Dance of the Peacocks: New Zealanders in Exile in the Time of Hitler and Mao Tse-tung* (Auckland: Random House/Vintage, 2003), p. 312.

19   Ibid., p. 308. According to McNeish, women were Milner's 'Achilles heel': he was 'particularly susceptible to them'.

20   Ball and Horner, pp. 327–8.

21   See Ball and Horner, pp. 327–8. The chief reporter and commentator on the Czech documents is Peter Hruby. See 'Secret Life of Agent 9006', *Courier Mail*, 30 November 1996, p. 30; and Hruby's unpublished 457-page manuscript, 'Dangerous Dreamers: The Australian Anti-Democratic Left'.

22   See Ball and Horner, pp. 327–8.

23   See Ian Milner, *Milner of Waitaki: Portrait of the Man* (Dunedin: John McIndoe, 1983).

24   O'Sullivan, p. 12.

25   Hall, p. 207.

26   Miroslav Holub, *Although* (London: Cape, 1971), p. 48.

27   See, for example, Ian Milner, 'Lydgate and the Heroic Aspiration in *Middlemarch*', in *Prague Studies in English*, 9 (1961), 23–39.

28   Ian Milner, 'The Genesis of George Eliot's Address to Working Men and its Relation to *Felix Holt, the Radical*', *Prague Studies in English*, 10 (1963), 49–54.

29   Ian Milner, 'George Eliot's Prague Story', *Prague Studies in English*, 15 (1973), 67–82.

30   *Prague Studies in English*, 13 (1969), 97–107.

31   Ibid., (1972), 65–73.

32   Hall, p. 176.

33   O'Sullivan, p. 33.

34   Ibid., p. 71.

35   Ric Throssell, *My Father's Son* (Melbourne: William Heinemann, 1989), p. 157.

36   See Ball and Horner, p. 272–3.

37   Ibid., p. 271.

38   *Straight Left: Katharine Susannah Prichard*, ed. Ric Throssell (Sydney: Wild and Woolley, 1982).

39   David McKnight, *Australian Spies and their Secrets* (Sydney: Allen and Unwin, 1994), p. 55.

40   Throssell, 1989, p. 239.

41   Ball and Horner, p. 214

42   Throssell, 1989, pp. 237–8.

43   Ball and Horner, p. 214

44 Ibid., p. 229.
45 Interview with David McKnight, Bondi, 19 May 2003.
46 Interview with Bill Tully, Canberra, 12 May 2003.
47 Richard McGregor, '"Spy" and Wife Die as One', *Australian*, 22 April 1999, p. 3.
48 'Key Petrov Identity Dies', *Age*, 22 April 1999, p. 2.
49 Richard McGregor, 'Red Stain Pursued Diplomat to his Death', *Weekend Australian*, 24–25 April 1999, p. 7.
50 Throssell's manuscripts and papers are held in the National Library of Australia.
51 Ric Throssell, *Wild Weeds and Wind Flowers: The Life and Letters of Katharine Susannah Prichard* (Sydney: Angus and Robertson, 1975).
52 Ric Throssell, *For Valour* (Sydney: Currency Methuen Drama, 1976).
53 Throssell, 1989, revised edn 1997, p. 374.
54 Ball and Horner, p. 323.
55 Throssell, 1989, revised edn 1997, p. 295.
56 Ibid.
57 Ric Throssell, *A Reliable Source* (Port Melbourne: William Heinemann Australia, 1990), p. 84.
58 Ric Throssell, *In a Wilderness of Mirrors* (Sydney: Left Book Club, 1992). See Oleg Kalugin, *Spy Master* (London: Smith Gryphon, 1994), p. 134.
59 Kalugin, p. 134.
60 O'Sullivan, p. 17.
61 Ric Throssell, *Tomorrow* (North Melbourne: EM Press, 1997), Acknowledgements.
62 Throssell, Ric. MS 8071, series 5, Box 20, folder 20. National Library of Australia.

Ten The Secret Lives of Spies and Novelists: Herbert Dyce Murphy and Patrick White

1 Sun Tzu, *The Art of War*, ed. Dallas Galvin (New York: Barnes and Noble, 2004), p. 207.
2 Ibid., p. 210.
3 Ibid., p. 211.
4 John Le Carré, *The Spy Who Came in From the Cold* (London: Gollancz, 1963), p. 149.
5 Stephen Murray-Smith, 'Murphy, Herbert Dyce (1879–1971)', *Australian Dictionary of Biography*, vol. 10 (Carlton: Melbourne University Press, 1986), pp. 637–8.
6 Moira Watson, *The Spy Who Loved Children* (Carlton: Melbourne University Press, 1997).
7 Heather Rossiter, *Lady Spy, Gentleman Explorer: The Life of Herbert Dyce Murphy* (Sydney: Random House, 2001).
8 Adrian Caesar, *The White* (Sydney: Pan Macmillan/Picador, 1999).
9 Murray-Smith, p. 637.
10 Watson, p. 61.
11 Rossiter, p. 78.
12 Ibid., pp. 78–9.
13 Murray-Smith, p. 637.
14 Rossiter, p. 87.
15 Watson, p. 62.
16 Ibid., p. 62.
17 Jennifer Sexton, 'Empire strikes back', *Australian*, 11 August 2006, p. 13.
18 Ibid., p. 13.
19 David Marr, *Patrick White: A Life* (Sydney: Random House, 1991), p. 544.
20 Ibid., p. 545.
21 Ibid., p. 562.
22 Ibid., p. 563.
23 Ibid., p. 581.

24 Ibid., p. 203.
25 Ibid., p. 220.
26 Ibid., p. 227.
27 Ibid., p. 224.
28 Ibid., p. 224.
29 Patrick White, *The Twyborn Affair* (London: Jonathan Cape, 1979, p. 67.
30 Marr, 1991, p. 203.
31 See Cahal Milmo, 'The double agents with poetic licence to kill?' *Canberra Times*, 3 March 2007, Forum B3. Auden and Burgess were friends and Auden was sought for questioning by MI5 over Burgess's disappearance from Britain in May 1951.
32 Bliss, Carolyn. *Patrick White's Fiction: The Paradox of Fortunate Failure* (London: Macmillan, 1986), p. 168.
33 White, p. 389.
34 Ibid., p. 374.
35 Ibid., p. 360.
36 Ibid., p. 383.
37 In her memoir *Truth at Last*, 'good-time girl' Keeler presents herself as an unwitting spy and a pawn in the Cold War (p. xiii).Christine Keeler, *The Truth at Last: My Story* (London: Sidgwick and Jackson, 2001).
38 White, p. 379.
39 John Colmer, *Patrick White* (London: Methuen, 1984), p. 79.
40 David Marr, ed., *Patrick White: Letters* (Sydney: Vintage/Random House, 1994), p. 502.
41 White, p. 423.

Eleven A Wilderness of Mirrors: Perspectives on 'The Spying Game' in Australian Literature

1 Bruce Bennett, 'In the Shadows: The Spy in Australian Literary and Cultural History'. *Antipodes*, 20.1 (June 2006), 28–37.
2 For example, AustLit: The Australian Literature Resource notes 16 literary items with espionage as a subject for the month of March 2006. A similar number of items is recorded most months.
3 Ric Throssell, *In a Wilderness of Mirrors* (Sydney: Left Book Club, 1992), p. 196.
4 Ibid., pp. 37–9.
5 William Colby, *Honorable Men: My Life in the CIA* (New York: Simon and Schuster, 1978), pp. 364–5, 377–8, 396.
6 Throssell, pp. 33–4.
7 Elizabeth Perkins, 'Three Post-Colonial Novels: Fiction and a Political Conscience?', *LinQ* 19.1 (1992), 143–9.
8 Throssell, p. 71.
9 Duane R. Clarridge, with Digby Diehl, p. 255.
10 Ibid., p. 268.
11 Desmond Ball and David Horner, *Breaking the Codes: Australia's KGB Network, 1944–1950* (Sydney: Allen and Unwin, 1998), p. 270.
12 The articles in the *Courier-Mail* and the *Age* both refer to Ball and Horner's book *Breaking the Codes*. Peter Charlton in the *Courier-Mail* notes that Ball and Horner 'established conclusively that [Katharine Susannah] Prichard [Throssell's mother] had been a Soviet agent and that Throssell's role could not be clearly differentiated from hers'. The *Age* more accurately summarises Ball and Horner's conclusion that 'it was unclear whether Mr Throssell was a Soviet agent or simply an unwitting source of information to his mother, who was a conduit to the Soviets'.
13 Interview Sydney, 19 May 2003. McKnight observed that the Petrovs had claimed that Throssell was working for the Soviets and that most of what the Petrovs said has been

borne out.

14　Frank Moorhouse, *Grand Days* (New York: Pantheon, c. 1993), p. 503.

15　Jane Stenning, 'Boundary Writers: Moral Pragmatism in Henry Lawson and Frank Moorhouse'. PhD thesis. University of Sydney, 2006, pp. 232–3.

16　Moorhouse, p. 504.

17　Ibid., p. 233.

18　Christopher J. Koch, *Highways to a War* (Kew, Vic: Reed Books/Minerva, 1995), p. 390.

19　Ibid., p. 393.

20　Ibid., p. 386.

21　Ibid., p. 391.

22　Ibid., p. 391.

23　Ibid., p. 429.

24　Ibid., p. 429.

25　John F. Sullivan, *Of Spies and Lies: A CIA Lie Detector Remembers Vietnam* (Lawrence: University Press of Kansas, 2002), p. 159.

26　Ibid., p. 26.

27　Christopher Andrew, with Vasili Mitrokhin, *The World Was Going Our Way: The KGB and the Battle for the Third World* (New York: Perseus, 2005), p. 88.

28　Janette Turner Hospital, *Due Preparations for the Plague* (New York: W. W. Norton, 2003), p. 49.

29　Ibid., p. 29.

30　Robert Birnhaum, Interview with Janette Turner Hospital in identitytheory.com. Posted 11 November 2003.

31　Brenda Niall, 'Loading the Dice', *Australian Book Review* (June/July 2003), p. 38.

32　See Richardson, *My Father*. The author's father 'disappears into the secret world' (p. 76) from which his son tries to retrieve him. The son generalises towards the end: '[A]s time passed, he replaced his doubts with convictions and became so absorbed in his war he forgot that happiness was part of wisdom' (p. 305).

33　*The 9/11 Commission Report: Final Report of the National Commission on Terrorist Attacks Upon the United States* (New York: W.W. Norton, n.d.).

Twelve Memory, Identity and Imagination in Secret Intelligence: Christopher Koch's *The Memory Room*

1　Christopher Koch, *The Memory Room* (Sydney: Vintage/Random House, 2007), p. 37.

2　Ibid., p. 45.

3　Ibid., p. 57.

4　Ibid., p. 70.

5　Evan Thomas, *The Very Best Men* (New York: Touchstone, 1996), p. xxx.

6　Nicholas Hasluck, *Somewhere in the Atlas. The Road to Khe Sanh and Other Travel Pieces* (Claremont: Freshwater Bay Press, 2007), pp. 37–117.

7　Koch, p. 161.

8　Ibid., p. 161.

9　Ibid., p. 164.

10　Ibid., p. 164.

11　Ibid., p. 173.

12　Ibid., p. 12.

13　Ibid., pp. 173–4.

14　Ibid., p. 174.

15　See Tom Allard, 'New ASIO Chief blew Cairo spy's cover"', www.theage.com.au.July172005.

16　Warren Reed, *Coe Cicada* (Sydney: Harper Collins, 2004), p. 415.

17   Koch, p. 144.
18   Ibid., p. 140.
19   Ibid., p. 177.
20   Ibid., p. 195.
21   Ibid., p. 210.
22   See Michael Thwaites, *Truth Will Out: ASIO and the Petrovs* (Sydney: Collins, 1980).
23   Royal Commission on Australia's Security and Intelligence Agencies, Canberra, 1983–4.
24   Koch, p. 379.
25   Ibid., p. 379.
26   Ibid., p. 417.
27   Ibid., p. 429.
28   Ibid., p. 431.
29   Wendy Jane Stevenson, 'An Obfuscated Career', *Journal of the Australian Institute of Professional Intelligence Officers,* 15.1 (2007), 32.
30   Ibid., pp. 32–3.
31   Personal correspondence from author to Bruce Bennett.

Thirteen Spies, Lies and Intelligence: Reconfiguring Asia-Pacific Literatures

1   James McAuley, *Collected Poems 1936–1970* (Sydney: Angus & Robertson, 1971), pp. 111–76.
2   Cassandra Pybus, *The Devil and James McAuley* (St Lucia: University of Queensland Press, 1999), p. 178.
3   Ibid., pp. 38–9; Michael Heyward, *The Ern Malley Affair* (St Lucia: University of Queensland Press, 1993).
4   Ibid., pp . 39–41.
5   Michael Thwaites, *Truth Will Out: ASIO and the Petrovs* (Sydney: Collins, 1980), p. 18.
6   Vladimir and Evdokia Petrov, *Empire of Fear* (New York: Doubleday, 1965).
7   Leo Braudy, *From Chivalry to Terrorism: War and the Changing Nature of Terrorism* (New York: Knopf, 2003), p. 534.
8   Chris Cunneen, 'Steward, Sir George Charles Thomas (1865–1920)', *Australian Dictionary of Biography*, vol. 12 (Carlton: Melbourne University Press, 1990), p. 81.
9   Ibid., p. 82.
10   Frank Cain, *The Origins of Political Surveillance in Australia* (Sydney: Angus and Robertson, 1983), pp. 1–36.
11   Chris Cunneen, *King's Men: Australia's Governors-General from Hopetoun to Isaacs* (Sydney: George Allen and Unwin, 1983), p. 141.
12   Cunneen, 1990, p. 82.
13   *Johnson's Dictionary: A Modern Selection,* ed. E. L.McAdam and George Milne (London: Macmillan, 1982), pp. 292–3.
14   Ban Kah Choon, *Absent History: The Untold Story of Special Branch Operations in Singapore 1915–1942* (Singapore: Raffles/SNP Media Asia, 2001), p. xii.
15   Ibid., p. xiii.
16   Ibid., p. 3.
17   Ibid., pp. 6–7.
18   Ibid., p. 8.
19   Ibid., p. 8.
20   Ibid., p. 182.
21   Ibid., pp. 183–7; Peter Elphick and Michael Smith, *Odd Man Out: The Story of a*

Singapore Traitor (London: Hodder & Stoughton, 1994).

22 Christopher Thorne, 'MacArthur, Australia and the British 1942–1943: The Secret Journal of MacArthur's British Liaison Officer', Parts I and II, *Australian Outlook,* 29.1–2 (April and August 1975), 53–67 and 186–210 [I, p. 54].

23 Ban, p. xiii.

24 Brewer, pp. 49–55.

25 Ross Peake, 'Arroyo to witness aid and defence agreements', *Canberra Times*, 31 May 2007, p. 5.

26 Natalie O'Brien, 'JI splinter groups now threaten Australians', *Australian*, 8 October 2007, p. 2.

27 Nicholas Hasluck, *The Legal Labyrinth* (Claremont: Freshwater Bay Press, 2003), p. 4.

28 Ibid., p. 56.

29 Ibid., p. 158.

30 Dudley De Souza, 'The Novels of F. Sionil José: Protagonists in Spiritual Exile', *A Sense of Exile: Essays in the Literature of the Asia-Pacific Region,* ed. Bruce Bennett (Nedlands: University of Western Australia, 1988), p. 156.

31 F. Sionil José, *Mass* (Manila: Solidaridad, 1983), p. 24.

32 Ibid., p. 139.

33 Ibid., p. 112.

34 Ibid., p. 153.

35 Ibid., p. 152.

36 Ibid., p. 167.

37 Ibid., p. 178.

38 Ibid., p. 189.

39 Ibid., p. 191.

40 Ibid., p. 216.

41 Ibid.

42 Ibid., p. 223.

43 Jose Y. Dalisay, *Killing Time in a Warm Place* (Pasig City: Anvil, 2006, new edn), p. 77.

44 Ibid., p. 87.

45 Ibid., p. 103.

46 Ibid.

47 Ibid., p. 137.

48 Ibid., p. 141.

49 Ibid., p. 191.

50 Ibid., p. 192.

51 Robert Drewe, *A Cry in the Jungle Bar* (1979; Sydney: Pan Macmillan, 1993), p. 49.

52 Ibid., p. 182.

53 Ibid., p. 153.

54 Ibid., p. 158.

55 Ibid., p. 179.

Fourteen Of Spies and Terrorists: Australian Fiction after 9/11

1 Kerryn Goldsworthy, 'Straight for the Throat', *Australian Book Review*, October 2006, p. 8.

2 Andrew McGahan, *Underground* (Crows Nest, NSW: Allen & Unwin, 2006), p. 298.

3 Goldsworthy, p. 9.

4 Richard Flanagan, *The Unknown Terrorist* (Sydney: Picador/Pan Macmillan, 2006). Reviews quoted in 2007 edition. Also New York: Grove.

5 Adib Khan, *Spiral Road* (Sydney: Harper Collins, 2007), pp. 14–15.

6 Ibid., p. 51.

7 Ibid., p. 59.

8   Ibid., p. 62.
9   Ibid.
10 Ibid., p. 63.
11 Ibid., p. 315.
12 Ibid., p. 174.
13 Ibid., p. 241.
14 Ibid.
15 Ibid., p. 325.
16 Adrian d'Hage, *The Beijing Conspiracy* (Camberwell, Vic: Penguin, 2007), pp. 72–3.
17 Ibid., p. 130.

Fifteen Australian Literature's War on Terror

1   'Iraq Poll', *The Chaser's War on Everything*, ABC TV, 9 May 2007.
2   Robert Drewe, *Grace* (Camberwell, Vic: Viking, 2005), p. 212.
3   Mark Dodd, 'AIDS worse than 9/11: Kirby', *Australian*, 21 February 2007, p. 1.
4   Chris Merritt, 'Judge is out of touch, out of line', *Australian*, 21 February 2007, p. 2.
5   *Spooks*, ABC TV, 11 May 2007.
6   Elizabeth Gosch and David King, 'Roche plots a quiet life', *Australian*, 18 May 2007, p. 2.
7   Emma-Kate Symons, 'A Win in France', *The Weekend Australian*, 17–18 March 2007, p. 24.
8   Sandy McCutcheon, *The Magician's Son* (Camberwell, Vic: Penguin, 2005).
9   Sandy McCutcheon, *In Wolf's Clothing* (Pymble, NSW: HarperCollins, 1997).
10 Sandy McCutcheon, *The Cobbler's Apprentice* (Carlton, Vic: Scribe, 2006).
11 Warren Reed, *Code Cicada* (Sydney: HarperCollins, 2004).
12 Reed, p. 45.
13 Reed, p. 159.
14 Reed, p. 415.
15 Richard Flanagan, *The Unknown Terrorist* (Sydney: Picador/Pan Macmillan, 2006).
16 Flanagan, 2006, p. 107.
17 Richard Flanagan, 'Out of control: the tragedy of Tasmania's forests', *Monthly*, May 2007, pp. 20–31.
18 Flanagan, 2006, p. 149.
19 Flanagan, 2007, pp. 20–5.
20 Margaret Throsby, Interview with Richard Flanagan, ABC Classic FM Radio, May 2007 (repeat of November 2006).
21 Throsby Interview.
22 Flanagan, 2006, p. 218.
23 Flanagan, 2006, p. 270.
24 Flanagan, 2006, p. 271.
25 Ibid., p. 271.
26 Janette Turner Hospital, *Orpheus Lost* (Sydney: Fourth Estate/HarperCollins, 2007).
27 Bron Sibree, 'Notes from the Underworld', *Courier Mail*, 5 May 2007, p. M18.
28 Turner Hospital, p. 60.
29 Sibree, p. M18.
30 Peter Pierce, 'A fine rendition: One of Australia's best novelists plumbs the depths of the war on terror', *Bulletin*, vol. 125, no. 21, 22 May 2007.
31 Peter Craven, 'Courting disaster', *Australian Literary Review*, 2 May 2007, p. 5.
32 Craven, 'Courting disaster', p. 5.
33 Turner Hospital, p. 202.
34 Mark McKenna, 'Patriot Act', *Australian Literary Review*, 6 June 2007, pp. 14–16.
35 McKenna, p. 14.

36 McKenna, p. 3.
37 Carl Thayer, 'Terrorism Studies: Dismal Science?' Unpublished paper, Canberra, 2007.
38 Michael Thwaites, *Truth Will Out: ASIO and the Petrovs* (Sydney: Collins, 1980), p. 18.
39 *The 9/11 Commission Report: Final Report of the National Commission on Terrorist Attacks upon the United States* (New York, W. W. Norton, 2004).

Index